W9-BVY-973

More advance praise for *Unplugged*

"Readers who were fascinated by Colby's previous book, *Long Goodbye*, will not be disappointed with this brilliant new offering. He has a rare talent for informing and enlightening his readers on complex subjects through narrative—and narrative that is not just readable but riveting."

—Douglas L. Wilson, author of *Lincoln's Sword* and winner of the Lincoln Prize

"I had planned to skim the manuscript to write a dust jacket blurb but found that I couldn't put this book down. Colby writes in a gripping way about a story that could tragically happen to anyone. He also provides a compelling argument for why we all need to anticipate and plan for what—for too many of us—is the unthinkable: our own mortality."

—Alan Meisel, Director, Center for Bioethics, University of Pittsburgh

"*Unplugged* folds a number of gripping stories–Karen Ann Quinlan's, Nancy Cruzan's, Terri Schiavo's–into a larger story that is even more gripping: the story of the march of medical technology and the disruptions it has wrought in our traditional ways of thinking about the end of life."

—Robert Hellenga, best-selling author of *Philosophy Made Simple*

"History suggests that every thousand years or so complex societies, globally considered, are called upon to wrestle with the fundamental human values underlying life and death, endeavor and belief—yet the tempo of these tumultuous and revelatory moments appears to be accelerating, along with the technological advances that punctuate the rhythm. Such is William Colby's theme in this impressively researched and gorgeously orchestrated book: here is what we thought to be true last year, last week, yesterday; and here is why such heartbreaking naiveté is no longer possible today. What is possible?

Read *Unplugged*; savor your most poignant memories; meditate on history; decide for yourself. William Colby is your steadfast guide."

—Robin Metz, author of *Unbidden Angel* and winner of the Rilke International Poetry Prize

"Bill Colby's perspective on dying in America is both unique and multi-faceted. His arguments before the U.S. Supreme Court helped shape the legal framework for end-of-life decision making. Perhaps, more importantly, since writing his first book, *Long Goodbye*, he has spoken to people across the country about their hopes and fears for their last chapter. *Unplugged* weaves together his knowledge, understanding, and compassion."

—Myra Christopher, CEO, Center for Practical Bioethics

"*Unplugged* is an insightful and unsentimental examination of the Terri Schiavo case. Bill Colby, who represented Nancy Cruzan's family, explains why it is so hard for our physicians and families to stop using medical technology (especially feeding tubes) when we are near the end of our lives, and tells us what we can do to improve our lives and the lives of our family members."

—George J. Annas, Chair of the Department of Health Law, Bioethics & Human Rights at Boston University School of Public Health and author of *The Rights of Patients*

UNPLUGGED

RECLAIMING OUR RIGHT TO DIE IN AMERICA

WILLIAM H. COLBY

AMACOM

AMERICAN MANAGEMENT ASSOCIATION

New York • Atlanta • Brussels • Chicago • Mexico City • San Francisco

Shanghai • Tokyo • Toronto • Washington, D.C.

*Special discounts on bulk quantities of AMACOM books are available to corporations, professional associations, and other organizations. For details, contact Special Sales Department, AMACOM, a division of American Management Association, 1601 Broadway, New York, NY 10019.
Tel.: 212-903-8316. Fax: 212-903-8083.
Web site: www.amacombooks.org*

Library of Congress Cataloging-in-Publication Data

Colby, William H., 1955–
Unplugged : reclaiming our right to die in America / William H. Colby.
p. cm.
Includes bibliographical references and index.
ISBN-10: 0-8144-0882-6
ISBN-13: 978-0-8144-0882-7
1. Terminal care—Moral and ethical aspects. 2. Right to die—Moral and ethical aspects. 3. Life and death, Power over—Moral and ethical aspects. I. Title.

R726.C637 2006
179.7—dc22

2006008004

Printing number

10 9 8 7 6 5 4 3 2 1

CONTENTS

FOREWORD

CONSIDER THIS. You're in an accident. Emergency personnel arrive and rush you to the hospital, all the while valiantly working to keep you alive. A distraught family member arrives at the emergency room an hour later and the doctor gives her the news—you are unconscious and your prognosis is uncertain. You may never wake up. You may never be able to breathe on your own. You will never walk or talk. You're hooked up to a ventilator that breathes for you since you can't breathe on your own.

A week later more of your loved ones have gathered. There's been no change in your condition and the prognosis is still bad. The doctors want to insert a tube to provide you with nutrition and hydration. One of your family members says "No" because of a conversation about Terri Schiavo that the two of you had. Another one says "Yes" because of her spiritual beliefs. Who decides? How will you live out the next days, weeks, months or perhaps years of your life? The simple answer in America today is, "It depends."

These questions are being asked every day in hospitals and nursing homes across this country. You might think this couldn't happen to you. You're young—but so was Terri Schiavo. You're healthy—but so was Nancy Cruzan. If you want a better answer for your own family than "it depends," then you need to read this book.

Bill Colby is one of the nation's foremost legal experts on end-of-life issues. In this book he takes readers on a fascinating, narrative journey through the development of law and medicine that affects our death and dying. He leads the reader to understand how dramatically medical technology has changed our society over the last 40 years, and how we could come to be in a place in the spring of 2005 where the country saw such societal discord over the case of Terri Schiavo. The book also sounds a call to action: The public is only beginning to confront these complicated questions, with technology continuing its march forward and the population of the country graying rapidly as well.

Do yourself and your family a favor—read this book. Think about how you want to live your life now, and what will be important as your life draws to an end. Talk about it. Ask yourself and others, "What would you want if you were in Terri Schiavo's situation?"

Once you've finished reading, recommend the book to someone you care about and ask them to read it. If they say "no," ask them to read it as a favor to you. Tell them you don't want to struggle to make decisions on their behalf if they are ever injured or seriously ill and can't speak for themselves. Just as importantly, take the advice in the book and fill out an advance directive—a living will or power of attorney for health care, or both.

It's your life. Thinking, talking and planning ahead—now, while you're able—is the least you should do for yourself and for those you love. No one can predict what their future will hold, but letting others know what kind of health care decisions you'd make if you were seriously ill can bring you and your loved ones peace of mind. That peace of mind might be the greatest gift you ever give.

As we say in the hospice world, it's not about dying—*It's about how you live.*

J. Donald Schumacher
President & Chief Executive Officer
National Hospice and Palliative Care Organization
Washington, D.C., January 2006

ACKNOWLEDGMENTS

MANY PEOPLE HELPED with this book. Thanks to those friends and colleagues who read different chapters and offered excellent suggestions and encouragement, or who assisted with research: Rob Adams, Wendy Baker, Heather Berry, Peter Bonadonna, Cindy Bruzzese, Peter Busalacchi, Susan Campbell, John Carney, Myra Christopher, Stephen Conor, Brookes Cowan, Dr. Joseph Fins, Sr. Rosemary Flanigan, Katharine Gregg, Nancy Hulston, Elizabeth Ihrig, Ann Jackson, Dr. Gordon Kelly, Don Lambert, Barbara Coombs Lee, Victoria Liston, Dr. Bernard Lown, Dr. Joanne Lynn, Elizabeth Metz, Galen Miller, Dr. John Muraskas, Dr. Steve Nigh, Fr. Kevin O'Rourke, Ed Peterson, Dr. Fred Plum, Susan Plum, Dr. Robert Potter, Jon Radulovic, Coco Regis, Rachel Reeder, Charles Sabatino, Claire Simons, Gwynn Sullivan, Linda Ward, and Chris Cruzan White.

Thanks also to my excellent book agents, and friends, Shannon Miser-Marven and Jan Miller, and to all of the people at AMACOM Books, who have treated this book as if it were important, which I appreciate. Thanks, too, to the Greater Kansas City Community Foundation for its support.

Special thanks to those who allowed their arms to be twisted, without a lot of effort on my part, to give significant amounts of time and energy to this project: Dr. Ann Allegre, Kathy Brandt, Dr. Ronald Cranford, Virginia Darby, Prof. Nancy Levit, Dr. Christian Sinclair, Lisa Veglahn, and Robin Metz. (If you care about the issues raised in this book, read *Unbidden Angel* by Robin Metz). And to Dr. Robert Milch, who not only edited diligently, but also counseled my family with my own mother, who died in October of 2005.

Last, thanks to my editor, Lon Otto, who worked tirelessly on successive drafts of the book, using his steady hand and sharp pencil to make the book better—exactly the type of editing touchstone, and friend, that a writer needs. And, as always, for Kelley, Zach, Anna, George, and Charley Colby, my touchstones in life.

Bill Colby, Prairie Village, Kansas, 2006

INTRODUCTION

ON SATURDAY, December 22, 1990, I drove my red and gray Ford Bronco slowly across the snow-packed two-lane roads down to Mt. Vernon, Missouri, to say goodbye to Nancy Cruzan and her family. Near the front steps of the state hospital, protesters huddled together against the frigid cold in a crude lean-to. They shouted "Save Nancy!" at me as I passed by.[1] Inside, I sat with the family around Nancy Cruzan's bed.

In March of 1993, I again walked past protesters, this time outside Barnes Hospital in St. Louis, and sat with Pete Busalacchi in the darkened hospital room next to the bed of his daughter, Christine. Or Chrissy, as he would say. Both father and daughter shared unnaturally red and bloodshot eyes, his from crying and lack of sleep, hers from the effects of dehydration.

Christine Busalacchi and Nancy Cruzan were dying, days after doctors had removed their feeding tubes. I was their lawyer. Their families had "won" the right to remove the feeding tubes from their unconscious daughters after years of litigation against the state of Missouri. No Cruzan or Busalacchi felt like they'd won anything.

And then in the spring of 2005, like many Americans, I watched the story of Terri Schiavo and her fractured family unfold in the media. Unlike most Americans, though, my initial shock at seeing the horrific destruction called the persistent vegetative state had come and gone years before, on the morning when I walked into Nancy Cruzan's hospital room for the first time. I will never forget that morning, standing there, stunned, nearly riveted to the floor of the hospital room. My education about the brain, how it works and how it can be destroyed, began that morning at Nancy's bedside.

In the years that followed, I saw many patients whom doctors had diagnosed as being in persistent vegetative states. So when I watched the video of Terri Schiavo in 2005, my reaction was not one of shock, but more of sadness, and on some level, understanding. By that point I had been thinking for nearly twenty years about the question that started coming at me more and more as I traveled around the country in 2004 and 2005: "What do you think is 'right' for Terri Schiavo?"

Remarkably, nearly every American saw the video footage of Terri Schiavo appearing to smile in response to her parents, Bob and Mary Schindler. For most, it was their first encounter with the persistent vegetative state. That video became a lightning rod, with many, including some governmental leaders, voicing opinions about what Terri Schiavo's apparent smile meant to them. Among the loudest and shrillest voices was then-federal House Majority Leader Tom DeLay, who said, "Mrs. Schiavo's life is not slipping away, it is being violently wrenched from her body in an act of medical terrorism."[2] Others made similar sensational statements.

Yet public opinion polls showed that the majority of Americans believed removal of the feeding tube was the right choice.[3] Likewise, when surveyed about general end-of-life questions, most Americans say that they want to die at home, free from the burdens of machines and pain, surrounded by loved ones. Studies show that our actual fate is usually the opposite: most dying takes place in institutions, with patients often tethered to unwanted technology, often isolated, and too often in pain.[4]

How can we have such fundamental societal disagreement on what was "right" for Terri Schiavo? How can we have such a chasm between what we say we want with our dying and what actually happens?

Blame medical technology. In many ways the questions raised about the proper medical treatment of Terri Schiavo are hard because they are so new in our culture. They have come to us quickly, in a tremendous rush of technological progress. Go back three-and-a-half decades and we wouldn't have been talking about Terri Schiavo being in a persistent vegetative state, because that diagnosis was not described in the medical literature until 1972. The technology simply didn't exist yet to keep human beings with such massive brain damage alive for an extended time. In that less-technological era, anyone with a serious illness generally wanted all of the medicines and machines that the medical team could bring to bear, because not much was available. Very sick patients either died or improved in a relatively short time.

Today, of course, the simpler time is gone. The idea of letting nature take its course has fallen by the medical-technological wayside. The whooping cough, tuberculosis, and pneumonia that used to "take us" are now tamed by vaccines and antibiotics that we take for granted. In response to extreme illness or catastrophic accident, the sophisticated emergency room and even more sophisticated intensive care unit can step in to alter nature's course. This altering happens every day, with medical teams applying an arsenal of machines and medicines that is incomprehensible to the lay person. Most of us are destined to live with chronic illnesses that advance slowly, conditions which we, together with our doctors, will beat back for years.

Sometimes, that medical beating back can produce wonderful results. In the early 1980s my dad had a triple bypass at the Mayo Clinic. The rapidly improving technology of that time (though primitive in ways compared to the tools today, just twenty years later), gave him another fifteen years of a great life. My family would not trade that time for anything, and we feel blessed by the advances in medical technology and doctoring skill that granted us that gift of years.

But understanding when medicine and technology can deliver such wonderful results and when it can deliver no satisfying results at all is a profoundly complicated question for doctors and patients alike. And it's a brand new question for humankind. The elderly in the U.S. today, and the huge demographic bulge of Baby Boomers following right behind them, are the first to face these issues. With technology advancing relentlessly, the questions will soon be coming at us with alarming frequency.

Most tragedies contain buried seeds of hope. The destruction of the relationships within Terri Schiavo's family and her public dying in the spring of 2005, such a complete tragedy for her family, gave the rest of us a great gift—the opening lines to a critical societal conversation: "What do you think was 'right' for Terri Schiavo? What would you want if you were in her shoes?" As the rancorous debate over the fate of Terri Schiavo showed, our political and religious leaders do not speak with one voice, nor do they necessarily have answers. They are pedaling to keep up just like the rest of us. But it's not really our leaders' job at all. It's ours.

Most people believe that "Schiavo" could never happen to them. On the one hand, that assumption is true—bitter court fights like *Schiavo* are the rare exception. In the state of Florida, for example, about 460 people die each day, most in institutions, most as a result of some decision.[5] And there is no daily rush to the courtrooms of Florida, asking judges to decide. On the other hand, like the husband and parents of Terri Schiavo, families face hard decisions every day in the hospitals and nursing homes of Florida. While they might not sink into a protracted legal dispute, these families often are troubled by doubt, guilt, indecision, and too often conflict, because they have little idea of what their loved one might want, or what they want for that loved one.

The basic questions found in the Schiavo dispute are not rare at all: They will soon touch every person in America in some way. These questions will not answer themselves. Would Mom want the respirator turned off? Is the decision to remove a feeding tube respecting life, or the opposite? Can religion help answer that question? Ethics? The law?

This book is not intended as an advocacy piece, though by the end of the book you will understand clearly what my views are about removal of treatment. Instead, it is meant simply to show the reader how one lawyer, after working in this area for many years, came to his own conclusions about the questions: "What do you think was 'right' for Terri Schiavo? What would you want if you were in her shoes?"

More importantly, it's meant to pose those questions for you. You may come up with different answers in your family than we have in mine. But don't we all owe it to those we love to spend the time needed to face these questions, head on, before it's too late?

PART ONE

CHAPTER 1

Terri Schiavo's Private Years

December 1963–January 2000

THE PUBLIC DISCUSSION of the *Schiavo* case was marked and marred by incredible negativity and name-calling. This sad state came about in part due to the proliferation of cable outlets on television and the apparent need for confrontational coverage to attract viewers. As the legal case built to its contentious conclusion throughout the spring of 2005, I was doing a lot of interviews. Over and over, television producers asked me in preparation for an appearance on their show, "Which side are you on?" They seemed perplexed when I said, "Neither."

Part of the problem is our culture itself, where civil discourse over hard questions—and even basic civility—has faded into angry talking heads on the radio and television. Part of the blame in the *Schiavo* case must go to the bitterly divided family, willing after years of fighting to say anything about the other side. In the cauldron of charges and countercharges that became the public face of the Terri Schiavo story, it was hard to know an individual fact. It was even harder to learn "the truth."

I represented parents in two similarly highly public cases, parents who in each case sought to remove a feeding tube from a daughter in a persistent vegetative state. One might assume that I would simply take up the side of Michael Schiavo, the husband who was seeking to have his wife's feeding tube removed. I did not. I have also represented and counseled other families in cases that never made it to the public eye. Some of those families sought to remove treatment, while others fought to keep it in place against a medical team that believed the treatment futile.

I also did not then, and do not today, take up the side of the parents. I do not come to the *Schiavo* case as an advocate at all. From years of working on cases like *Schiavo*, I realize that at a very basic level it is impossible for us to understand—in any real way—what either the Schiavo or Schindler families have endured. Families I've talked with who *can* understand, like the Cruzans and Busalacchis, watched the news coverage of this fractured family and picked no side. Their hearts went out to parents and husband alike.

But while we cannot fully comprehend until we've been there, we can still learn from this tragedy. I have tried to sift through the history of the legal case to find as much fact as possible. My goal is to provide some understanding of the medical information developed and relied upon over the years in the court system. Conspiracy theorists on both ends will likely find this account unfulfilling and incomplete by their reckoning. There are several books out there for those interested in partisan accounts.[1] And I mean no offense to either Michael Schiavo or the Schindlers in anything written here. Their war continues with books of their own published in the spring of 2006.[2] I only hope they can someday find peace.

My focus is on how society grappled with this case. I've tried to look through the lens of those who were simply there because that was their job—the investigating police officer, the doctor and nurses who cared for her, the judges to whom the case fell by random assignment, the medical examiner assigned an autopsy for which the whole world waited. I've relied on original documents like trial transcripts, depositions, and judicial opinions, and I've filled in with newspaper accounts and interviews that I've conducted, too.

In the spring of 2005, literally millions of Americans were talking about Terri Schiavo. Though no longer at that fever pitch, the discussion continues today all across this country. The following account of the case seeks to provide a basic understanding of the medical and legal facts our court system used to resolve the dispute over Terri Schiavo. This part of the book is long, covering three chapters. Since any discussion of the right to die today often starts with Terri Schiavo, I thought it was important to try to tell her story in as straightforward and complete a way as I could. If we can come to a better understanding of the key aspects of the legal case in *Schiavo*, we will be better able to answer with our own families the questions that many have pondered in the wake of this tragic case: "What do you think was 'right' for Terri Schiavo? What would you want if you were in her shoes?"

TERRI SCHIAVO'S FIRST 26 YEARS

Terri Schiavo was born on December 3, 1963 to Bob and Mary Schindler. She grew up in a middle-class suburb of Philadelphia, the oldest of three children. She was shy in high school and struggled with her weight. By her senior year at the all-girls Archbishop Wood Catholic School, her weight at times reached 250 pounds on her 5 foot, 3 inch frame.[3] She did not attend school dances or her senior prom, and though Terri did not complain, her mother always sensed that her weight "bothered her."[4]

After high school, Terri Schiavo enrolled in Bucks County Community College with plans to work with animals in some way.[5] She also went on the NutriSystem diet and lost about 100 pounds.[6] Shortly after that, she met and began dating another Bucks County student, Michael Schiavo, her first real boyfriend. They dated for about two years and married on November 10, 1984.[7] They spent their honeymoon at the condo owned by Terri's parents in St. Petersburg Beach, Florida.[8]

Terri and Michael Schiavo enjoyed a large extended family in the Philadelphia area. Michael was the youngest of five brothers, and Terri and Michael were always going to birthday parties and kids' events. Terri was best friends with her sister-in-law, Joan, married to Michael's brother, William. Terri's brother, sister and parents also lived in the Philadelphia area, and Terri and Michael enjoyed a close family relationship on Terri's side, too.[9]

By 1986, "fed up with the weather" in Philadelphia, the Schiavos accepted the offer of Terri's parents to take up permanent residence in their St. Petersburg Beach, Florida condo.[10] Not long after that, Terri's parents and siblings moved to Florida as well. In 1989, Terri and Michael Schiavo began to meet with an obstetrician for infertility treatment. Terri saw the doctor for over a year, but had no success getting pregnant. Her weight by this time had dropped to 110 pounds.[11] Her mother, worried, confronted her daughter about how thin she had grown. Terri told her mother, "I eat, Mom, I eat."[12]

TERRI SCHIAVO'S COLLAPSE

In the early morning hours of February 25, 1990, Michael Schiavo arrived home from his work on the late shift as a restaurant manager. At some point several hours after he'd been home, Terri Schiavo suffered a cardiac arrest. The investigating officer's report filed by St. Petersburg police officer Rodney Brewer includes this description: "Husband stated he was awakened this morning when he heard a thud. He thought his wife had fallen down and got up to check on her. He found her unconscious on the floor and called paramedics."[13]

At a trial ten years later, in January of 2000, on the witness stand Michael gave this account of that night: "I got home late from work that night. I came in the house. Terri woke up. She heard me. I gave her a kiss good night. She gave me a kiss good night. A few hours later, I was getting out of bed for some reason and I heard this thud. So I ran out into the hall and I found Terri on the floor. I knelt down next to her and I turned her over because she sort of fell on her face. On her stomach and face.

"I turned her over going, 'Terri, Terri. You okay?' She kind of had this gurgling noise. I laid her down and ran over and called 911. I was hysterical. I called 911. I called her brother, who lived in the same complex as we did. I ran back to Terri. She was not moving. I held her in my arms until her brother got there. I rocked her. I didn't know what to do. I was hysterical. It was a horrible moment."[14]

Terri Schiavo had suffered a cardiac arrest; her heart had stopped. Paramedics arrived, and Michael Schiavo heard one say, "She is flat line, start CPR!"[15] In addition to manual CPR and drugs like epinephrine (to jump start the heart) and lidocaine (to suppress ventricular fibrillation, the deadly, wildly erratic, squirming of the heart), they also had to shock her with defibrillation paddles seven times.[16] Ultimately, they were able to restart her heart,[17] and she was rushed in the ambulance to Humana Northside Hospital in St. Petersburg. Michael Schiavo rode in the back of the ambulance with Terri.[18]

Officer Brewer inspected the apartment and interviewed firefighters and paramedics on the scene after the ambulance left. His report indicated that he found nothing unusual in the apartment and no apparent trauma to Terri Schiavo's head or face when he saw her in the hospital. At the hospital, he interviewed Michael Schiavo, who had no explanation for Terri's collapse. He could think of no reason she would want to commit suicide, and she had no history of heart disease or allergies to medication. He did tell the officer that she had been having "female problems" and had been "tired lately and not feeling well."[19] Michael Schiavo huddled all night in the hospital waiting room together with Terri's parents, Bob and Mary Schindler, sitting, talking quietly, waiting for news.[20] Both her parents and her husband said later that they never suspected that she had an eating disorder.[21]

The First Three Years

Terri Schiavo stayed in Humana Northside until May 12, 1990, almost three months.[22] Though her eyes opened, she did not recover consciousness during that time.[23] Over the first sixteen days, with Terri in the intensive care unit (ICU), Michael did not leave her. He either slept next to her, or more often, caught naps on the waiting room chairs.[24] After that he went home at times, but spent most of every day with Terri.

Humana Northside discharged Terri Schiavo to the College Harbor nursing home in May.[25] After two months there, Michael moved her to Bayfront Rehabilitation Center for another two months, and then, in September, Michael tried to take Terri home to care for her. Mary Schindler, Terri's mother, worked side by side with Michael Schiavo to care for Terri, but after only three weeks, the two concluded that Terri had too many needs and they returned her to the College Harbor facility.[26] During this summer, Michael also was appointed Terri's legal guardian by Judge Robert Michael in St. Petersburg.[27] This appointment was a formality to help Michael deal with insurance and medical records. Her parents did not contest the appointment nor would they have had reason to do so.

Over the course of these seven months in different institutions, Terri received extensive occupational, physical, and speech therapy. These therapies with a profoundly brain-injured patient are extremely basic. It is not the picture of physical therapy that might come to mind, like an aide walking alongside a patient with recent knee surgery, coaxing movement. Instead, the patient is lifted from bed and strapped upright in a special chair. A therapist will stand in front of the patient and repeatedly seek compliance with one-step commands, such as, "Can you blink your eyes for me?" Or family members talk with the patient to try to unlock the damaged brain. Michael Schiavo recorded the voices of family members on a Walkman, for example, and played those voices for Terri through headphones. Small spoonfuls of pureed food may be placed in the patient's mouth, in hopes of stimulating taste or the memory of how to swallow.

The arms and legs of profoundly brain-injured patients start to atrophy and stiffen, drawing in slowly toward the trunk. Doctors call this drawing in "contracture." A part of the therapy is very basic range-of-motion exercise, trying to stop the often-inevitable stiffening. Michael Schiavo explained some of the simple range-of-motion exercises and care in the fall of 1992 as he watched a video of the two of them: "I'm drying out her hands there," he said, watching. "Since she's contracted, you have to keep them dry, because infection can set in."[28]

Despite the attempted therapy, Terri Schiavo showed no improvement. Tests continued to show that Terri could not swallow, and neurological exams reported that she remained unresponsive. The formal diagnosis by the doctors was called the persistent vegetative state.[29] The persistent vegetative state is a relatively new syndrome, defined in 1972 by Drs. Plum and Jennett in the prestigious British medical journal, *The Lancet*. Cases existed before 1972, but around that time doctors began seeing a marked increase in the number of cases due to advancing medical technology—the development of portable respirators, the invention of CPR in the mid-1960s, and other innovations in both basic and advanced life support. The technology ultimately changed not only how doctors thought about consciousness, but how they defined death itself.[30]

The human brain is often likened to a mushroom, with the cerebral hemispheres being the top of the mushroom, and the brainstem being the mushroom stem. Thinking and consciousness occur in the cerebral hemispheres; the brainstem houses what medical textbooks call the body's "vegetative functions"—breathing, digesting food, producing urine, and some basic reflexes. The diagnosis of different conditions depends on what parts of the brain are still working.

In "brain death" the patient has lost all brain function, including brainstem. The heart and lungs continue to function only with mechanical support. In 1970, Kansas became the first state to redefine death, by statute, to include brain death. (Brain death is discussed in Chapter 5).

Patients in a "vegetative state" are not brain dead; they retain relatively normal brainstem function. The brainstem can survive significantly longer without oxygen and remain intact. The upper, "thinking" part of the brain begins to suffer damage after four to six minutes without oxygen. Patients in a vegetative state are nonetheless unconscious just like patients who are brain dead. They appear awake, but are unaware. Their eyes may move around the room, the patients may smile, grimace, make noises, or cough. While these actions appear to be representative of consciousness, they are not—patients in a vegetative state have no thinking, no feeling, no consciousness.

"Coma" is a diagnosis falling between brain death and the vegetative state. The brainstem retains some function, but it's more limited than in the vegetative state. Patients in a coma may need assistance breathing, for example, and they will remain in a sleep-like state. Coma also typically is limited in duration, seldom lasting more than two to four weeks. By that time, the patients either regain some consciousness, die, or enter the vegetative state.

Historically, when a vegetative state lasted more than a few weeks, the diagnosis was changed to a "persistent vegetative state," sometimes also called "PVS." When the vegetative state has been caused by oxygen deprivation to the brain, it is considered a permanent condition if the patient has not emerged within three months.

In 2002, doctors from New York identified another category, which they named the "minimally conscious state." Patients in the minimally conscious state might be described as being slightly outside a vegetative state, with some definite but limited awareness, like giving appropriate yes or no answers or following simple commands.

The diagnoses of vegetative state and persistent vegetative state are clinical ones, made by the doctor after careful and extended observation at the bedside. CT scans, electroencephalograms, and other laboratory studies can help confirm a diagnosis, but the diagnosis itself is made clinically.

Dr. Ronald Cranford, a neurologist who testified as an expert witness in both the *Cruzan* and *Schiavo* cases, set the bar for this medical diagnosis incredibly high when he testified in *Cruzan*: "If there is any small amount of thinking or feeling or awareness or consciousness, then the patient is not in a persistent vegetative state. This is a complete lack of consciousness."[31]

Unfortunately, that was exactly the condition in which Terri Schiavo's parents and husband still found her seven months after her cardiac arrest. In response, Michael Schiavo investigated experimental therapies. In the late fall of 1990, he flew Terri to San Francisco, where a doctor implanted platinum electrodes—an experimental thalamic stimulator—in her brain. Michael stayed with Terri in California throughout the fall and early winter, returning to St. Petersburg in January of 1991.[32]

Back in Florida, Terri was moved into the Mediplex Rehabilitation Center in Bradenton, Florida, where she received 24-hour skilled care and more rehabilitation.[33] Michael worked hand-in-hand with Mary and Bob Schindler in their efforts to rehabilitate and care for Terri. But after months of trying, doctors at Mediplex told Michael Schiavo that "there was nothing more they [could] do for Terri."[34] So on July 19, 1991, after seventeen straight months without success in their efforts to try to rehabilitate Terri Schiavo, Michael Schiavo transferred her to Sabal Palms Health Care Center, a nursing home in Largo, Florida.[35]

THE MEDICAL MALPRACTICE SUIT

In early 1992, lawyers Glenn Woodworth and Gary Fox filed a medical malpractice suit on behalf of Terri and Michael Schiavo against both the obstetrician/gynecologist and the family doctor who had been treating her for infertility. Their claim was that the two doctors had failed to diagnose Terri's eating disorder—bulimia nervosa—and had failed to refer her to specialists for treatment.[36] Bulimia is a disease that causes its victims to overeat and then later vomit, a practice known as binging and purging. The human heart needs to maintain a balance in the body's electrolytes, which can be upset by excessive vomiting. According to Gary Fox, one of the Schiavos' attorneys in the malpractice suit, "that is what happened to Terri. One night, Terri purged, which caused her potassium level to drop low enough to cause a heart attack."[37]

At the medical malpractice trial in Clearwater, nearly three years after Terri Schiavo's cardiac arrest, Bob and Mary Schindler and Michael Schiavo were united, as they had been since that night. In fact, Bob, Mary, and Michael had lived together in Florida until the previous May. Mary Schindler testified in support of Michael: "He's there every day," she said. "He is loving, caring. I don't know of any young boy that would be this attentive. . . . He's just been unbelievable. And I know without him there is no way I could have survived all this."[38]

Knowing that if a jury blamed Terri for hiding her condition it could reduce any award, the Schiavos' lawyers offered to settle the case for $250,000 shortly after the trial began. The doctors rejected the offer.[39] Days later, the jury came back with a verdict of more than $6.8 million in total damages, which was reduced to about $2 million, since the jury also found Terri 70 percent at fault for the eating disorder.[40] Ultimately, after payment of attorneys' fees and expenses in the case, Michael Schiavo received about $300,000 for the loss of his wife's companionship, and Terri Schiavo received $700,000, which was paid into a trust fund set up for her by the court. The money was paid in early February of 1993.[41] That's when the trouble between Michael Schiavo and the Schindlers began.

The Valentine's Day Family Split

On February 14, 1993, now three years after Terri's collapse, Michael arrived at her Largo nursing home with two dozen roses, set them down, and began studying. Terri Schiavo had been placed into her medical lounge chair, upright, and Michael sat in front of her with his books at a small table. He was taking classes to become a nurse so that he could care for Terri on his own. Bob and Mary Schindler arrived for a scheduled dinner with Michael and they soon began to talk about the money.[42]

Years later, the parties remembered very differently what happened that night. Bob Schindler testified that he had asked Michael Schiavo a few weeks before Valentine's Day about their "agreement" that Michael would share part of the jury award with the Schindlers.[43] Bob Schindler recalled that Michael said he'd "get back to" him on the matter. Bob Schindler testified that he asked Michael in the room that Valentine's Day night, "Have you reconciled how we're going to settle this thing?"

Michael Schiavo recalled later that Bob Schindler pointed a finger at him and said, "How much money am I going to get?"[44] Michael admitted that he lied to Bob then "to shut him up" and said, "Look, I gave all my money to Terri. I don't have any money." According to Schiavo, Bob Schindler then turned, pointing at Terri, and said, "How much money is she going to give me?"[45] Schiavo responded by telling Bob Schindler that he would have to "call the guardianship; I'm not the guardian over her property." Michael said at this point Bob swore at him and stormed out of the room, and Michael followed him.

Bob Schindler recalled later that he said, "Michael, you made an agreement with my wife and myself that you were going to share that money with us," and that Michael responded, "I am the husband. I'll make all the decisions. You have nothing to say." Bob Schindler remembered that he then responded, "Well, you made a commitment. What about your integrity?" At that, Schindler said, Michael Schiavo erupted. He pushed the table with his books out of the way, picked one up and threw it against the wall and stormed at Schindler, fists clenched.[46] Mrs. Schindler stepped in between the two men to stop a fight. Whatever exactly was said that night, a heated argument took place, Bob Schindler and Michael Schiavo nearly came to blows, and the Schindlers left. Michael Schiavo and his in-laws never spoke to one another again.

The relationship soured quickly. Michael instructed the nursing home that they could not discuss Terri's medical status with the Schindlers. The Schindlers began arranging their visits to Terri so that they would not be there at the same time as Michael. In June, Michael Schiavo hired a lawyer to write the Schindlers a letter about $644 they owed him.[47]

On July 16, 1993, Bob and Mary Schindler wrote Michael Schiavo a letter, telling him how it upset them to be excluded from making decisions about Terri's care. They also reminded him that he had made a commitment to use the award proceeds to enhance Terri's long-term care, including buying a house so that the Schindlers could live with Terri and care for her.[48] The letter concluded, "On a long-term basis, we would like you to consider giving Terri back to us, so we can give her the love and care she deserves. Logically and realistically you still have a life ahead of you. Give this some thought. Are you ready to dedicate the rest of your life to Terri? We are! Let us know your fellings [*sic*]."[49]

At the end of July, receiving no response from Michael Schiavo, Bob and Mary Schindler sued in a Florida court to have Schiavo removed as Terri's legal guardian.[50] Judge Thomas Penick appointed a local lawyer, John H. Pecarek, as *guardian ad litem*. The job of the *guardian ad litem* is to investigate the allegations and report back to the judge. The *guardian ad litem* acts as an advocate for the incapacitated person (in this case Terri Schiavo) and examines whether the guardian (Michael Schiavo) is acting in her best interest.

A deposition of Michael Schiavo taken on November 19, 1993, revealed that he had come to believe that Terri was not going to recover. Terri's treating physician, Dr. Patrick Mulroy, had entered a do-not-resuscitate (DNR) order in Terri's medical chart following conversations with Michael Schiavo. A DNR order provides that in the event of cardiac arrest, the medical team will not use CPR or other resuscitation techniques to restart the heart. (These orders are discussed in detail in Chapter 8.)

In addition, that fall Terri had developed a urinary tract infection, and after talking with Dr. Mulroy, Michael had requested that the staff at Sabal Palms not treat the infection with antibiotics. The Schindlers' lawyer, James Sheehan, asked Schiavo about his conversation with Dr. Mulroy.[51]

"I talked to him about what he felt Terri's future was," Schiavo testified. "And he told me that Terri is basically going to be like this for the rest of her life, and I was trying to make decisions on what Terri would want." Sheehan asked Schiavo how he determined what Terri would want. "She was my wife," Schiavo answered. "I lived with her. We shared things. We shared a bed. We shared our thoughts." Michael told Sheehan about an uncle who emerged from a coma, but was dependent on his mother for care. Schiavo testified that Terri said, "I would never want to live like that. I would want to just die."[52] The nursing home had objected to Michael's instructions, however, claiming that the law compelled them to treat the infection. Michael Schiavo allowed the infection to be treated.

Schiavo also testified that day in November of 1993 about a conversation he'd had just the day before with another doctor, Dr. Harrison, who had performed an electroencephalogram (EEG) on Terri, a test to try to measure the electrical activity in her brain. Dr. Harrison sat Michael Schiavo down and talked with him about not treating the next infection, or removing her feeding tube. "[Dr. Harrison] said to me that this woman died four years ago."[53] Schiavo testified that he said about removal of the feeding tube at that time, "I couldn't do that to Terri."[54]

Three months later, on March 1, 1994, Judge Penick held a hearing in the case. The *guardian ad litem*, John Pecarek, both testified and delivered a written report to the court. That report concluded that no basis existed to remove Michael Schiavo as guardian, that he had been meticulous in his care for Terri and demanding of the staff—a "nursing home administrator's nightmare"—which resulted in Terri receiving extra attention.[55] Advocates for the Schindlers later pointed out the contradiction of meticulous care and refusing to treat a potentially deadly infection. After the hearing, the Schindlers amended their petition and sought to continue the litigation, but fearing high legal fees, they voluntarily dismissed their lawsuit in the fall of 1995, and Michael Schiavo remained Terri's guardian.[56]

The relationship between Michael Schiavo and Bob and Mary Schindler then settled into a fragile truce with periodic skirmishes for a couple of years, until the spring of 1998, when the fight began in earnest.

THE PETITION TO REMOVE TERRI SCHIAVO'S FEEDING TUBE

On May 11, 1998, Michael Schiavo filed a petition in the probate court in Pinellas County, seeking authorization to remove Terri's artificial life support. His lawyer was George Felos, a Tampa Bay-area solo practitioner who had represented the family of Estelle Browning in a 1990 right-to-die case that went to the Florida Supreme Court. One month later, the court appointed a second *guardian ad litem*, Richard L. Pearse, to investigate the case. Mr. Pearse filed his 16-page report six months later on December 30, 1998.

Pearse reported to the judge that Dr. Jeffrey Karp had performed the most recent neurological evaluation on Terri. Dr. Karp noted "an absence of voluntary activity or cognitive behavior, and [an] inability to communicate or interact purposefully with her environment." He called the condition a "chronic vegetative state" and concluded that, based on the duration of the condition, "her chance of any improvement to a functional level is essentially zero."[57] Her primary physician, Dr. Vincent Gambone, concurred in that assessment.

Pearse noted that Mary Schindler believed that Terri reacted to her, which Mrs. Schindler "ascribes to some kind of low-level cognitive function." Nursing home staff who saw similar reactions, described them as "random and not predictably in response to any specific stimulus."[58]

The report also chronicled for the judge the falling out between the Schindlers and Michael Schiavo, the amount of money involved in that falling out, Michael Schiavo's aggressive treatment for Terri for four years after the accident, and then his change of course when he concluded that Terri was not going to recover consciousness. Pearse outlined what Michael Schiavo had told him about a conversation he and Terri had on a train trip from Pennsylvania to Florida in the 1980s. They had talked about her uncle who suffered severe injuries in a car wreck. Terri told Michael "that if she were ever in a situation of being artificially maintained that she wanted the life support removed."[59]

Pearse concluded his report by recommending that the judge deny the petition to remove life support. He found a conflict of interest because of the money Michael Schiavo stood to inherit at Terri's death, and found Schiavo's credibility compromised by the timing of his decision. He had sought aggressive care until receiving the large malpractice award, at which point he refused consent to treat an infection. Pearse also stated that if the judge on reviewing the evidence did not have similar concerns, then under Florida law "the feeding tube should be withdrawn."[60]

Almost ten months later, on September 27, 1999, the lawyer for the Schindlers, Pam Campbell, took a two-hour deposition of Michael Schiavo. Sitting in a small conference room in a court reporter's office were Campbell, Michael Schiavo, his lawyer George Felos, a court reporter, and Mary Schindler.

Pam Campbell wasted no time, beginning the questioning by asking Michael Schiavo about his girlfriend, Jodi Centonze. Campbell confirmed that Schiavo and Ms. Centonze had begun living together in 1995, and that they had recently bought a house together. After that, the deposition focused extensively on Terri Schiavo's medical history. Schiavo told Campbell that he still visited Terri, now over nine years after the cardiac arrest, once or twice a week for an hour to hour and a half. He told her that he never saw any kind of response from Terri in all of the visits over the entire nine years. He said that now they often sat in her room as he watched *The Price Is Right* on television and that he would dry her hair and put away her clean laundry that he'd done at home.

In response to a question about any hospitalizations during the past six years, Schiavo could not remember specifics, but he told Campbell that Terri had had her gall bladder removed, a D&C (dilation and curettage), a toe amputated (a result of compromised circulation), and said she'd "been hospitalized I believe two or three or four times for urinary tract infections."[61]

To end the deposition, Campbell asked Michael Schiavo if he'd been paid to serve as his wife's guardian. He told her he'd received no money, only reimbursement for supplies. She closed by asking him about the Schindlers:

Q: Have you considered turning the guardianship over to Mr. and Mrs. Schindler?

A: No, I have not.

Q: And why?

A: I think that's pretty self-explanatory.

Q: I'd like to hear your answer.

A: Basically I don't want to do it.

Q: And why don't you want to do it?

A: Because they put me through pretty much hell the last few years.

Q: And can you describe what you mean by hell?

A: The litigations they put me through.

Q: Any other specifics besides the litigation?

A: Just their attitude towards me because of the litigations. There is no other reason. I'm Terri's husband and I will remain guardian.[62]

The First Trial

Four months later, on January 24, 2000, Florida probate judge George Greer took the bench on Monday morning for the trial of *In Re: The Guardianship of Theresa Marie Schiavo, Incapacitated*. There was no jury; the case would be decided by the judge. Over the course of a full week, Judge Greer heard from eighteen witnesses, including family, friends, and medical providers for Terri Schiavo. He watched videotapes, reviewed CT scans, and received extensive medical records.[63] The courtroom was mostly empty. A polite, church-going Baptist and a conservative Republican described by a friend as a member of the "Religious Right," Judge Greer likely had no idea that day of the path ahead of him.

After brief opening statements from George Felos and Pam Campbell, Felos called Michael Schiavo as his first witness. Felos and Schiavo spent a little over an hour telling Judge Greer Terri's story to that point. At the end of that testimony, the judge gave everyone a morning break. As she left the courtroom, Campbell saw a reporter from the *St. Petersburg Times*, Anita Kumar, in the courtroom. Kumar was the lone reporter there.[64]

"What are you doing here?" she asked the reporter, surprised.[65] In the two years since it was filed in 1998, the case had not yet generated any real news.

Assembled back in the courtroom before testimony resumed, George Felos asked the judge if they could approach the bench. He and Pam Campbell walked to the judge's dais, Felos leaned in, and spoke quietly. "Your Honor, my client requests that the proceedings not be recorded by the media, and he believes that it would impair the privacy rights of the ward and we make that request."

"What is the legal basis for that? Is there any authority for keeping the media out of here?" asked the judge.

"I have not researched the issue, Your Honor. I have no case to present."

Felos and Judge Greer discussed juvenile proceedings, and incompetency hearings, where the media can sometimes be excluded. The judge did not think those cases applied.

"This is different," he said. Then he turned to the Schindlers' lawyer. "Do you know of any authority?" he asked Campbell.

"I don't know any," she replied. "While I'd like to see it agreed to, I don't know of any legal authority that we could."

The judge made up his mind. "Absent authority, I don't know how I can ask them to leave," he said. He offered to give the lawyers an extended recess, to see if they could prevail upon the reporter to leave. The lawyers decided just to proceed.[66]

CHAPTER 2

Terri Schiavo's Public Years

January 2000–March 31, 2005

ON FEBRUARY 11, 2000, two weeks shy of the ten-year anniversary of Terri Schiavo's collapse, Judge Greer ruled that her husband could stop tube feeding. The judge made the ruling in a ten-page, single-spaced written opinion, published thirteen days after the week-long trial ended. (The decisions of judges are called "opinions," but they are not opinions in the usual sense of the word, like "I don't like that shade of green"—they are rulings.)

Judge Greer spent only one paragraph of the entire opinion on Terri Schiavo's medical condition, concluding "beyond all doubt," based on the testimony and medical records, that she was in a persistent vegetative state, with "no hope of ever regaining consciousness."[1] Mrs. Schindler had testified that Terri responded to her, and the judge had watched videotape of their interaction. He also heard from other family members who did not think she responded, and from nurses and doctors with the same reaction. He concluded, "The overwhelming credible evidence is that Terri Schiavo has been totally unresponsive since lapsing into the coma almost ten years ago, that her movements are reflexive and predicated on brainstem activity alone, that she suffers from severe structural brain damage and to a large extent her brain has been replaced by spinal fluid. . . . The testimony of Dr. Barnhill establishes that Terri Schiavo's reflex actions such as breathing and movement shows merely that her brain stem and spinal cord are intact."[2]

The judge spent the bulk of his ten pages trying to determine what, given that irreversible condition, Terri Schiavo's wishes would be if she could speak. Five witnesses testified to conversations they'd had with Terri Schiavo about life support. Mrs. Schindler, and a childhood friend of Terri's, Diane Meyer, recalled conversations with Terri about the famous Karen Ann Quinlan case from New Jersey, decided by the New Jersey Supreme Court in 1976. Mrs. Schindler remembered watching television coverage with Terri, and Terri saying, "Just leave her alone. Leave her. If they take her off, she might die. Just leave her alone, and she will die whenever."[3] Diane Meyer testified, "One of the things Terri said is, 'How did they know Quinlan would want this?' "[4]

On cross-examination, George Felos handed to Mary Schindler newspaper clippings about the *Quinlan* case that showed that the court battle had taken place in 1976. Felos pointed out that Terri would have had to have been only about twelve years old when these conversations happened.[5] No one could remember the dates exactly, but Mrs. Schindler and Diane Meyer thought that Terri was a teenager when the conversations took place.

Judge Greer wrote that Diane Meyer testified her conversation happened in 1982, but Meyer and Terri had talked about Karen Quinlan in the present tense. "The court is mystified as to how these present tense verbs would have been used some six years after the death of Karen Ann Quinlan," the judge wrote.[6] Years later as the media light intensified, the lawyers and judge learned that they'd had the facts wrong—the New Jersey Supreme Court did authorize the removal of Karen Ann Quinlan's respirator in 1976, but once it was removed, she breathed on her own. Her feeding tube remained in place, and Karen died nearly ten years later, on June 11, 1985, of pneumonia.[7]

Three witnesses for the petitioner testified about a different outlook from Terri Schiavo. Michael Schiavo told the judge about a train trip from Florida back to Philadelphia after Terri's grandmother had died. According to Michael, Terri said to him on that train, "If I ever have to be a burden to anybody, I don't want to live like that." Schiavo said Terri had made similar statements once while watching a television show about people on feeding tubes.[8]

Michael Schiavo's sister-in-law, Joan, married to his older brother William Schiavo, also testified. Joan and Terri were good friends. Joan said that she had talked about the right to die with Terri at least twelve times. One time the conversation started as they watched a movie about a man in a coma. Many times it came up as they talked about a friend who had to remove a feeding tube from a baby. Joan summed up Terri's view this way: "If that ever happened to one of us, in our lifetime, we would not want to go through that. That we would want it stated in our will we would want the tubes and everything taken out."[9]

Another of Michael's brothers, Scott Schiavo, testified about his conversation with Terri at the Buck Hotel in Langhorne, Pennsylvania, over lunch in 1988. The family had gathered following the funeral of a Schiavo grandmother who had spent her final days hooked up to machines, against her wishes. Terri told Scott Schiavo at that table, "If I ever go like that, just let me go. Don't leave me there. I don't want to be kept alive on a machine."[10]

In weighing this evidence, Judge Greer reasoned that statements Terri Schiavo had made about others (the Karen Quinlan discussions and the repeated talks with Joan Schiavo about the removal of a feeding tube from a baby) were not as useful as statements Terri had made about what she would want for herself in a particular situation. He found the statements made to Michael Schiavo and Joan Schiavo after watching television, and to Scott Schiavo at the funeral luncheon, were more reliable. The judge concluded that, taken together, the statements rose to the level required by Florida law of clear and convincing evidence of her intent.[11]

Terri Schiavo's statements fit with testimony the judge heard from experts about what most people want—to try treatment "for a while," but not to leave the treatment in place for an extended time with no hope of improvement. "That implicit condition has long since been satisfied in this case,"[12] the judge wrote, and he granted Michael Schiavo's petition.

The next day the story hit the front page of the *St. Petersburg Times* with a headline that read, "Judge: Schiavo's Life Can End." The almost 1200-word story was accompanied by a color photo of Michael visiting Terri.[13] Soon after, *People* magazine and *Dateline NBC* arrived, and the bitter, private family dispute began to make its journey into the public eye.[14] Bobby Schindler, Terri's younger brother, said at the time, "If Terri knew what this had done to this family, she would go ballistic."[15] And the courtroom battles and publicity were only beginning.

Shortly after receiving the trial court decision, Michael Schiavo moved Terri from her nursing home to the Hospice House Woodside in Pinellas Park, Florida. The facility is run by a large Florida nonprofit hospice named The Hospice of the Florida Suncoast. Hospice care typically takes place in a person's home, but some hospice organizations have inpatient facilities like Woodside. Wherever the patient is, the philosophy of hospice is to focus on relieving symptoms and supporting patients who have a limited life expectancy of six months or less, as well as supporting their families. The medical focus switches from curing to comforting.

The Palm Gardens nursing home where Terri had lived the prior six years (she moved from Sabal Palms to Palm Gardens in 1994) had grown concerned about security and unwanted notoriety after the trial verdict, so Michael had Terri moved after Judge Greer handed down his decision. The Schindlers went back to the judge to oppose this move to hospice.

"To me, it's quite clear what's going on here," said Bobby Schindler, Terri's brother. "He wants her to die before the appeal can go through." The Schindlers ultimately agreed to the hospice when Schiavo lawyers said that they would inform the Schindlers before Michael made any decision to withhold treatment.[16]

THE FIRST APPEAL

The Schindler's appeal of Judge Greer's decision went to the Florida Second District Court of Appeals. This is the level of appellate court between the trial and supreme court in a state. As with most cases, a three-judge panel was assigned to the case. During the appeals process, Terri Schiavo's feeding tube remained in place. Judge Greer had entered an order called a *stay*. With a stay, a lower court decision is not implemented until the parties have the chance to go to an appeals court to seek relief from the lower court order.

Those three judges read written briefs from the parties, heard oral argument, and deliberated. Nearly one year after the trial, on January 24, 2001, the judges issued a ten-page, double-spaced unanimous opinion, affirming Judge Greer's decision to permit the removal of Terri's feeding tube. Judge Altenbernd, who wrote the opinion in which Judges Parker and Blue concurred, began like this: "Theresa has been blessed with loving parents and a loving husband."[17]

The opinion marveled at Michael Schiavo's devotion, and likewise admired Terri's parents: "No one questions the sincerity of their prayers for the divine miracle that now is Theresa's only hope to regain any level of normal existence. No one questions that they have filed this appeal out of love for their daughter."[18] The judge also wrote that while the Schindlers and Michael Schiavo had each become suspicious that the other was motivated by the money from the malpractice lawsuit, the appellate court did not see that motivation in the trial record. "Michael and the Schindlers simply cannot agree on what decision Theresa would make today if she were able to assess her own condition and make her own decision."[19]

The appellate court concluded that Judge Greer had clear and convincing evidence of Terri Schiavo's wish for a "natural death" when faced with "not a few weeks in a coma, but after ten years in a persistent vegetative state that has robbed her of most of her cerebrum and all but the most instinctive of neurological functions, with no hope of a medical cure but with sufficient money and strength of body to live indefinitely . . ."[20]

The decision by the court of appeals triggered a flurry of filings by the Schindlers in different courts, which lasted throughout the spring of 2001.[21] One by one, the different courts turned down these requests, culminating on Wednesday, April 18, 2001, when the Florida Supreme Court said it would not hear an appeal in the case.[22] With the feeding tube scheduled for removal on Friday at 1:00 p.m., the Schindlers' lawyers scrambled to stop it. That Friday morning, a federal district judge in Tampa, Richard Lazzara, granted the Schindlers a stay until the following Monday, to give them the chance to exhaust all possible appeals. On Monday, Justice Anthony Kennedy of the U.S. Supreme Court refused to stay the case for a review in the highest Court.[23] The Schindlers got the word about 4:00 p.m.

"They're so devastated," said a family friend. "It's a sin; they were hopeful up until the very last minute."[24] One of their lawyers said he did not know of any other legal avenues. "That's the end of the line," he said. George Felos told reporters that Michael Schiavo was relieved to have the final word that the U.S. Supreme Court had refused to hear the Schindlers' appeal. "He is in a state of shock that the legal proceedings are at an end," Felos said.[25]

ARTIFICAL NUTRITION AND HYDRATION DISCONTINUED

The next afternoon, on Tuesday, April 24, 2001, Terri Schiavo's artificial nutrition and hydration was discontinued.[26] The feeding tube surgically inserted in her stomach was not removed; instead Michael Schiavo simply instructed doctors to stop the tube feeding.[27] The hospice team continued to provide comfort care.

Two days later, on Thursday, the Schindlers filed a completely new lawsuit in the general civil courts of St. Petersburg. The suit sought an order for emergency resumption of tube feeding based on newly-discovered evidence. The papers claimed that a former girlfriend of Michael Schiavo's would testify that Schiavo had told her that he and

Terri had never discussed Terri's wishes and that Michael Schiavo therefore may have committed perjury at the trial before Judge Greer. Affidavits of Mr. Schindler and a private investigator, describing what the witness told them, were attached to the filing.[28] The lawsuit also sought monetary damages for the mental anguish Schiavo had caused the Schindlers.

Under the normal procedures for case assignment, the papers went to Judge Frank Quesada on the afternoon of April 26, 2001, and he scheduled an emergency hearing for 7:15 that Thursday evening.[29] As the court of appeals wrote later, "Judge Quesada was given an unenviable task in this case. Late in the day he received an emergency motion involving the life of a young woman."[30] He knew little of the case, and the pleadings and affidavits before him were hastily and "poorly drafted."[31] The judge issued his order to resume tube feeding about an hour after he'd begun the hearing, at 8:30 that evening; hospice staff resumed feeding within minutes of that order.[32] The front-page headline of the *St. Petersburg Times* the next day reported the decision: "Doctors Resume Feeding Schiavo."[33]

The former girlfriend, whom Bob Schindler and the private investigator had described in their affidavits, Cindy Shook, told a reporter that the Schindlers had taken her statements out of context, claiming that all she remembered was Michael Schiavo saying that he did not know whether Terri would have wanted to stay in a nursing home or move to her parents' home. Shook told the reporter that, contrary to the affidavit of Bob Schindler, she had not talked with Michael about life support.[34] It did not matter—the court system was once again engaged.

THE FLORIDA APPEALS COURT (*SCHIAVO* II AND *SCHIAVO* III)

The same three judges who heard the first *Schiavo* appeal listened to oral arguments from the lawyers again on June 25, 2001.[35] They issued an eleven-page, single-spaced opinion seventeen days later. The opinion appeared to give the Schindlers a chance at a new trial based on "significant new evidence or substantial changes in circumstances arising after the entry of the judgment."[36] The court gave as examples of evidence that might warrant a new trial the discovery of a lost living will, or medical research discovering a complete cure for what had previously been thought to be a terminal condition.

Back in the trial court, Judge Greer quickly dismissed the Schindler petition as not meeting that standard for new evidence. He once again set a date for removal of the feeding tube—October 9.[37] The Schindlers headed back to the court of appeals in mid-summer of 2001 and with different lawyers: Patricia Fields Anderson and Lawrence D. Crow.[38] The Schindlers argued that Terri Schiavo needed an updated medical exam.[39] This new petition had doctors' affidavits attached, including one from Dr. Fred Webber of Clearwater. Dr. Webber claimed that he had "treated patients with brain defects similar to Mrs. Schiavo's [and that] in most cases, using cardiovascular medication style of therapy, my patients have shown some improvement."[40]

While the appellate court "expressed skepticism," it hesitated, noting the difficulty for judges untrained in medicine to reject medical affidavits without additional evidence.[41] The court issued its third opinion in the case, and ordered Judge Greer to conduct a new trial, with five doctors—two from each side, and one independent—to assess Terri Schiavo's current medical condition, and the "probable efficacy" of the new medical treatments discussed in the Webber affidavit.[42] For the time being, the Schindlers had won.

THE SECOND TRIAL: OCTOBER 2002

It would take a full year before that new trial happened. During that time, Michael Schiavo's lawyer went to the Florida Supreme Court in an effort to stop the trial, arguing in essence that there were no new treatments or new questions about Terri's medical condition.[43] The parties also attempted to mediate their dispute. On December 19, 2001, a court-appointed mediator shuttled back and forth between the two groups in a day-long effort to resolve the case. They did not reach agreement, but Pat Anderson, the Schindlers' lawyer, said she "remained hopeful." They were discussing the idea of having doctors examine Terri again and come to a definitive diagnosis. Ultimately, the two sides could not agree on doctors, and George Felos filed a notice with the Florida Supreme Court in February 2002, indicating that the talks had reached an impasse.[44]

Eight months later the parties were back in front of Judge Greer for the new trial, which began on October 11, 2002, and ended on October 22. The trial was mainly medical testimony and generated surprisingly little public attention. On the first morning of trial the judge saw hours of videotape, some of Terri appearing to smile at her mother. "Obviously, there's awareness there," Bob Schindler said to a reporter that day. "She's not in a vegetative state." Michael Schiavo had a different reaction: "She's done that for thirteen years," he said, describing the reactions as involuntary. "It proves nothing."[45] The doctors over the next several days had similar contradictory opinions.

Judge Greer, who listened to it all, issued his nine-page, single-spaced order one month after the hearing, on November 22, 2002. In the opinion, the judge tackled two questions: Terri Schiavo's medical condition, and the promise for her of new treatments. The judge noted that all five doctors brought impressive credentials, including board certification, and that all had prepared well. Much of the testimony revolved around the extensive videotape of Terri Schiavo. In one particular sequence she appears to smile at her mother; in another, her eyes appear to follow a balloon held by her father. The judge found that such "actions were neither consistent nor reproducible."[46]

He wrote that Terri Schiavo appeared to have the same look on her face when a doctor rubbed her neck and when she simply was being examined by another doctor; that Mr. Schindler tried many times to have her follow the balloon, without success; and that she did not respond consistently to Mrs. Schindler.

The judge also raised questions about one of the expert witnesses for the Schindlers, Dr. William Hammesfahr, a neurologist. The doctor testified that "he was able to get Terri Schiavo to reproduce repeatedly to his commands." But Judge Greer wrote that between Dr. Hammesfahr and Mrs. Schindler, they gave Terri 111 commands on the video, and asked her 72 questions, eliciting "few actions that could be considered responsive."[47] The judge concluded that the evidence "overwhelmingly" supported the diagnosis of a persistent vegetative state.

The "real issue," according to Judge Greer—the main charge from the appellate court above—was to discover whether new treatments could "significantly improve her quality of life."[48] The judge defined "new treatment" as any treatment that had not been tried with Terri before. Dr. William Maxfield, a radiologist, testified that hyperbaric therapy offered a "significant probability" that Terri Schiavo would improve in her cognitive ability. Dr. Peter Bambakidis (the independent expert chosen by the court), and Dr. Ronald Cranford and Dr. Melvin Greer (no relation to Judge Greer), the two doctors chosen by Michael Schiavo, all neurologists, had referred patients for this therapy, but none with a brain injury like Terri's. They testified that the therapy would have no effect on her. The judge also noted that the treatment was over a century old, and yet there was no case study in the medical literature of treating a vegetative-state patient with hyperbaric therapy.[49]

Dr. Hammesfahr told Judge Greer that "only rarely" did patients treated with his vasodilatation therapy fail to improve and that he should be able to get Terri to talk. He told the judge that he had "treated about fifty patients in the same or worse condition than Terri Schiavo since 1994" and that he had success in all but one case. Judge Greer found it "inconceivable" that a doctor could make such an astounding claim, and then not produce case studies, test results, video, or any other supporting evidence: ". . . Surely the medical literature would be replete with this new, now patented, procedure," he wrote. But Dr. Hammesfahr testified that he knew of no articles linking the procedure and treatment of the vegetative state. The judge also noted that the doctor's clinic was operated on a cash-in-advance basis.[50]

Judge Greer wrote that the court of appeals in *Schiavo* III had directed him to find whether a "preponderance of evidence" existed that the new treatment proposed offered "sufficient promise of increased cognitive function in Mrs. Schiavo's cerebral cortex so as to significantly improve her quality of life." The judge concluded, "There is no such testimony, much less a preponderance of the evidence to that effect." He denied the Schindler motion for Relief from the Judgment, and set January 3, 2003, at 3:00 p.m., for the withdrawal of artificial life support.[51] Shortly after that, however, Judge Greer once again granted the Schindlers a stay of his order so that they could appeal his decision.[52]

Any efforts at mediating the dispute were completely shattered in the days leading up to Judge Greer's opinion. On November 12, 2002, lawyers for the Schindlers filed a motion asking the judge to delay issuing his opinion. They claimed that a newly-discovered medical record, a 1991 bone scan, showed that Terri Schiavo had been beaten, which caused her vegetative state. George Felos replied that the bone scan showed the type of degenerative loss that doctors would expect from someone who had been paralyzed for that amount of time. "What it is, is garbage," an angry Felos told reporters.[53] Any chance at compromise was finished.

SCHIAVO IV: JUNE 2003

Six months later, now fourteen years after Terri Schiavo's collapse, the court of appeals issued its fourth opinion in the case. At this stage, the court received briefs filed on behalf of the Schindlers by different advocacy groups, mostly disability rights and anti-abortion groups such as the International Task Force on Euthanasia and Assisted Suicide.[54] The appellate judges expressed surprise that Dr. Fred Webber, "who was so critical in this court's decision to remand the case" in *Schiavo* III, did not testify in the latest trial.[55] (Dr. Webber was the Clearwater doctor who had submitted an affidavit in the previous appeal, *Schiavo* III, in which he claimed that he had seen improvement in patients like Terri Schiavo by using cardiovascular-medication style therapy.)

The appellate court also noted that while the two doctors for the Schindlers did not agree with the diagnosis of PVS, they did agree that Terri Schiavo had "extensive permanent damage to her brain," their sole contention being that she had "a small amount of isolated living tissue in her cerebral cortex."[56]

The court reasoned that in all likelihood the case had received the most detailed presentation of "medical evidence" of any guardianship court in history. It concluded that the initial trial decision, now almost three-and-a-half years old, was right: Terri Schiavo remained in a permanently unconscious, persistent vegetative state, and her clear wish in such case would be to have the feeding tube removed. The judges also tried to put themselves in the Schindlers' shoes: "Each of us, however, has our own [children]. If Mrs. Schiavo were our own daughter, we could not but hold to such faith," that some awareness remained.[57]

It appeared that the Schindlers were finally out of options. On July 9, 2003, the court of appeals refused to reconsider its decision. One month later the Florida Supreme Court refused to review the decision. The Schindlers tried federal court, but federal judge Richard Lazzara quickly dismissed the suit, ruling that the Schindlers had no basis to come to federal court.[58] On Tuesday, October 14, 2003, the Florida Court of Appeals refused to block Judge Greer's order to discontinue artificial nutrition and hydration.

On Wednesday, October 15, 2003, at 2 p.m., artificial nutrition and hydration was stopped for the second time. This time, doctors completely removed the feeding tube that had been surgically implanted in Terri Schiavo's stomach.[59] The Schindlers' attorney, Pat Anderson, said, "There's nothing left to do legally."[60]

OPERATION RESCUE AND THE BIRTH OF TERRI'S LAW

But rumblings had been coming from arenas other than the courts for several days. Governor Jeb Bush of Florida had filed papers in the federal lawsuit in support of the Schindlers, and Florida legislators were discussing the case. Activists were also pondering their options.

Four days before the feeding tube was removed, on Saturday, October 11, 2003, Mary Parker Lewis, a staffer for conservative radio host and former presidential candidate Alan Keyes, along with Phil Sheldon, a conservative activist, had telephoned Randall Terry, founder of the anti-abortion group, Operation Rescue. They told Terry that he needed to head south, to St. Petersburg. Soon the three had tracked down Bob Schindler by cell phone. Randall Terry explained the publicity Operation Rescue could create. Schindler said to Terry, "Please come."

On Sunday night, Randall Terry arrived in St. Petersburg with his media assistant. They sat down with the Schindler family and others and sketched out a simple plan: protest vigil, media attention, and significant pressure applied directly to Governor Bush, an anti-abortion Republican.[61] On Monday, Randall Terry held a press conference. On Tuesday, he released to the press a videotape of Terri Schiavo that her parents had secretly filmed, in violation of an order of Judge Greer. In front of the hospice house where Terri Schiavo was a patient, protest groups began to form.[62] Bob Schindler later said when explaining how the protests began, "Our family asked Randall Terry to come, and we gave him carte blanche to put Terri's fight in front of the American people. He did exactly what we asked, and more."[63]

In Tallahassee, the Florida state capital, e-mail and phone calls began to pour in with messages from people pleading for Terri Schiavo's life: "If a person in Florida stopped feeding and watering their dog, they would be punished for cruelty to animals. This is a human life we are talking about here," wrote a woman from Phoenix, Arizona in an e-mail to Governor Bush.[64] The governor later said that 160,000 people contacted him.[65] Pressure was building.

On Sunday, October 19, 2003, four days after the removal of Terri Schiavo's feeding tube, Republican lawmakers in Florida talked by phone about ways to take up the *Schiavo* case in a special legislative session on economic development that was scheduled to begin the next day. As Governor Bush opened the special session that Monday and talked to legislators about his plan to attract the biomedical Scripps Research Institute to Florida, key lawmakers were exchanging handwritten notes with ideas for changing Florida law to allow for reinserting Terri Schiavo's feeding tube.[66] Outside the legislative chamber, lawyers and staffers for the governor and lawmakers were debating options and drafting bills.

The law came to life with lightning speed. At 7:44 p.m. on Monday evening, Gov. Bush added a bill for Terri Schiavo to the special session agenda. Minutes later, Republican representative John Stargel from Lakeland rose to explain the bill on the House floor. The law was quite simple, allowing the governor fifteen days to order a feeding tube reinserted for a patient who did not have a living will. After limited debate, the House passed the bill at 10:10 p.m. A Senate committee heard the bill first thing on Tuesday, October 21, 2003, and approval of a slightly-revised version of the House bill came from the full Senate around 3:30 p.m. by a 23-15 vote. The Florida House passed the new version by a 73-24 vote around 4 p.m., and the Governor signed the bill into law at 4:30.[67]

Around 5:00 p.m., Bob Schindler spoke by cell phone to Governor Bush. At 5:36 p.m., Pat Anderson, the Schindlers' attorney, forced her way through the crowd at the hospice and handed one of the five Pinellas Park police officers blocking the hospice entrance a copy of Governor Bush's order that the feeding tube be reinserted. The crowd of about 100 protesters cheered and began to sing "Amazing Grace." Around 6:30 p.m., an ambulance arrived and soon took Terri Schiavo to Morton Plant Hospital, flanked by police cruisers.[68] The atmosphere resembled a sports celebration gone awry, as television news coverage that evening appeared to capture what looked like a beer bottle smashed over the ambulance as it left.[69]

Terri Schiavo's longtime physician, Dr. Victor Gambone, refused to insert the feeding tube and resigned as her doctor rather than take part in the procedure.[70] Hospital officials had difficulty finding a doctor to insert the tube, though one ultimately was found, and the procedure was performed to reinsert the feeding tube around 11:00 p.m.[71] The doctor's name was not released.

From all sides, reaction came swiftly to the law that people soon began to call "Terri's Law." The unprecedented legislative intervention and ordering of the feeding tube reinsertion moved the dispute firmly onto the national front page. Michael Schiavo, who had shied away from the media for years (in an effort to maintain his wife's privacy, according to his lawyer), made the decision to speak publicly on CNN's *Larry King Live* on Monday, October 27, 2003. Schiavo appeared pale, tired, and angry. When Larry King asked why he didn't simply move on with his life, Schiavo said, "This is Terri's wish, this is Terri's choice. And I'm going to follow that wish if it's the last thing I can do for Terri."[72]

BACK TO THE COURTS

The next day Schiavo's lawyers began a new legal battle, challenging Terri's Law as unconstitutional.[73] The litigation over Terri's Law took over a year. The media attention was fairly muted during this drawn-out legal process. During the winter of 2003–04, the new Schindler-Bush legal team and the Schiavo lawyers skirmished over a variety of issues: Could Governor Bush conduct new depositions? Should the new trial judge for this constitutional case, W. Douglas Baird, be disqualified?

The chief judge of the trial courts appointed an independent *guardian ad litem*, Jay Wolfson, to investigate the case, as required by Terri's Law. It would be the third *guardian ad litem* appointed in the dispute, now stretching more than a decade. This guardian's report was 38 pages and essentially concluded that Judge Greer had gotten the decision right.[74] The Bush-Schindler team disputed the quality of the report and the independence of the *guardian ad litem*.[75]

In the end, the dispute over the report did not really matter. On May 6, 2004, Judge Baird struck down Terri's Law as unconstitutional. In an at times stinging 22-page rebuke the judge, a Republican, concluded: "It is difficult to imagine a clearer deprivation of a judicially vested right by retroactive legislation than that which has occurred in this case."[76] He ordered Governor Bush's order void and enjoined him from any further action under Terri's Law.

Governor Bush appealed the order, and Michael Schiavo moved to have the appeal taken directly to the Florida Supreme Court (to skip over the intermediate appellate court). That court agreed, and set August 31, 2004, to hear oral arguments.[77] In the courtroom in Tallahassee, Michael Schiavo sat with his brother Brian. Across the aisle, sat Bob and Mary Schindler with Terri's brother and sister. The two sides of Terri Schiavo's family listened, as the seven judges on the raised bench at the front of the courtroom questioned the lawyers. Out front, protesters gathered, including wheelchair-bound members of an Illinois disability-rights group named Not Dead Yet. One protester held a sign reading, "Commute Terri's Death Sentence."[78]

Speaking to reporters outside after the oral argument, Michael

Schiavo bristled. "If this case is so important to the governor, where is he?" Schiavo said. "I don't see him anywhere."[79]

The unanimous ruling of the seven judges came quickly, on September 23, 2004. All seven judges agreed that Terri's Law violated the constitutional requirement of separation of powers. "The cornerstone of American democracy known as separation of powers," the court wrote, "recognizes three separate branches of government—the executive, the legislative, and the judicial—each with its own powers and responsibilities."[80] The court explained the historical underpinnings of the Constitution, and how its drafters sought to avoid the tyranny of unfettered legislative power in England in favor of a more controlled government in America. In Terri's Law, the court saw that separation blurred. "[I]t is without question an invasion of the authority of the judicial branch for the Legislature to pass a law that allows the executive branch to interfere with the final judicial determination in a case. That is precisely what occurred here," with Terri's Law.[81]

Governor Bush announced plans to appeal this decision to the United States Supreme Court, and the Florida courts ordered the feeding tube to remain in place pending the outcome of that appeal. The administrative branch also sought to maneuver around the court orders by attempting to have the Department of Children & Families (or DCF) enter the case, claiming that they were required to investigate claims of abuse. In addition, the Schindlers filed in Florida courts various claims, including the plea that recent pronouncements from the Vatican and the promise of new medical procedures or experimental treatments should prompt Judge Greer to change his decision.[82]

Once again, however, their options were dwindling. On January 24, 2005, the U.S. Supreme Court refused to review Terri's Law.[83] With the final stay about ready to expire, Judge Greer held a hearing on February 23, 2005, with lawyers for both sides present. His order, issued two days later on Friday, February 25, suggested that he believed the legal process had more than run its course. He stated that he would grant no further stays and that no further hearings were needed. He would set "a date certain" for removal of the feeding tube, "so that last rites and other similar matters can be addressed in an orderly manner."[84] He set the date for Friday, March 18 at 1:00 p.m.

On March 7, 2005, the Schindlers appealed this order to the Florida Court of Appeals. On March 10, Judge Greer issued an order denying the Florida Department of Children & Families permission to intervene in the case.[85] On March 16, the court of appeals rejected the Schindlers' appeal. The judges again expressed sympathy, as parents, for the Schindlers, but concluded, "Not only has Mrs. Schiavo's case been given due process, but few, if any, similar cases have ever been afforded this heightened level of process."[86] The court concluded that "given the lack of merit in the issues pursued in this appeal" it would issue its opinion immediately, without stay, and without the option to seek rehearing.[87] (A rehearing is the procedure of going back to an appellate court to request that it reconsider its opinion because it made a mistake of some kind.)

On Thursday, March 17, the Florida Supreme Court turned down an effort by the Florida Department of Children & Families to intervene in the case to investigate claims of abuse to Terri Schiavo. Justice Anthony Kennedy of the U.S. Supreme Court also turned down a request for an emergency stay of proceedings pending appeal.[88]

On the legislative front in Tallahassee, Bob and Mary Schindler met with Governor Jeb Bush and also with key lawmakers, urging new legislation. The Florida House passed a second Terri's Law to block removal of the feeding tube by a 78-37 vote.[89] But in the state Senate a group of Republican senators had grown hesitant after the heavy public criticism of the first Terri's Law. The new legislation went down in a 21-16 vote in the state Senate.[90] The state legislators went home for their Easter recess. All Florida options—judicial, legislative, and executive—finally appeared to have run out.

THE FEDERAL CONGRESS AND PRESIDENT OF THE UNITED STATES

While the drama unfolded in Florida, federal lawmakers in Washington, particularly anti-abortion lawmakers, had been watching the *Schiavo* case closely. As options dwindled in the Florida courts and government, members of the U.S. Congress scrambled to pass legislation before the two-week Easter recess began at the end of the day on Thursday.[91] Powerful House Majority Leader Tom DeLay led the effort. Quickly, the House was able to pass a bill that would move the *Schiavo* case to federal courts. But senators pushing the legislation in their body could not generate similar support, so the bill stalled. Most federal lawmakers headed for planes leaving Washington. A handful of representatives and senators remained, however.

In the early morning hours of Friday, March 18, House leaders announced that they would issue congressional subpoenas to trigger federal protection for Terri Schiavo. When the state courts opened in Florida later that morning, lawyers from the Office of General Counsel of the U.S. House of Representatives filed a motion to intervene in the state case, as well as a motion to delay the removal of the feeding tube, which was scheduled for 1:00 p.m. that coming afternoon. They requested an immediate oral argument on the motions.[92] The motions were based on subpoenas from the House Committee on Government Reform that U.S. Marshals were serving in Florida that morning on Terri and Michael Schiavo, two doctors and a hospice administrator. The federal House committee had scheduled a field hearing in Terri Schiavo's hospice for one week later, on March 25. The subpoenas ordered that Terri Schiavo be present at that hearing, with her feeding tube in working order.[93]

Judge Greer called an emergency hearing in Clearwater, and lawyers for the federal House of Representatives, Michael Schiavo, and the Schindlers, together with reporters, crowded into a conference room. Judge Greer did not attend in person, instead remaining in an undisclosed location under armed guard. At 12:30 p.m., he reached the conference room by cell phone and started the hearing. It ended quickly. Judge Greer told the lead federal government lawyer: "And while you're only asking for nine days, counselor, I must remind you that the order you want me to modify is over five years old. So there's been lots of time, if Congress wished to investigate, they certainly could have done that. I don't think legislative agencies or bodies have any business in a court proceeding. And, accordingly, I'm going to deny your motion to intervene . . . [T]he fact that your committee chose to do something today doesn't create an emergency, sir. I'm sorry. My order will stand."[94]

The hearing concluded at 1:34 p.m., and at 1:45 p.m., a doctor at the hospice removed Terri Schiavo's feeding tube. Michael Schiavo did not watch; he waited outside his wife's room. When a staff person told him that the tube had been taken out, he came to his wife's bedside and wept.[95] In Washington that afternoon, Tom DeLay said during a press conference, "It's not over." Late Friday, House Republicans "were told to remain accessible throughout the weekend."[96]

Over cell phones and behind closed doors, leaders from both the House and Senate scrambled to draft emergency legislation. By late Saturday it appeared they had reached that goal. In a rare Saturday night session of the U.S. Senate that was attended by only three senators, Senate Majority Leader Bill Frist, Mel Martinez from Florida, and John Warner from Virginia, Senator Frist said, "Under the legislation we will soon consider, Terri Schiavo will have another chance."[97]

The next day, Palm Sunday, all three branches of the federal government sprang to action. The proposed federal law, titled "For the relief of the parents of Theresa Marie Schiavo," came before emergency sessions of both the House and the Senate. The main thrust of the law was to provide a new trial for Terri Schiavo in federal court. Again, the three senators took the floor on Sunday, and they passed the bill by unanimous vote in a ten-minute session.

The House of Representatives met for four minutes, and the bill did not come to a vote because eight Democratic House members stood ready to block the bill under rules in place for weekend sessions. The House leadership announced that the vote would come shortly after midnight when the voting rules changed.

After notice of the midnight vote that early Sunday morning, March 20, Republican lawmakers scrambled to return to Washington in time. President George W. Bush had spoken with his brother, Florida Governor Jeb Bush, on Friday. On Sunday, the president cut short his vacation and returned to Washington from his Texas ranch. He told staff to wake him as soon as the bill was ready to sign.[98]

The clerk's office at the federal court in Tampa agreed to open at midnight to accept the new lawsuit that the Schindlers' lawyers planned to file. All six federal judges in Tampa agreed to be on call that night. The case would be assigned randomly by computer, as all new cases were.[99]

The debate in the U.S. House on Sunday evening was frequently emotional, often uninformed, and at times both. The congressmen mispronounced Terri Schiavo's name and badly distorted her medical diagnosis. Tom DeLay, the public face of the extraordinary federal legislative effort, stood and said, "A young woman in Florida is being dehydrated and starved to death. For 58 long hours her mouth has been parched and her hunger pains have been throbbing. . . She is alive. She is still one of us. And this cannot stand."[100] The final vote passed, 203-58, at 12:41 a.m. Clerks then rushed it to the White House for signing. President George W. Bush signed the law at 1:11 a.m.[101]

At 3:46 a.m. on Monday, March 21, lawyers for Terri Schiavo's parents filed their motion in federal court in Tampa. The case fell by random assignment to U.S. District Judge James D. Whittemore, a 1998 Clinton appointee. The judge scheduled a hearing for 3:00 that afternoon, which lasted for about two hours. His courtroom was full; reporters from around the world waited in a long line to get in, and about 40 protesters gathered out front holding signs that read, "Save Terri Schiavo."[102] At the end of those two hours, the judge said that he would not rule immediately.

All of the parties in the case seemed stunned by the events of the last few days. Michael Schiavo spoke again on *Larry King Live* and said that he was taking the case "day by day." Bob Schindler told reporters, "I'm numb, I'm just totally numb. This whole thing is hard to believe."[103] Indeed, the world around Terri Schiavo seemed to take a collective deep breath that Monday night, waiting for the ruling from Judge Whittemore. They did not have to wait long.

At around 6:30 a.m. on Tuesday, March 22, the judge issued his 13-page opinion, denying the request by the Schindlers to have the tube reinserted.[104] The judge wrote that this "court appreciates the gravity" of such a decision, but he concluded that the Schindlers had not shown a substantial likelihood of success on the merits of their federal claim that the Florida courts had not protected Terri Schiavo's constitutional rights—a critical requirement to receiving preliminary injunctive relief.

The Schindlers appealed quickly, filing papers at the federal court of appeals in Atlanta late that Tuesday morning. That court gave Michael Schiavo's attorneys four hours to file a response. At the court of appeals, lawyers for the federal government also filed papers, urging the court to order reinsertion of the feeding tube.[105] Again no word came immediately from the federal court that afternoon, and the parties and the media waited.

Outside the Hospice House Woodside, the scene was tense and emotional. Mary Schindler, now nearly always flanked by two brown-frocked friars on one side and Randall Terry on the other, stood in front of television cameras with about 100 protesters crowded around her. She pleaded with the Florida legislature, "Please, Senators, for the love of God, don't let my daughter die of thirst," she cried out. Then, overcome, she fell into the arms of one of the friars.[106]

Early on Wednesday, March 23, events began to unfold in many places. At 2:30 a.m., the federal court of appeals issued a 2-1 decision refusing to reinsert the feeding tube. The two judges in the majority called Judge Whittemore's decision of the day before "carefully thought-out," and they noted that the federal Congress had considered and rejected a more aggressive law, one that would have *required* the federal courts to issue an injunction to reinsert the feeding tube. Judge Charles R. Wilson, a former U.S. Attorney in Tampa, wrote in his dissent that he believed the new federal law did, in fact, require the federal courts to consider the Schindlers' claims "with a fresh set of eyes," and that required reinserting the feeding tube.[107] The voting ran counter to the political expectations of many. Judge Wilson in dissent had been appointed by President Bill Clinton to the bench, and Judge Carnes in the majority had been appointed in 1992 by the first President Bush.[108]

As the day progressed, other doors appeared to close one by one. In Tallahassee, the state Senate again voted down legislation; the final vote was 21-18 against the proposed new Terri's Law this time. The debate was emotional and at times angry. Senator Mike Haridopolos said that if Terri Schiavo were on death row, starving her would be unconstitutionally cruel and unusual. "We voted to end a life," he said. Senator Jim King, one of the group of nine Republicans who had opposed the new Terri's Law in the face of incessant political pressure, responded angrily, "To be kept alive like that against your wishes is truly cruel and unusual punishment. If we were Terri Schiavo, is there anyone amongst you that would like to continue as she is? I think not." After the vote, the Senate recessed and the state senators headed home to their families for Easter.[109]

Downstairs in the same building, Governor Jeb Bush spoke at a press conference. Amazing rumblings had been coming from Tallahassee that the state Department of Children & Families (DCF) might seize Terri Schiavo. "Is your goal to take custody of Schiavo?" a reporter asked the governor. The governor paused, then turned and summoned his chief legal counsel, Raquel Rodriguez, to the podium.

"DCF could take protective custody of Ms. Schiavo; I'll leave it at that," Rodriquez answered. Later that morning, the DCF moved to intervene again in the court proceedings before Judge Greer. DCF claimed that they had received reports of abuse of Terri Schiavo that they were required to investigate. They also asserted that a neurologist from the Mayo Clinic in Tallahassee, Dr. William Cheshire, had been in Terri Schiavo's room on March 1 and that he believed that Terri Schiavo was in a minimally conscious state, not a persistent vegetative state.

That morning, Schiavo's lawyers talked by phone with two Pinellas Park police officers who told him that they believed that state police officers were escorting DCF workers to the hospice to take custody of Schiavo. The lawyers went immediately to Judge Greer who called yet another emergency hearing. In a remarkable confrontation between the judicial branch and the executive branch of a government, the judge issued a restraining order barring DCF from removing Terri Schiavo from the hospice, and ordering "each and every singular sheriff of the state of Florida" to take actions necessary to enforce the order.[110] No confrontation materialized.

That afternoon, the entire twelve-member federal appellate court in Atlanta denied by a vote of 10-2 a request to rehear the decision made by the panel of three judges of the court hours earlier. The

Schindlers' attorneys prepared an emergency motion to the U.S. Supreme Court.

The Schindlers had their answer from the Supreme Court by about 10 a.m. on Thursday, March 24, a one-sentence order that denied relief. Quickly, the Schindlers' lawyers went back to the federal trial court, and Judge Whittemore, with new filings. The judge held a tense three-hour hearing that Thursday night.

When the Schindlers' lawyer, David Gibbs, who is also the President of the Christian Law Association, called Michael Schiavo a "murderer," Judge Whittemore cut him off. "That's the emotional aspect of this case, and the rhetoric that does not influence this court. We have to follow the rule of law and that's what will be applied," said the judge.[111] He ended the hearing at 9:25 p.m., saying he would stay until the order was written: "I'll be here as long as necessary."

By the next morning, Good Friday, Terri Schiavo was approaching one week without the feeding tube, and Judge Whittemore again ruled against the Schindlers. Late that day a three-judge panel in Atlanta agreed. The Schindlers said that they were done filing federal appeals. They filed a new motion in the state trial court that afternoon, though, claiming that Terri had told a lawyer that she wanted to live. Barbara Welter, a lawyer with the Gibbs law firm, claimed that on March 18, she had told Terri Schiavo that the fight could end if Terri "could articulate one sentence: 'I want to live.'" The motion claimed that Terri Schiavo "became very agitated" and vocalized "AHHHHHHH WAAAAAAA!" but she could not complete the statement. No supporting affidavits from health care workers in the room were submitted to buttress Barbara Welter's claim. Judge Greer denied the motion on Saturday morning.[112] Mr. Schindler urged protesters, whose numbers had swelled now to several hundred, to go home and spend Easter with their own families. But most stayed, and they grew louder and angrier.

For weeks, the protesters had been taunting hospice staff and others entering the hospice with catcalls of "Murder!" On Easter Sunday, they goaded police, shouting "Nazis" and "cowards." Arrests began after dawn, and by late Sunday, 37 people had been arrested.[113] Long before, however, protest leaders had contacted police about arrest "protocols," and the arrests were peaceful and "well choreographed," according to a police spokesman.[114] Governor Bush told CNN on Easter Sunday that he had no further power to intervene. A priest gave Terri Schiavo communion, placing a drop of wine on her tongue with an eyedropper. And thirty protesters laying flowers at Michael Schiavo's home were greeted by the sprinkler system.[115] The grade school across the street from the hospice was scheduled to reopen on Monday at the end of their spring break. School officials made the decision to hold school elsewhere, given the "unstable situation." On Sunday afternoon, a gym teacher could be seen hauling balls and hula hoops in a wheelbarrow from the school to his car.

The week began with all sides waiting and watching Terri Schiavo, who looked peaceful or distraught, depending on which side was talking with the media. On Tuesday, the Reverend Jesse Jackson arrived at the hospice at the request of the Schindlers. He prayed with the family and made calls to state legislators. Lawyers for the Schindlers decided to make a final effort in the federal courts, filing a new appeal in Atlanta. But Wednesday brought news that the court of appeals had again rejected the Schindlers' requests, and later that day the U.S. Supreme Court also refused, for the sixth and final time, to take on the case.[116] The court of appeals opinion included a lengthy concurring opinion by Judge Stanley F. Birch, Jr., a 1990 federal court appointee by the first President Bush. Judge Birch, a social conservative, chided the action by President George W. Bush and the federal Congress: "When the fervor of political passions moves the executive and legislative branches to act in ways inimical to basic constitutional principles, it is the duty of the judiciary to intervene."[117]

At the hospice, though, the focus was on Terri. Michael Schiavo and his brother, Brian, stayed up through the night in Terri's room, leaving only when the Schindlers visited. The Schiavo brothers told stories about Terri, and rubbed her arms and legs, which were cold and mottled, the skin turning bluish as blood pooled, unable to return to the heart. They talked about her loud, infectious laugh.

As morning dawned on Thursday, March 31, Bobby Schindler fought for one more chance for him and his sister, Suzanne, to visit their sister Terri. Mr. and Mrs. Schindler had made their last visit days earlier, finding it too painful. Bobby Schindler, visibly angry, said to a police officer, "Can you ask him to leave for like half an hour? Ask him that. Give us a half hour."[118] Just after 7:30 a.m., Bobby Schindler and his sister, Suzanne, accompanied by Father Frank Pavone, came to Terri's room. Hospice workers told the Schindlers that it would not be much longer. Conflicting stories emerged about Bobby having an altercation with an officer over trying to stay in the room when told he had to leave, but he did leave, and a hospice nurse hurried Michael and Brian Schiavo back into the room.

Michael Schiavo held Terri and spoke to her, as Brian Schiavo rubbed his brother's back and said, "It's going to be all right." Schiavo's lawyers, and a handful of hospice workers also stood nearby.

At 9:05 a.m., nearly thirteen days after her feeding tube had been removed, Terri Schiavo died. Michael and Brian stayed alone with Terri, and then left to move to another room, so that the Schindlers could come in. Both men were crying. Bob and Mary Schindler and their children, Bobby and Suzanne, stood around the bed, also crying. Hospice workers who had cared for Terri throughout the years of argument stood around her in a circle, holding hands, as a hospice pastor prayed.[119]

In front of the Hospice House Woodside, protesters cried and reporters conducted their last interviews. At 11:25 a.m., two white vans, one a decoy, left the hospice. The van transporting Terri Schiavo's body headed for the Pinellas-Pasco Medical Examiner's Office.

That afternoon, word came from the Vatican that Pope John Paul II had taken a turn for the worse, spiking a fever. Almost instantly, the 24-hour news cycle switched to the Pope, and Terri Schiavo was gone.

CHAPTER 3

The Autopsy of Terri Schiavo

THOUGH NEARLY ALL of the television cameras shifted their focus to the gravely ill Pope the day Terri Schiavo died, her death did not stop the bitter fight between her husband and the Schindlers. They feuded publicly about burial versus cremation, whether to have a memorial service, and who might attend or even receive notice of such a service. Hanging onto the dispute to the very end, they even fought over where her remains, or cremains, would be buried. And many Schindler supporters viewed the final line on Terri Schiavo's tombstone—"I KEPT MY PROMISE"—as a last vindictive slap at her parents by Michael Schiavo.[1]

Her death also did not stop the societal battle that had grown up around her case. In the last months of Terri Schiavo's life, the public attention focused on her case was extraordinary, significantly more than the *Quinlan* and *Cruzan* cases before it. The advocates on either side fought battles large and small—from disputes over the most basic, and seemingly incontrovertible facts in the case, to construction of grandiose (and far-fetched) conspiracy theories. Both sides waited with anticipation for the autopsy report.

Dr. Jon Thogmartin, the Pasco-Pinellas County Chief Medical Examiner, understandably was under extraordinary public pressure over this autopsy. Surprisingly to some, the autopsy examined both Terri Schiavo's medical condition and also the potential causes of her condition. The 39-page written report is meticulously thorough, painstakingly unbiased, and about as close to an independent assessment of the facts as possible.

The depth of the report is impressive. Beyond the 39-page narrative, the report catalogued the additional medical work done as part of the autopsy: 58 pre-autopsy x-rays; 28 more x-rays at the end of the autopsy; 72 photographs (external) and 116 (internal); detailed dissection of the brain, neck, spine; multiple microscopic samples; examination of the central nervous system by a board-certified neuropathologist; examination of the heart tissue by a forensic pathologist with special expertise in cardiovascular pathology; genetic testing; complete toxicology testing; and examination of the vitreous humor chemistry (the clear gelatinous substance that fills the eyeball between the retina and the lens). As part of the death investigation, the medical examiner also reviewed the extensive court, medical, and other records, including the public and the confidential files of the Division of Children & Families and various law enforcement documents.[2]

Dr. Thogmartin's narrative report sought to answer some of the most frequent and contentious questions from the public debate over Terri Schiavo. Neither "side" in that debate liked or agreed with all of the doctor's answers.

Did bulimia cause Terri Schiavo's cardiac arrest and collapse in February of 1990? To a layperson, bulimia seems like the most logical answer. Terri Schiavo went from 250 pounds on her small, 5 foot 3 inch frame, to less than half that weight; she ate lots of salad, drank gallons of iced tea, and worried about her weight. Michael Schiavo and Bob and Mary Schindler, presenting a united front, claimed in court in November of 1992 that the doctors had missed the diagnosis of bulimia, and a jury believed them and awarded millions of dollars. In the hospital after the cardiac arrest, Terri Schiavo had low potassium levels, a marker for bulimia. Moreover, cardiac arrest is a complication of bulimia.[3]

Dr. Thogmartin did not find this information definitive. His concluding narrative summary is eight pages long, and he spends three pages, or nearly half the summary, examining the bulimia claim. Dr. Thogmartin reasoned that Terri Schiavo's low potassium levels measured in the emergency room on the morning of February 25, 1990 could have resulted from her cardiac arrest and subsequent emergency use of epinephrine and fluids, which can affect potassium levels. He noted that other cases in his office, where such resuscitation efforts had failed, showed potassium levels like Terri Schiavo's with a whole range of causes of death in those cases other than bulimia.

Coupled with the lack of any witness who had ever seen her binge and purge, and with no other signs of bulimia present except the weight change and potassium, Dr. Thogmartin did not find bulimia a likely cause, malpractice verdict or not.[4] He did write that the excessive drinking of iced tea (which contains caffeine) might have contributed, but that was unlikely unless Terri Schiavo also took a stimulant containing caffeine, and the report found no evidence of such a stimulant.

Did the bone scan done during her attempted rehabilitation in 1991 provide evidence of physical abuse that might have caused her cardiac arrest? In the final media frenzy as the different court and legislative doors closed, this claim became a mainstay of conservative cable television personalities. The autopsy report concluded that this theory had no basis. To the contrary, the 1991 bone scan appeared exactly as a doctor would expect from that of a patient who had been severely brain damaged and essentially bedridden for over a year.[5]

On February 5, 1991, a year after her collapse, Terri Schiavo was admitted to Mediplex in Bradenton, Florida for additional attempts at physical therapy. Her knees became red and swollen, and doctors at

Mediplex ordered x-rays, which showed severe degenerative changes but no fractures. Her Mediplex doctors ordered a bone scan "to rule out heterotopic ossification (HO), infection, or trauma." HO is abnormal growth of bone in soft tissue.

One month later, she went to Manatee Memorial Hospital for the scan. The scan request form listed Terri Schiavo as having a "closed head injury." The report of the bone scan completed by Manatee Memorial staff and radiologists stated that "the patient has a history of trauma" in the history section. Thogmartin reviewed the medical records, a deposition of the radiologist taken in late 2003 by the Schindlers' lawyers years after the Manatee visit, and a 2003 report from Florida DCF that investigated the charges of abuse. Thogmartin concluded that the suggestions of "trauma" simply came about from the routine filling out of a medical report by Manatee staffers with "little or no knowledge of the admitting diagnosis or clinical situation of Mrs. Schiavo."

Bone scans show the degree of metabolic activity in a bone. The March 1991 bone scan of Terri Schiavo revealed "focal abnormal areas," including ribs, knees, ankles, thigh, and various parts of the spine. Subsequent x-rays taken of those areas revealed one likely fracture, in the first lumbar vertebrae (lower back). Dr. Thogmartin concluded that that fracture was "much more typical of osteoporosis," a common complication of prolonged paralysis rather than any type of abuse. Moreover, that fracture was not present on the many x-rays and physical exams done of the neck, back, and head of Terri Schiavo in the days and weeks after her cardiac arrest; those early x-rays showed no evidence of trauma. Dr. Thogmartin concluded that "by far" the likely explanation of the trauma on the bone scan was the paralysis.[6]

Did the autopsy confirm the diagnosis of persistent vegetative state? Yes and no. PVS is a clinical diagnosis made by observation at the bedside over an extended period of time. The autopsy could neither refute nor confirm a clinical diagnosis. Thogmartin wrote, "Neuropathologic examination alone of the decedent's brain—or any brain, for that matter—cannot prove or disprove a diagnosis of persistent vegetative state or minimally conscious state."[7] The autopsy did show, however, a profoundly damaged brain, with changes that were "striking in their appearance, and global in their distribution."[8] Terri Schiavo's brain "was grossly abnormal," weighing 615 grams, less than half the weight expected for a woman her age. By comparison, "the brain of Karen Ann Quinlan weighed 835 grams at the time of her death, after ten years in a similar persistent vegetative state."[9]

Interestingly, the autopsy made the point that the "neuronal loss in her occipital lobes" indicated "cortical blindness."[10] The point presumably was that the anatomic changes in Terri Schiavo's brain, both gross and microscopic, were so complete in the area that controls vision that from the view of a neuropathologist, the dead tissue in the visual cortex confirmed that Terri Schiavo was blind. Dr. Thogmartin included this fact in the paragraph immediately below the paragraph on persistent vegetative state, intimating that the finding of cortical blindness supported the diagnosis of PVS. In some ways that conclusion is true, but emphasizing the fact of her blindness is in other ways confusing.

A patient reliably diagnosed with PVS by definition has lost *all* neocortical function—she cannot see, but she also cannot hear, speak, think, or remember. Yet doctors don't say the PVS patient is demented, amnestic, aphasic, or deaf. The diagnosis instead is complete loss of consciousness. Possibly Dr. Thogmartin added this line due to the videotapes and the claim that Terri Schiavo could see and smile at her mother. His conclusion is that she could not—that part of her brain was simply gone.

Could Terri Schiavo eat by mouth? No. "In fact, the records and findings are such that oral feedings in quantities sufficient to sustain life would have certainly resulted in aspiration," or secretions and food improperly going into the lungs, causing pneumonia.[11]

■ ■ ■

Trying to write history, one gathers as much data and information as possible and then sorts through it, weighing which information is most reliable. Then the writer has to decide how to reconstruct those facts into a coherent account, telling the truest story possible. That's what I've tried to do in these chapters covering Terri Schiavo's final twenty years.

It strikes me that the key outline of the story found in this account is fairly straightforward: In the early morning hours of February 25, 1990, 26-year-old Terri Schiavo collapsed onto the floor in her apartment. She had suffered a cardiac arrest, emergency personnel were called, and it took Herculean efforts, including seven shocks with defibrillator paddles, to restart her heart.

We know that she had lost massive amounts of weight in the years prior to her cardiac arrest, that she drank excessive amounts of iced tea, and that her husband, supported by the testimony of her parents, won a multi-million dollar lawsuit against her doctors for failing to diagnose her bulimia. Few of the classic signs of bulimia were present, however. No one saw her binge and purge, for example. The medical examiner later was not persuaded that bulimia had caused her cardiac arrest regardless of that malpractice verdict.

After the award of that large amount of money, the relationship between Terri Schiavo's husband and her parents soured almost immediately and turned very bitter very quickly. Within months, Michael Schiavo had refused Terri's parents certain access to her, and within months they had sued, claiming he was not fit to be Terri's legal guardian. We also know that three-and-a-half years after Terri's cardiac arrest, Michael made the decision with Terri's doctor that a do-not-resuscitate order would be entered in Terri's medical chart and that he did not want her urinary tract infection treated.

In 1998, eight years after her cardiac arrest, Michael sought court permission to remove Terri's feeding tube, and her parents intervened and opposed the request. Over the ensuing seven years, the Schindlers and Michael Schiavo battled through extensive trials, depositions, hearings, and appellate court arguments. Two times artificial nutrition and hydration was stopped and started again, and then stopped one last time.

The media grew interested, and anti-abortion activists courted Terri Schiavo's parents who enlisted their help. The media attention escalated, with the case becoming the lead story of the national news for an extended period of time. Ultimately, the Florida state legislature, the federal Congress, the President of the United States, and the Pope weighed in. Most Americans saw video of Terri Schiavo appearing to smile at her mother. For most, it was their first exposure to what doctors called a persistent vegetative state.

Terri Schiavo died on March 31, 2005, thirteen days after a doctor had removed her feeding tube. The autopsy showed that her cerebral cortex had been utterly destroyed many years earlier by the long period without oxygen following cardiac arrest in 1990. The diagnosis of permanent unconsciousness, or persistent vegetative state, reached by so many doctors over the years, was most likely exactly right. Advocates drawn to the case disputed this conclusion, claiming that certain reactions exhibited some consciousness, even if profoundly limited. Likewise, her parents, brother, and sister, so completely engulfed by this tragedy and court fight, will likely never believe that assessment of her medical condition. Nor will Michael Schiavo ever likely feel much "winning" in the final outcome of the protracted, bitter legal battle with her parents.

And we know at least one other fact: The rest of us can benefit from taking the time to talk about Terri Schiavo, whatever our beliefs about her condition and her case.

PART TWO

CHAPTER 4

The Ascent of Medical Technology

FROM THE TIME I began working on right-to-die cases in the spring of 1987 until today, the only real way that I've had any luck in making sense of the complicated legal, medical and ethical issues raised by a case like Terri Schiavo's is to put those issues into some kind of historical context. This context also helps illustrate how new the questions posed by the *Schiavo* case are in our culture and how quickly these questions have come upon all of us. There are many ways to tackle such a task, but I want to do it with the stories of three doctors.

1959, DR. BERNARD LOWN

At 2:30 a.m. on November 3, 1959, a phone call from an emergency room nurse woke Dr. Bernard Lown in his apartment in Brookline, Massachusetts. A patient whom he had treated for about ten weeks for ventricular tachycardia was back in the emergency room.[1] Ventricular tachycardia is the prolonged, rapid beating of the heart which results from the heart's internal electrical system malfunctioning. The patient, whom Dr. Lown called Mr. C to honor patient confidentiality, came to the ER in the middle of the night in no real discomfort other than rapid palpitations, his heart racing at about 170 beats per minute (BPM).[2] This same routine had been playing out for about ten weeks, and Dr. Lown thought that Mr. C could tolerate the racing heart for several hours without problems. He pulled himself out of bed, bundled against the middle of a November night in Massachusetts, and drove to the hospital.

Dr. Lown had graduated from Johns Hopkins Medical School in 1950 and then headed north to Boston's Peter Bent Brigham Hospital to start a fellowship in the rapidly changing field of cardiology, the study of the human heart. Dr. Lown worked under cardiology pioneer Dr. Samuel Levine. Shortly after his arrival in Boston, Lown began cutting-edge research work on the uses of the drug digitalis for correcting abnormal heart rhythm. He also ran a study on the innovative and controversial idea of treating heart attack victims in chairs, upright, rather than with bed rest. While most of the medical establishment saw taking these patients out of bed as heresy, Drs. Lown and Levine were able to lower the mortality rate for these patients from 33 percent to 11 percent.[3]

In November of 1959, Dr. Lown confronted the hard case of Mr. C's ventricular tachycardia. Doctors in 1959 had no real treatment for ventricular tachycardias. They experimented with three different drugs: antiarrythmics quinidine and Pronestyl, and Dilantin, an anticonvulsant. The drugs, however, often proved ineffective. Worse than that, they could send a patient on a downhill course far more quickly than the underlying heart problem. Trying different approaches on Mr. C, Dr. Lown had learned that giving Pronestyl in a massive intravenous (IV) dose each week would restore his normal heartbeat. That restoration came after a stressful hour, as the negative side effects of the drug battled for control. Mr. C would turn blue, his breathing would grow rapid and strained and his lungs would fill with congestion. Then almost magically, the positive effects of the medicine won the battle each week, a normal thump-thump of a heartbeat returned, and soon Mr. C would be standing, smiling, shaking hands all around.

But in the early morning hours of Tuesday, November 3, 1959, the large dose of Pronestyl did not work. Mr. C's heart rate increased from 170 BPM to 212 BPM, and his blood pressure dropped so low that it was hard to measure. He remained in that condition for a day. On Wednesday, Dr. Lown tried Dilantin, without success, and Mr. C's heart began to show signs of heart failure. By Friday, the staff stopped trying to take his blood pressure, and his lungs filled with congestion that did not respond to diuretic medicines. Mr. C remained conscious and fell into long bouts of coughing and gasping each time he tried to speak, his eyes wide with despair and fear.

With the options he'd used in the past exhausted, Dr. Lown thought about alternatives. He'd learned in medical school of the amazing advance at Case Western Reserve in Cleveland in 1947, when Dr. Claude Beck had accomplished the first successful defibrillation of a human heart. A 14-year-old boy who had cardiac arrest during thoracic surgery had his heart restarted when Dr. Beck, after opening his chest, applied common 110-volt household current directly to his heart, using a device that looked like a lamp cord connected to two tablespoons.[4] Dr. Beck's dictum had soon begun to be spread throughout the fledgling world of modern cardiology: Many hearts are "too young to die."[5]

Closer to home, Dr. Lown also knew about the pioneering work of Dr. Paul Zoll at the adjoining Beth Israel Hospital in Boston. Dr. Zoll had made news in the mid-1950s by shocking a stopped heart back to life by using an electrical current passed through an invention called an AC defibrillator. He applied this shock directly to the chest, without the need to cut the patient open as Dr. Beck had done. Lown had never seen the procedure performed and wasn't sure where to find one of the devices. Yet he wondered if such a shock could work on a patient whose heart was still beating—a living patient. He tried to reach Dr. Zoll but the doctor was out of town and couldn't be found. A coworker of Dr. Zoll's told Lown that they had only used the treatment on those in full cardiac arrest, patients who were already considered dead.

Dr. Lown plunged on. He found an AC defibrillator in the surgical department of the hospital. He didn't know of any doctors who had used it yet, and assumed that cardiac surgeons had ordered the device after learning of Dr. Beck's and Dr. Zoll's work. The device was a large, heavy box that plugged into the wall and transferred wall current to the patient. The dial went from 0 up to 750 volts.

He took Mrs. C out into the hallway and told her what he wanted to try and explained that the experiment could very well kill Mr. C. He fretted over what he did not know: What voltage level? If the first shock did not work, should he try again? Would the oxygen nearby explode? Would the flesh burn? Did Mr. C need anesthesia?

Fearing that they were running out of time, and worried that an anesthesiologist who was one of the more junior doctors, like himself, could not take this risk, Dr. Lown called the head of the anesthesia department, Dr. Roy Vandam. Lown explained the experiment. Dr. Vandam hung up and came racing down the hallway to the room, carrying a small canister of nitrous oxide (the anesthetic known today as "laughing gas") ready to help. On his heels came the medical director of the facility, determined to stop the procedure in its tracks.

"Do you have any experience with defibrillators? Has anyone in the world tried this?" the medical director asked. Lown said "No" to both questions. The director insisted that Lown obtain clearance from the hospital lawyer before proceeding, but Lown, judging himself nearly out of time, refused. As a compromise, he wrote a note in the medical chart that the hospital bore no responsibility and that it all landed directly on him.

Dr. Vandam stepped forward with the nitrous oxide and put Mr. C under. Dr. Lown set the machine to 400 volts. Forty-six years later, when recalling that day, Dr. Lown said, "To this day I am mystified why I chose 400 volts, I just did." He lifted the two silver-plated electrical paddles and lowered them to Mr. C's chest. Vandam nodded to him, everyone in the room stepped back, and Dr. Lown pushed the button, shooting 400 volts into Mr. C's chest.

For about a minute, the needle of the electrocardiogram bounced wildly, delivering no news. But Dr. Lown bent over Mr. C and used a technology that he considered among the most important and sophisticated in the cardiologist's black bag—a stethoscope—and he heard a sound from Heaven, the slow, rhythmic beating of the human heart.

Amazingly, Mr. C soon awoke, smiling. The next day he walked on his own. Peter Bent Brigham Hospital had been the scene of a true medical miracle.

Soon, however, the miracle fell apart. Dr. Lown approved a trip to Miami for Mr. and Mrs. C for a well-deserved holiday, and three weeks after being shocked, Mr. C found himself in a Miami hospital with a racing heart, a thousand miles away from Dr. Lown's paddles. Lown pleaded over the phone with the head of cardiology at the hospital, but that doctor refused to even consider using such an untested, experimental procedure in his hospital. That refusal turned the next eighteen hours into a medical nightmare of mishaps and blunders.

Dr. Lown urged Mr. C to find a way back to Boston. At Miami airport, all airlines refused to transport such a sick person. Through colleagues, Lown tracked down the chairman of the board of Eastern Airlines, and Mr. C was soon in the air to Boston. But fog covered the city, and the plane had to divert to a suburban New York airport. The waiting ambulance driver misunderstood his mission, and he took Mr. C the wrong way, into New York City. When they finally turned around and headed north, the fog slowed their progress to a crawl.

Mr. C arrived at Brigham near 8 a.m., nearly dead. This time the shock went wrong, and the paddles sent Mr. C into ventricular fibrillation, or V-fib, the deadly, out-of-control, arrhythmic contraction that turns the heart muscle into a squirming, shivering valentine that circulates no blood. Repeat shocks did nothing. Lown called for a scalpel, cut open Mr. C's chest, and applied internal paddles directly to his heart, shocking the muscle back into rhythm. But the damage this time had been massive, and Mr. C did not leave the hospital for six weeks. He died at home shortly after that.

Bernard Lown wanted to learn from this experience. He began to investigate alternating current and the dangers it posed, both to conscious patients like Mr. C and to "dead" patients like those Dr. Zoll worked on. He studied these patients, did experiments on dogs, and concluded that alternating current was dangerous to the heart in either low or high doses. So he began experimenting with direct current (DC) and the endless wave form options it offered, and eventually he learned something extremely useful—a shock with direct current could correct V-fib, where alternating current could not. Soon after came Dr. Lown's invention of the DC defibrillator.

In the early 1960s, Lown set out to develop the first coronary intensive care unit (ICU) in the world, building on the idea that if V-fib could be detected within minutes, the outcomes would be much better. He scouted around for funding, space, and institutional support. In his research, however, he came to learn that he would not be first. A coronary ICU was already up and running in, of all places, Kansas City, Kansas.

1964, DR. ROBERT POTTER

Dr. Robert Potter began his internship at Bethany Medical Center in Kansas City, Kansas in 1964, a heady time at the hospital. In the early 1960s, Dr. Hughes Day, a cardiologist, had begun experimenting with the innovations reported in the medical literature—electrical shock to a fibrillating heart from the outside of the chest; the new concept of closed-chest massage or cardio-pulmonary resuscitation (CPR), first written up in the summer of 1960; and the new electronic monitoring of patients. They built mobile crash carts that could carry some of this specialized equipment to patients on the general medical floors quickly. Unfortunately, Dr. Day's initial results were disappointing, mainly because nurses and doctors on the general floors did not know how to interpret the information or perform the CPR, and by the time a cardiologist arrived, the damage had been done.

Dr. Day came up with the idea for a completely separate area for heart patients, which he "proposed to call a *coronary care unit*."[6] In the summer of 1961, the John A. Hartford Foundation agreed to provide Dr. Day a sizable grant to develop this unit, which opened on May 20, 1962. Dr. Day commandeered a large area on the second floor of the hospital that had been used as a county ward for the elderly on public assistance. The unit had eleven beds, each within its own glass cubicle, a chair next to each bed, and a nursing station in the center. Each cubicle was equipped with an electrocardiogram (EKG) monitor that fed heart readings to the central nursing station nearby, and at a time when few doctors knew the technique, the nurses on the coronary care unit were specially trained in CPR and defibrillation.

From the CCU at Bethany came the now-famous call over the hospital loud speaker of "Code Blue!" Dr. Day later wrote that they chose that terminology for the emergency call because the patients in cardiac arrest were cyanotic, or turning bluish due to lack of blood flow. Robert Potter and some of the other new doctors thought it might have come from the color of the new "crash carts" at Bethany, which had been painted gunmetal blue.[7]

The initial crash carts, in fact, were built by Dr. Potter's father, who ran a sheet metal fabrication shop.[8] Bethany had two carts for the new CCU, both of which were equipped with an Ambu bag (a flexible bag attached to a mask, invented in 1953, and used to manually send air into the lungs);[9] defibrillator paddles; a bed board to move patients quickly; and endotracheal tubes (a flexible tube put down the windpipe to force air directly into the lungs).

They always kept at least one of the crash carts in the CCU. Often when the carts came back from the general medical floors they were broken. The early monitors were made of tubes and soldered wire, and if they had to be rolled to a site, an expansion joint on the floor or bump into the wall could jostle wires loose, and they would not work once plugged in back at the CCU. The early defibrillators on these machines were huge by today's standards, weighing about a hundred pounds (today they can weigh less than five pounds). Often, they were perched on carts that were unstable under that kind of weight, and it wasn't uncommon to round a corner in a hurry, and have the whole contraption tip over—hence the name "crash cart."[10]

Some patients in the CCU at Bethany required respirators. Though available, the technology was still in its infancy, and the machines were primitive by today's standards. Bethany had two respirators in the hospital at the time, which looked like green lunch boxes made of thick glass, sitting atop a rolling steel tripod.[11] Often called "the Bird," the devices had been invented by a doctor from California, Forrest Bird, and were made by the Puritan-Bennett company. On the rare occasion on Tuesday nights in the mid-1960s when handsome Richard Chamberlain, Dr. Kildare, ran into a case on NBC that he could not fix, he might turn to a nurse and shout, "Get me the Bird!" The nurse would hurry out and rush back in, rolling the green glass lunchbox-looking contraption on a steel tripod.[12]

The Birds in the CCU at Bethany in 1964 could control volume and rate of airflow, but not pressure. What's more, they did not yet have automatic switches. Interns or nurses would sit with the machines at the bedside in shifts up to three hours, flipping a switch every five or six seconds to shoot a blast of air in the body, then turning it off. The CCU could sustain patients for only a few days if they were not able to wean them from the respirator.[13]

The machines, however, did not seem primitive then. They were amazing, and it was an amazing time to be a young doctor. Dr. Potter had the chance to rub elbows with some remarkable physicians—physicians like the famous cardiologist from Boston, Dr. Bernard Lown, who came to Kansas City to see the fledgling CCU. And the magic and power of "bringing someone back" is something Dr. Potter would describe years later, his eyes moist, as something "almost indescribable." In a town like Kansas City, Kansas, where many people know each other, everyone knew in 1964 that the young Dr. Potter had "saved" the owner of the local hardware store. For the next ten years, until the death of the store owner, the two men shared a special bond, evident each time Potter walked into that store and the men smiled at one another.

After his one-year internship at Bethany, Dr. Potter did a residency at General Hospital in Kansas City, Missouri, before shipping off for a tour of duty with the Kansas National Guard. In January of 1970, he returned home to Kansas and back to Bethany Medical Center where he began to teach medicine.

Between the time he left Bethany in 1965 and his return in 1970, much was changing in the world of emergency medicine and in the world all around. Tension over the Vietnam War simmered on college campuses across the country. Shortly after Dr. Potter's return, that tension would explode most famously at Kent State University in Ohio where National Guardsmen shot and killed four protesters on May 4, 1970. Closer to home, protesters at the University of Kansas set the student union on fire in April of that year, and in July, violence erupted between the police and campus protesters that ended in the deaths of two of the protesters.[14]

Women and doctors in Massachusetts sued the government over a law that sent the doctors to jail if they prescribed a new method of birth control that everyone was calling "the Pill." Russian satellites still circled over our airspace at night, a constant reminder of our vulnerability, and kids in school squatted under their desks in the event of a nuclear war with the Soviets. And in the middle of all this social bedlam, a hopeful America sat transfixed by the unlimited possibilities that emerged from the grainy, black-and-white television images of Neil Armstrong's July 21, 1969 walk on the moon.

Changes in medicine were coming quickly, too. In 1966, the National Academy of Sciences–National Resource Council convened a meeting on the new technique called cardiopulmonary resuscitation, or CPR. Out of this meeting came the recommendation that doctors and other health professionals begin training to learn CPR, and that a supervised trial be conducted to see if laypersons could learn the technique as well.[15]

In June of 1967, a federal task force recommended development of a national emergency telephone number and that pay phones be set up so that a victim could call the operator without using money. "The victim of a robber careful enough to steal his last dime cannot now use the public telephone," the task force report stated.[16] The first 911 call came to a special red telephone at the Haleyville, Alabama police station. The call was answered with this emergency greeting: "Hello?"[17]

In 1966, President Lyndon Johnson signed the National Highway Safety Act, which established the National Highway Safety Administration. As part of that federal law, states were required to establish training programs for ambulance drivers. In Miami, Florida, the fire department started the country's first paramedic training program in 1969, and the first successful out-of-hospital defibrillation of a heart attack victim occurred in Miami shortly after that.[18]

And on December 3, 1967, in Cape Town, South Africa, Dr. Christiaan Barnard conducted the first human heart transplant. A teenage auto accident victim, Denise Darvall, was brought to the hospital where 53-year-old Lewis Washkansky was waiting. Dr. Barnard later said, "I did not want to touch this girl until she was conventionally dead, a corpse. I felt we could not put a knife into her until she was truly a cadaver."[19] Immunologist M.C. Botha, standing at the bedside as he watched the first heart transplant unfold, remembered his amazement at seeing Washkansky hooked to the heart bypass machine, awaiting the healthy heart. He also recalled his utter fascination when Washansky's diseased heart, removed from the body and set aside, "did not appear to want to stop beating."[20] The medicine given to Washkansky to prevent his immune system from attacking the new heart also suppressed his body's ability to fight off other illnesses. Eighteen days after the operation, Washkansky died of double pneumonia.[21] He reportedly said during those eighteen days, "I'm the new Frankenstein."[22] The field of transplantation would soon demand changes in the law, as discussed in the next chapter.

At Bethany Medical Center in 1970, Dr. Robert Potter saw evidence of this change in the field of medicine all around him, but he also saw that there was still much work to do. Respirators now had automatic switches among other improvements, but they had grown to the size of dishwashers and were not portable; a patient dependent on a respirator was destined to remain in an institution for life. When "Code Blue" came over the loudspeaker, all doctors at Bethany were required to respond. Dr. Potter often ran the five floors of the hospital because the elevators were so slow and, unfortunately, the crash cart at times was on the slow-moving elevator. Once in a room he might find it crowded with twenty people—interns, nurses, residents, doctors—with no one exactly sure what to do.

Still, the advance of knowledge was relentless and amazing, and Dr. Potter saw many "miracles." He also began to see and think more about a dark side to this growing technology. In the early 1970s, a 42-year-old Croatian laborer came to Bethany Medical Center with heart problems. Dr. Potter was able to restore the man's regular heartbeat after an event of V-fib, but the *man* did not come back. He lay in bed, eyes open, unaware. For three years, Dr. Potter visited Mr. X in his nursing home room weekly. "I felt guilty every time I saw him," Potter said. "Guilty for having created the situation with my almost successful technology." Eventually Mr. X succumbed to pneumonia.[23]

1972, DR. FRED PLUM

At Cornell Medical School, on the Upper East Side in New York City, another bow-tied, bespectacled doctor—a neurologist—was thinking about his own Mr. Xs. Dr. Fred Plum had grown up as a doctor right in the midst of the coming of the age of medical technology.[24] He began his medical internship at age 25 in the New York General Hospital in the late 1940s, during the height of the polio epidemic. Polio struck terror throughout the country, crippling and killing children, and doctors had no idea what caused the disease. Baffled public health officials closed swimming pools in the summer and schools in the winter, and cautioned parents to keep children home, clean, and well fed.[25]

In the late 1940s, at a time when many hospitals would not accept polio patients for fear of contagion, Dr. Plum and his colleagues made the radical decision to group all of the serious polio patients on one large floor of twenty-eight patients so that they could monitor them more closely. This polio treatment area at New York General Hospital essentially became one of the first ICUs. The room looked like a bizarre landscape, with fifteen black iron lungs scattered around the room, the heads or head and shoulders of the patients sticking out of the end of each, depending on their height. Thirteen other polio patients not in iron lungs were also on that floor. The iron lung was the first modern respirator (invented by Harvard medical researcher Philip Drinker in 1927). The inventors used an iron box about the size of a subcompact car and two vacuum cleaners.[26] The iron lung worked on negative pressure, creating a vacuum inside the steel cylinder by removing air, so that weakened lungs could expand.

In the early 1950s, Plum and his colleagues began experimenting with the development of techniques to force air directly into the patients' lungs using a three-inch metal pipe, surgically inserted into the front of the throat, connected to a crude tank respirator. This technique caused their death rate to drop, so "we had everybody tracheotomized," Dr. Plum said. Soon after that, the advent of the Salk and then the Sabin vaccines began to erase the disease altogether. At its height in 1952, there were 58,000 cases in the United States.[27] By 1964, that number had dwindled to 121 cases.[28]

Plum saw all of the developments—from early iron lungs, to the Salk vaccine, to Dr. Lown's discoveries, to CPR, to modern respirators. He saw many miracles of recovery. But by 1972, like Dr. Potter with Mr. X in the room at Bethany, Dr. Plum was seeing the dark side of the attempted recoveries, too, as patients were brought back from the brink of death but were left alive and awake but unaware. He wondered exactly how long these patients could live in this condition. He also wondered what to write in their charts and what name to give the condition when talking with the patients' families.

The literature already contained the early hints of these patients. French doctors in 1957 had written of *coma vigile*, or vigilant coma, in severe typhoid patients.[29] One article described a girl with a brain tumor as having *akinetic mutism*, but while she was mostly silent, she sometimes whispered in monosyllables and her condition was reversed by draining fluid from the tumor. A German psychiatrist named Kretschmer had coined the name *apallic syndrome* as early as 1940 to describe a gunshot victim who appeared awake, but unaware; however, the name never caught on in English-speaking medicine.

At a cocktail party at the meeting of the World Neurology Congress in London in 1972, Dr. Plum and Dr. Bryan Jennett, a neurosurgeon from the University of Glasgow, started talking about these patients, the lack of a satisfactory diagnosis and name, and the need for precise criteria to meet the diagnosis that they were contemplating. They decided to write an article together which appeared in *The Lancet* later that year. The title of the article was "A syndrome in search of a name."[30] The name they coined for it was *persistent vegetative state*.

The chance to talk about this new syndrome in a venue beyond a medical journal came to Dr. Plum four years later. In Landing, New Jersey on April 15, 1975, another set of parents received the phone call in the night that all parents dread. A 21-year-old woman had arrived unconscious at the ER at Newton Memorial Hospital. When her parents arrived that night, they found their daughter in a coma, hooked to a respirator through a tube in her mouth and with a pliable tube down her nose. Though news reports would later speculate that drugs were involved, tests performed that night revealed only therapeutic doses of aspirin and Valium in the young woman's system; the screen for all other drugs was negative. Friends reported that she'd been dieting aggressively, hadn't eaten anything all day, and had had a few gin and tonics that night before starting to nod off. Her friends put her in a bed, and when someone later checked on her and found her not breathing, they called "the rescue squad." A policeman arrived first, ran upstairs, and pulled the young woman off the bed to the floor. He started mouth-to-mouth resuscitation and the woman began to breathe again.[31]

In the hospital later that afternoon, with the patient hooked up to a fairly small respirator that provided air through a black mouthpiece, the doctors told her family that she was struggling to breathe, had pneumonia, and needed emergency surgery. Right there in the ICU, with her sister watching, doctors cut a hole in the woman's throat. Blood covered her bed as the doctors inserted a plastic tube into the hole and then connected the tube to a much larger respirator, an MA-1, sitting on the floor next to the bed. The MA-1 was about two feet wide, three feet deep, and three feet tall. The machine would pump air into the woman's lungs, and then stop so that she could take a breath on her own. But sometimes she would breathe at the same time the machine pumped, causing her to choke. A loud buzzer would then sound, calling a nurse.[32] The patient raised up in the bed whenever this happened, eyes popping open and arms flailing.

The large respirator continued to breathe for the young woman over the days and weeks ahead, but she did not regain consciousness. Ultimately, her parents, Joe and Julie Quinlan, began to ask a question never really asked before in human experience: Should they turn off the respirator, which could not return their daughter to "living" life, and allow their daughter, Karen Ann Quinlan, to die?

The question made its way into the New Jersey court system, and Dr. Fred Plum was one of the experts who testified about this new diagnosis called persistent vegetative state. Dr. Plum told the judge that it described "a subject who remains with the capacity to maintain the vegetative parts of neurological function but who, as best as can be determined in every possible way by examination, no longer has any cognitive function."[33] The next expert doctor, Dr. Sidney Diamond of Mount Sinai Hospital in New York, was more graphic: "I'm sorry if the description causes any anguish to the family," he said. "She was lying in bed, emaciated, curled up in what is known as flexion contracture. Every joint was bent in a flexion position and making one tight sort of fetal position. It's too grotesque, really, to describe in human terms like fetal."[34]

Ultimately, the New Jersey Supreme Court ruled that Karen Ann Quinlan had a constitutional right to privacy that her father could exercise on her behalf. But to the surprise of everyone—including the treating doctors who were learning about this new diagnosis like everyone else involved—when the doctors turned off her respirator, Karen Ann Quinlan breathed on her own. For ten more years she lived, awake but unaware, until she died from pneumonia on June 11, 1985.[35]

In the wake of the *Quinlan* case, the federal Congress in 1978 passed a law to establish a President's Commission for the Study of Ethical Problems in Medicine and Biomedical and Behavioral Research.[36] It was obvious that society needed to learn more. Congress gave the President's Commission a wide-ranging assignment to report on issues from informed consent to access to health care. At its first meeting in January of 1980, the commission decided to start at the end, to try to define or redefine *death* itself.[37]

They heard incredible testimony, like the story of Dr. Ron Wright, the deputy chief medical examiner for Dade County in Miami, Florida. Dr. Wright had persuaded a judge to hold a hearing in the winter of 1978 at a Miami hospital. He brought the judge into the ICU and convinced the judge that families in Miami were being charged $2,000 a day to keep the brain-dead bodies of their loved ones on machines in the ICU.[38]

The commission issued its first 166-page report, titled "Defining Death," in July of 1981. A hefty 554-page companion report, "Deciding to Forego Life-Sustaining Treatment," was delivered to the president on March 21, 1983.[39] The report dealt with questions like the *Quinlan* case, and how society should make decisions to withhold or withdraw treatment that the patient, or her family, did not see as a benefit.

Perhaps President Reagan and his staff began digging into these lengthy treatises about death and dying that March day in 1983, but it's likely that education of our governmental leaders came more slowly. Likewise, the American public had not yet seen the actual faces of this brave new medical-technological world. The public never saw a picture of Karen Ann Quinlan after her accident—we saw the yearbook photo of a beautiful young woman. Her parents did not allow reporters in her room, and they turned down huge sums of money for such photographs. (One photographer tried to sneak into her room disguised as a nun.)[40]

News accounts described Karen as being in a coma. In newspapers, sketch artists who had never seen Karen drew pictures of a peaceful Sleeping Beauty.[41] But the picture the world saw—on the covers of magazines, plastered onto TV screens by the three national television networks, and often in newspapers—was her black-and-white high school yearbook photo.

On March 21, 1983, when the president received the lengthy commission report about foregoing life-sustaining treatment, the American public had really not yet thought much about these questions. The public had certainly never seen a still photo of a patient in a persistent vegetative state, let alone a video.

On that March day in 1983, the two faces that would ultimately help teach America that the persistent vegetative state did not in any way resemble a high school yearbook photo were still young faces of hope. Just three days earlier, in blue-collar southwestern Missouri, 25-year-old Nancy Cruzan had finally been taken home by her family after two months and ten days in an acute care and then a rehabilitation hospital. Her eyes were open, but she was unaware of the world around her as she had been since the accident that had caused her condition.[42] Her family played music, talked to her, brought her dog to the hospital—they were willing to try anything, still hopeful two months after the accident that Nancy might respond and emerge from this open-eyed unconsciousness.

And outside Philadelphia that spring in 1983, a 19-year-old community college student named Terri Schindler was falling in love with the first boy she ever kissed, fellow student Michael Schiavo, a world of possibilities in front of her.

The Law and the Right to Die

THE LAW GROWS out of the needs of society. Our environment grew polluted from factories and cars, so Congress studied the issue and passed the Clean Air Act of 1970 and the Clean Water Act of 1972 to address the problem. As society has grown more complicated and dependent on technology, the laws needed to govern that society have expanded. Like the rapid developments in the medical technology, the complexity and sheer volume of new laws has increased exponentially in the last thirty years.

The laws that govern death and dying provide a perfect case study of this exponential growth. These laws also help illustrate how the law is intertwined with the technology that it seeks to regulate; the law does not exist in a vacuum. The case of Terri Schiavo is the most recent and most public example, but advances in medical technology have required the law to come up with many answers. The best way to understand the law, as with medicine, is to examine it in its historical context.

DEFINING DEATH AND THE LAW

For most of human history, when we were dead, we were dead. Our hearts, lungs, and brains all stopped at roughly the same time. There wasn't a need to define death, in the law or otherwise; it just was.

Then in 1967, the world heard about Dr. Christiaan Barnard in South Africa transplanting a human heart. Closer to home, Dr. Thomas Starzl in Colorado performed the first successful liver transplant that same year from one human to another.[1] In Boston, doctors had also started work in the new world of surgical transplants. These transplant doctors and their anesthesiologists wanted guidance on a profound question: At what moment could they remove organs from a patient whose heart was still beating?

In response to that question, Dr. Henry Beecher wrote a letter to the dean of the Harvard Medical School, suggesting the need for a committee. Patients in need of new organs were dying, and other patients with no hope of recovery had such organs. Medicine and society needed to create new criteria for death.[2] The Harvard Brain Death Committee formed, and this group gathered around a conference table in Cambridge, Massachusetts to discuss another extraordinary question: Was man's understanding of the meaning of death, essentially unchanged through all of recorded time to that point in 1968, now obsolete?

The committee published their conclusions in an article in the *Journal of the American Medical Association (JAMA)* that year titled "Report of the Ad Hoc Committee of the Harvard Medical School to Examine the Definition of Brain Death. A Definition of Irreversible Coma."[3] The report explained the purpose of the Ad Hoc Committee:

> Our primary purpose is to define irreversible coma as a new criterion for death. There are two reasons why there is need for a definition: (1) Im-

> provements in resuscitative and supportive measures have led to increased efforts to save those who are desperately injured. Sometimes these efforts have only partial success so that the result is an individual whose heart continues to beat but whose brain is irreversibly damaged. The burden is great on patients who suffer permanent loss of intellect, on their families, on the hospitals, and those in need of hospital beds already occupied by those comatose patients. (2) Obsolete criteria for the definition of death can lead to controversy in obtaining organs for transplantation.[4]

Dr. Henry Beecher understood the inexact nature of their mission. "At whatever level we choose to call death, it is an arbitrary decision. Death of the heart? The hair still grows. Death of the brain? The heart may still beat. The need is to choose an irreversible state where the brain no longer functions. It is best to choose a level where, although the brain is dead, usefulness of other organs is still present. This we have tried to make clear in what we have called the new definition of death."[5] Dr. Beecher also understood that their inquiry went well beyond the medical and scientific: "Can society afford to discard the tissues and organs of the hopelessly unconscious patient when he could be used to restore the otherwise hopelessly ill, but still salvageable individual?" he asked.[6]

Of course, change and progress—in law or medicine or any field—are not delivered seamlessly to all states and cities at one time. In fact, it's quite the opposite. The *JAMA* article about the Harvard committee helped launch the discussion in society. But not all doctors, or all laypeople, understood the issues in the detail presented in the report—and the conclusions in the report were certainly not written into the law in any states yet. Transplants simply began to happen in hospitals with no laws in place, just as there had been no law telling Dr. Lown that he could shock the chest of a patient to try to restore a heartbeat in 1959. Transplant doctors, like Dr. Lown, simply practiced medicine that made good sense and took some reasonable experimental risks in otherwise hopeless situations.

In 1970, Kansas became the first state whose legislature passed a law defining death to include brain death.[7] A physician-legislator proposed the law, and it passed without much discussion.[8] In 1972, law professor Alexander Capron (now director of ethics at the World Health Organization in Geneva, Switzerland) and Dr. Leon Kass (appointed by President Bush in 2001 to chair the President's Council on Bioethics), wrote a law review article that proposed a model statute that was shorter and less confusing than the new Kansas law.[9] Over the next ten years, many states debated these issues in their state legislatures and passed a variety of laws defining death.

Courts were involved, too, shaping the common law in places where statutes did not exist. The common law is judge-made law that grows as judges resolve disputes in society and write opinions explaining what law or rule they applied to resolve a particular dispute. In Virginia, a man suffered head injuries in a workplace accident and was taken to the hospital, unconscious. Doctors attempted surgery on the head injuries without success. They concluded the man was brain dead, turned off his respirator, and then removed his heart and kidneys for transplantation. His brother later sued the doctors for damages under Virginia's wrongful death act. (Wrongful death laws basically allow survivors of a person killed either intentionally or due to negligence to sue the wrongdoer for money.)

The doctors initially filed a motion asking the judge to dismiss the case. He refused. In the opinion denying the motion to dismiss, the judge wrote that the "definition" of death was the "all vital bodily functions" test found in the few other common law cases that existed. Since the injured worker's heart was still beating when the doctors turned off the respirator, his brother might have a claim against the doctor for wrongful death.

The case went to a trial and ultimately to a jury. The testimony during the trial apparently altered the judge's understanding of the definition of death. He gave the jurors this rather lengthy instruction to apply in reaching their verdict:

> You shall determine the time of death in this case by using the following definition of the nature of death. Death is a cessation of life. It is the ceasing to exist. Under the law, death is not continuing, but occurs at a precise time, and that time must be established according to the facts of

> each specific case. In the facts and circumstances of this case, you may consider the following elements, none of which should necessarily be considered controlling, although you may feel under the evidence, that one or more of these conditions are controlling: the time of the total stoppage of the circulation of the blood; the time of the total cessation of the other vital functions consequent thereto, such as respiration and pulsation; the time of the complete and irreversible loss of all function of the brain; and, whether or not the aforesaid functions were spontaneous or were being maintained artificially or mechanically.[10]

A fairly weighty question for a jury of laypeople in 1972. Not so easy today, either. The jury ruled in favor of the doctors. More common law was created.

This ten-year mishmash of laws is what led the previously mentioned President's Commission for the Study of Ethical Problems in Medicine and Biomedical and Behavioral Research, established by an act of Congress in 1978, to tackle first the task of defining death. Ultimately, the commission decided to write a completely separate report on that question alone, which it delivered to Congress on July 9, 1981.[11]

From that first meeting of the Harvard brain death committee in 1968 to the 1981 report of the President's Commission to the public dying of Terri Schiavo in 2005, American society has learned something of brain death. In many ways, though, any full understanding of this concept is in its infancy. Over and over on the nightly news, both local and national, commentators called Terri Schiavo brain dead. Even a publication with editorial control as rigorous as *The Wall Street Journal* made this mistake.[12] Of course she was not, because if a person is brain dead, she's dead. By law. Unless she's in New Jersey or New York.

As recently as 1993, the legislature in New Jersey struggled with the question of defining brain death differently for groups in society whose religious beliefs vary. Under New Jersey law today, a doctor can have two human beings in exactly the same medical condition, lying on beds next to one another in an emergency room—and one patient is dead, the other alive if the second patient meets the religious exception to brain death under state law.[13] When does the soul leave the body? When do we enter Heaven? Do we? The law has no great wisdom for answering these mysteries of death.

It's not just the law, though. We don't even have the words in our dictionaries to describe this technological no man's land. Consider Phillip Rader. In the fall of 1988, the Missouri Supreme Court had actually scheduled two arguments dealing with death for the same morning: the first was the case of Nancy Cruzan, which would take control of my own professional life for the next three years, and the second was the case of Phillip Rader.

On the Tuesday before Thanksgiving in 1987, 17-year-old Phillip Rader entered a south Kansas City hospital for the third and final corrective surgery to repair a cleft palate. The family expected that the hospital would discharge him that weekend, and that he would be back in school the following week, driving his brown, mint-condition 1979 Trans Am, his face already healing, the final vestiges of his cleft palate gone.

Phillip's surgery went well according to the doctors, but his recovery was difficult. Pain and nausea kept him awake much of the night Tuesday. At some point in the early morning hours Wednesday, he stopped breathing. A respiratory technician found him and called a "Code Blue" over the hospital intercom. Doctors rushed in and Phillip was resuscitated. The length of time he went without oxygen, however, was unknown. His electroencephalogram (EEG) taken immediately after the incident was abnormal but showed signs of some electrical life in the brain. Five hours later, his heart stopped again, and this time the EEG after the event found no electrical activity, described in Phillip's medical chart as electrocerebral silence.

That day the doctors told Phillip's family the horrific news, that Phillip was brain dead. They discussed organ donation and an autopsy. "They were very emphatic that he was dead and there was no hope for recovery," John Rader, Phillip's father, said. The problem was that Phillip was still breathing, and his heart still beating, albeit with the assistance of a respirator, feeding tube, medicine, and monitors. His parents believed their son was alive and refused permission to withdraw the machines. "We look at him and we still see Phillip," Mr. Rader said. "There might be something that they've overlooked."

The hospital complied, and with aggressive nursing care and careful monitoring, Phillip's body persisted. By June, more than six months later and still with no resolution, the frustrated medical team had had enough. They brought the issue to court. Kansas City judge Tom Clark held an emergency bench trial (no jury, only a judge). Seven doctors, including two brought in by the parents, told the judge that Phillip met the Missouri statutory definition of brain death, passed by the state six years earlier in 1982.

His mother still did not believe it. She testified that Phillip's blood pressure elevated 95 percent of the time when she entered the room. His face flushed. "I *know* he knows we are there," she told Judge Clark. Phillip's father testified, "It is a matter of time before he will awake and rise. We believe that Phillip can hear us. Parents, they can perceive these things where medical authority can't."

On July 7, 1988, Judge Clark issued a reluctant opinion, which began with the words, "With sadness and regret." He ruled in favor of the hospital, concluding it could turn off the respirator, and he gave the family ten days to appeal. Within days, the Missouri Supreme Court had set the morning of September 29 to hear arguments in *Cruzan* and *Rader*, one after the other. The irony the court would face in the two cases on September 29 was amazing. Phillip Rader's doctors said he was dead, but his mother told the judge, "I *know* he knows we are there," and she asked the judge to leave the respirator and feeding tube in place. Nancy Cruzan's doctors (and state officials) said she was alive, but her father told the judge, "My daughter died the night of the accident," and he asked the judge to remove her feeding tube.

As the argument date approached, the *Rader* case took some strange twists. By August 3, 1988, the day the court announced it would hear arguments in *Cruzan* and *Rader* on the same morning, Phillip Rader had been brain dead for over eight months, and still his heart pumped on. The *Kansas City Times* reported that the longest previous case of someone being sustained after brain death was four and a half months. One doctor told me that parts of the young man's body had actually started to decompose even though his heart somehow continued. No one knew how much longer he could go.

On August 5, Phillip Rader turned eighteen (unless he was already dead as the hospital contended). That event added an interesting legal question. Under Missouri law, Phillip was by definition emancipated on that date, and his parents no longer spoke on his behalf. Did the parents now need to seek a guardianship in probate court to continue speaking for him? Did the parents have rights as parents any longer, or were they now limited to the narrow powers of the guardianship laws? Had Phillip's accident somehow "frozen him in time" for purposes of decision-making by his parents? We actually made exactly this argument to the Missouri Supreme Court two years later in the *Busalacchi* case.

Things grew stranger. On August 16, Mr. Rader came into Phillip's fourth floor hospital room and found that Phillip's life-support systems had been sabotaged; the feeding tube was in a trash can, and bruises were evident around Phillip's neck where someone apparently tried to jerk out his breathing tube. Police were called, and they discovered that a mentally-disturbed patient from another floor had ventured into Phillip's room. The police detective told Phillip's mother that the police could do nothing about the woman, though, because under Missouri law Phillip was already considered dead. Doctors reinserted the feeding tube.

Two weeks later, on August 31, Phillip's heart stopped again. This time efforts to revive the heart failed. That left Nancy Cruzan and her family and me, their lawyer, on our own to tell the Missouri Supreme Court about the elusive line between life and death, to try to explain a world where a newspaper could run a headline on the day Phillip's heart stopped: "Brain-Dead Youth Dies."[14] (The role of the *Cruzan* case in this societal evolution is discussed in the next chapter.)

THE BIRTH OF THE LIVING WILL

Luis Kutner began practicing law in Chicago in 1930. By the 1960s he was one of the best-known human rights lawyers in the country. He co-founded Amnesty International in 1961, and founded the World Habeas Corpus project to fight unwarranted imprisonment around the world. Kutner was also a member of a group called the Euthanasia Society of America.[15] A prolific writer, Kutner in 1969 published an article in the *Indiana Law Journal*, which proposed a new document that he named "the living will."[16]

The article was considering another question never posed before: What if a patient might not really *want* a medical treatment, but the patient could no longer say so? Kutner was not thinking about patients who were brain dead, whom the law had begun to define, by law, as dead. He was thinking about the Mr. Xs of Dr. Plum and Dr. Potter.

He came up with the idea of the living will, which would specify circumstances in which a person might not want continued medical treatment in the future. In 1969, the Euthanasia Society began handing out copies of Kutner's document.[17]

State legislatures, however, did not immediately embrace the concept of a state living will law. The first attempts to pass such a law in Florida in 1968 and 1973 were opposed by the Florida Catholic Conference.[18] A California lawyer-legislator faced similar opposition to a proposed law in his state in 1972. But in 1976, in the wake of public attention after the decision of the New Jersey Supreme Court in the *Quinlan* case, the legislature in California was able to pass the nation's first living will law.[19]

Like state laws defining death, state laws providing for living wills did not develop uniformly. The National Conference of Commissioners on Uniform State Laws is a government-funded group of scholars, lawyers, and other experts, with the mission of drafting model bills for states to adopt in hopes of making state laws more uniform.[20] In the early 1980s, they proposed a uniform law for living wills. But as different state legislatures left their own marks on the draft law, any hope of uniformity from state to state evaporated.

In Missouri, for example, the Missouri Catholic Conference lobbied diligently to narrow the effect of the proposed law. When it finally passed in 1985, a Missouri statutory living will would apply only if the writer of the document was about to die regardless of any medical treatment. Feeding tubes were specifically excluded from medical technology considered medical treatment in Missouri.[21] Three years earlier in 1982, Missouri had passed a law defining death to include the new definition of brain death.[22] But it took the *Cruzan* case, beginning in 1987, to show that these two statutes had not resolved all of Missouri's end-of-life questions, not by a long shot.

THE U.S. SUPREME COURT AND THE RIGHT TO PRIVACY

The advance of medical technology also forced the U.S. Supreme Court to consider some hard questions. During the 1950s, Margaret Sanger, the founder of Planned Parenthood, raised hundreds of thousands of dollars for research into an oral contraceptive. In 1960, the Food & Drug Administration approved the first oral contraceptive, Envoid-10, popularly known as "the Pill."[23] In November of 1961, a doctor and the executive director of a Planned Parenthood clinic in Connecticut were charged under a Connecticut state law that made it a crime for any person to assist, abet, or counsel another in the use of "any drug, medicinal article or instrument for the purpose of preventing conception."[24] The crime carried jail time of 60 days to one year. Eventually the dispute made its way to the U.S. Supreme Court. The Court ultimately ruled that Connecticut had moved into a private area where the state could not go.

Though the word "privacy" does not appear in the U.S. Constitution, the Court nonetheless found in *Griswold v. Connecticut*, the case about the birth control pill, that Americans have privacy rights. The Court reasoned that "specific guarantees in the Bill of Rights have penumbras, formed by emanations from those guarantees that help give them life and substance. Various guarantees create zones of privacy . . . The present case, then, concerns a relationship lying within the zone of privacy created by several fundamental constitutional guarantees."[25] So, far from breaking the law, the Baby Boomers in 1965 learned that they had a constitutional right to the Pill.

Eight years later, the Supreme Court tackled this right to privacy head on in the famous abortion case, *Roe v. Wade*. The Court in *Roe* struck down a Texas law that made abortion a crime. The Court said:

"This right of privacy, whether it be founded in the Fourteenth Amendment's concept of personal liberty and restrictions upon state action, as we feel it is, or, as the District Court determined, in the Ninth Amendment's reservation of rights to the people, is broad enough to encompass a woman's decision whether or not to terminate her pregnancy."[26]

That decision came down on January 22, 1973. On May 14, 1973, the National Right to Life Committee was incorporated, and in June, the committee held its first national convention in Detroit, attracting right-to-life activists from around the country.[27] The battle was joined. Over the next twenty years, the Court worked—struggled, some would argue—through various cases trying to define the boundaries and shape of this right to privacy as it applied to abortion, the rights of homosexuals, and other complex social issues, including, in 1990, the right to die.

AUTONOMY AND INFORMED CONSENT

The so-called "right to die" was born in the New Jersey Supreme Court in 1976 in Karen Ann Quinlan's case. As this new right began to spread to other states, the right was sometimes linked in those written opinions to the right to privacy, but nearly always linked to the common law concepts of informed consent and autonomy. Entire books have been written about these rights. But like the rest of the issues around the right to die, these concepts did not begin to take on real importance and shape until medical technology began its advance. The U.S. Supreme Court would acknowledge this fact in 1990 when it confronted the right to die in the case of Nancy Cruzan: "Until about 15 years ago and the seminal decision in *In re Quinlan*, the number of right-to-refuse-treatment decisions was relatively few,"[28] Chief Justice William Rehnquist wrote.

The doctrine of informed consent grew from the common law concept of assault and battery; a person who touches another without consent or legal justification commits a battery. "Every human being of adult years and sound mind has a right to determine what shall be done with his own body; and a surgeon who performs an operation without his patient's consent commits an assault, for which he is liable in damages."[29]

Philosophers and scholars have written about autonomy for centuries. A pronouncement from an 1891 decision of the U.S. Supreme Court in *Union Pacific Railroad v. Botsford*, is often used to describe autonomy: "No right is held more sacred, or is more carefully guarded, by the common law, than the right of every individual to the possession and control of his own person, free from all restraint or interference of others . . ."[30]

These early discussions of autonomy and informed consent, though, usually dealt with patients refusing treatment for religious beliefs. Before the early 1970s, when doctors had limited treatment options and patients overwhelmingly wanted to try all of those options, questions of autonomy and consent at the end of life really did not come up or even matter.

For example, the American Hospital Association (AHA) first approved its *Statement on a Patient's Bill of Rights* on February 6, 1973. That statement decreed as a matter of AHA policy that, for the first time, patients had both the right to information necessary to give informed consent and "the right to refuse treatment to the extent permitted by law and to be informed of the medical consequences of his action."[31]

The concept of informed consent grew complicated as the technology grew more complex and medical options multiplied. And a new question arose: How could doctors obtain consent, or refusal of consent, from one who could no longer speak? As medicine developed the tools to be able to maintain a person in an unconscious state, like Karen Quinlan, Nancy Cruzan, and Terri Schiavo, the law fumbled through these hard issues.

Judges tried to reason that an unconscious patient like Karen Quinlan retained her right to autonomy, which included the right to refuse unwanted medical treatment. But if she could not speak for herself, how would her constitutional and common law rights be exercised? Can a person in a permanent coma exercise rights at all? To exercise my right to vote I can go to the poll and make a choice; a person in a coma cannot do that, so does she really have that right anymore?

In an effort to solve this issue, judges devised the concept of "substituted judgment." Using this concept, a substitute decision maker exercises the right of the incapacitated person by trying to determine what the person would want if she could speak, based on what she said prior to incapacity and how she has lived her life. In the absence of that information, the law at times moved to a "best interest standard," that is, trying to determine what was best for the patient.

This question was not so difficult when Dr. Lown was talking to Mr. C's wife about a last-ditch, brand new procedure—shocking the chest with paddles. It becomes profoundly difficult when trying to decide what is "right" for a patient in a persistent vegetative state.

■ ■ ■

None of this fairly academic discussion about substituted judgment or best interest or battery or autonomy came up on February 7, 1983, when a nurse at Freeman Hospital in Joplin, Missouri asked Joe Cruzan to sign a consent form authorizing the surgical procedure to insert a gastrostomy tube directly into his 25-year-old daughter Nancy's stomach, about three weeks after the car wreck that ultimately left her in a persistent vegetative state. The concept of the less invasive surgery for a PEG tube, invented in Cleveland in 1979 (discussed in Chapter 11), had not yet made its way to Joplin, Missouri—the proposed surgery was a full surgical gastrostomy.

That consent form, like those of most hospitals in America in 1983, ten years after the endorsement of the concept of informed consent by the American Hospital Association, included this language near the top:

> The nature and purpose of the operation, possible alternative methods of treatment, the risks involved, and the possibility of complications have been fully explained to me. No guarantee or assurance has been given by anyone as to the results that may be obtained.

To "fully explain the risks involved" to the unconscious patient's father that day, the physical as well as emotional risks, the nurse would have needed wisdom and foresight that few people possess. Joe Cruzan did not discuss the language of the form or any risks with the nurse. He did not talk about trying the treatment for a period of time to see if it could serve as a bridge to recovery. He did not talk about the nature of a feeding tube as medical treatment. No one told him that by giving this permission, he had forfeited the right to undo that permission and remove the feeding tube.

Joe did not even read the form closely; he simply signed the paper. None of what it said really mattered at the time. As Joyce Cruzan, Nancy's mother, told *National Public Radio* correspondent Nina Totenberg years later, "We didn't read anything we signed; if they said we needed to do it, we signed it. When it's just been three or four weeks after the accident you think, you know, there's a good chance she's going to get better." Joe always said, "We would have signed anything. We were just waiting for Nancy to wake up."[32]

CHAPTER 6

The Case of Nancy Cruzan

BEGINNING IN THE SPRING OF 1988, Nancy Cruzan began the second chapter in the education of the American public about the right to die. Three major cases over thirty years have shaped public opinion on this issue and all of them involved young women: Karen Ann Quinlan, Nancy Cruzan, and Terri Schiavo. I don't say this to diminish the anguish or importance of all of the other families who have been through public right-to-die cases: Hugh Finn, Robert Wendland, Paul Brophy, Daniel Delio, and many more, including my client and friend Pete Busalacchi, the father of Chris. But *Quinlan*, *Cruzan*, and *Schiavo* are the three cultural lightning rods around which our policies and ideas formed.

With Karen Ann Quinlan in 1976, the societal discussion was

abstract in many ways, probably for two reasons. Since the public saw the ubiquitous black-and-white high school yearbook photo of Karen, and the media talked about and their sketch artists drew pictures like Sleeping Beauty, the public really saw nothing of the disquieting picture of a destroyed brain that is the reality of the persistent vegetative state.

Perhaps more importantly, though, society likely wasn't ready even to contemplate such hard realities. Our education about this new, advancing medical technology—its miracles and its nightmares—was like early elementary school; the public was working hard to grasp the basics, only counting, not multiplying yet. Most of us still wanted our doctors to "do everything." No one really was concerned about what that meant because in 1976 "everything" wasn't much yet.

In the spring of 1988, the *Cruzan* case brought photographs and video of the persistent vegetative state to America. The Cruzans had agreed to allow Elizabeth "Betsey" Arledge, a producer of documentaries for PBS's *Frontline*, to film their journey through the process. Arledge had contacted a group in New York called the Society for the Right to Die about potential right-to-die cases, and the Cruzans were on their list because Joe Cruzan had phoned the Society looking for information. Arledge picked the Cruzans from a list of families around the country in large part because of timing: the Cruzans were about to start down the road of dealing with "the system."[1]

Eventually, the PBS series *Frontline* aired three separate documentaries on *Cruzan* over a four-year period (*Frontline* had never before expanded beyond a single documentary on a subject). They also allowed Ted Koppel and *Nightline* to show parts of the *Frontline* video, and many other news stations around the country then used that video without permission. The videotape took the public into Nancy's hospital room and "showed" the viewers the questions that were confronting the Cruzan family.

By the time of the first trial in *Cruzan* in March of 1988, the public probably was ready in some ways to start seeing these pictures. Families were beginning to experience stories of loved ones who died "on machines" that they didn't really want, some state legislatures had passed living will laws, and a few other cases like Karen Ann Quinlan's had made their way into the courts, and in some cases the press.

Like the *Schiavo* case later, though, it took an unusual turn of events to move the story onto the national page. That would happen in *Schiavo* when the Florida legislature passed Terri's Law and the governor ordered her feeding tube reinserted. It happened in *Cruzan* on July 3, 1989, when the U.S. Supreme Court agreed to hear the case. For the following year-and-a-half, the American public talked about Nancy Cruzan and the right to die.

The huge difference between the *Cruzan* and *Schiavo* cases is that the Cruzan family was united in their belief that Nancy Cruzan would want the feeding tube removed. In many other ways, however, the cases, and stories, are similar. I was the lawyer for the Cruzan family for nearly four years, from the first trial to Nancy's death. When I first became involved in the summer of 1987, Nancy Cruzan already had been in persistent vegetative state for four years. Nancy had been in a single-car accident, and like Terri Schiavo, had suffered anoxia, or lack of oxygen to the brain. As I reconstructed the night of the accident, I concluded she may have gone as long as thirty minutes without oxygen before paramedics resuscitated her.[2]

In hindsight, it was clear that she suffered a permanent loss of consciousness by the side of that road as a result of the anoxia. Families in those horrific situations, of course, don't have the benefit of hindsight. It took the Cruzans years before they really understood her condition, first trying to coax a recovery from Nancy, then learning about a diagnosis as counter-intuitive as "eyes-open unconsciousness," and ultimately coming to terms with the reality of the persistent vegetative state. Faced with that reality, they concluded that if Nancy could speak with them, she would say, "Let me go."[3]

Soon after coming to that decision, the Cruzans talked with the head of the state hospital, and learned that the hospital would not remove the feeding tube without a court order. Joe Cruzan talked with the probate judge about simply taking Nancy home to remove the tube, and the judge told Joe that an overly-zealous prosecutor could charge him with murder if he did. As a result, we ended up in a trial court with the Missouri Attorney General, the General Counsel of the Missouri Department of Health, and a *guardian ad litem* lawyer appointed by the trial judge on the other side. Ultimately, Nancy's case ended up before the U.S. Supreme Court.

On July 3, 1989, the Supreme Court put the issue of the right to die up for national debate when it agreed to hear the appeal of the Cruzan family. Immediately with that announcement, people began to line up on either side of the issue. Groups with an interest in cases before the Court can file what are called *amicus*, or friend-of-the-court, briefs. These briefs basically tell the Court why the group has an interest in the case, what expertise they might bring to the questions presented, how many people they represent, and how those people recommend the Court resolve the case in question.

In *Cruzan*, the Court received over twice as many of these briefs as they had in *Roe v. Wade*, the landmark abortion case. Twenty separate briefs went to the Court in support of the Cruzans, and many of those were signed by multiple parties. When the membership was added together, the briefs represented the voices of millions of Americans. Those voices came from across the country and from all walks of life, such as the American Medical Association, United Methodist Church, the American Geriatrics Society, the National Hospice Organization, as well as many others.[4] The same number of briefs came to the Court opposing the Cruzans. Several came from the fringes, but two very powerful societal forces aligned against the Cruzans: the U.S. Conference of Catholic Bishops (discussed in Chapter 12), and the Solicitor General of the United States, who at the time was former federal judge Kenneth Starr.

The Court set the date for oral argument for December 6, 1989. Throughout the fall, on television and radio, in barbershops, on golf courses, in churches, at medical schools, the public was talking about this case: What was this new condition that the television anchors were calling by its acronym, PVS? What exactly was a feeding tube? What were these documents called living wills? And, what was "right" for Nancy Cruzan?

That discussion continued in 1990, and then ignited once again on June 25, 1990, when the U.S. Supreme Court issued its ruling in

Cruzan. The final vote in the case split 5-4, and five of the nine justices wrote their own separate opinions: the majority opinion, two concurring opinions, and two dissents.[5] As sometimes happens with complicated Supreme Court opinions, the interest groups on both sides found something to claim as victory.

The main opinion, written on behalf of the five-justice majority by Chief Justice William Rehnquist, ruled against the Cruzans. The Missouri Supreme Court had found that unless Nancy Cruzan had left clear and convincing evidence of her wish to remove the feeding tube, it had to stay in place. Chief Justice Rehnquist wrote that this Missouri ruling did not violate the federal Constitution. The Court did not endorse the Missouri heightened evidentiary standard, but merely concluded that that standard did not violate the Constitution. Right-to-life groups and others supporting the state applauded this ruling.

Supporters of the Cruzans, however, cheered the recognition by the Chief Justice that competent people have a constitutional right, a liberty right, to refuse medical treatment. The Court had never directly recognized this federal right before.[6] They also were encouraged by the Court's conclusion that artificial nutrition and hydration is medical treatment like a respirator or dialysis or any other device that's taken the place of a natural function that's been lost. Five of the nine justices acknowledged this medical fact explicitly, and the remaining four implicitly.[7]

Chief Justice Rehnquist also provided grounds for the Cruzans to have a new trial, based on "the discovery of new evidence regarding the patient's intent."[8] We went back to southern Missouri for that new trial the following November. Three friends of Nancy's testified about conversations they'd had with Nancy about living on life support. These friends contacted the parents after hearing about Nancy's accident and lawsuit through the extensive media coverage. Unlike the first trial, this time the Missouri Attorney General and Department of Health chose not to oppose the family, or to even participate in the trial.

Though the Cruzans' story played out in the court system, in many ways it was not about the law. In the two and a half years between the first trial in March of 1988 and the last trial in November of 1990, the public understanding in Missouri about the right to die had grown dramatically. Public opinion polls in 1990 showed overwhelming support for the Cruzans. That summer, 88% of Missourians when polled said that they supported the decision made by the Cruzan family, and 99% of doctors surveyed agreed that it was ethically appropriate to removed a feeding tube from a permanently vegetative patient at the request of the patient's family.[9] Public education, understanding, and acceptance ultimately played as important a role as the law.

As with the *Schiavo* case, the public acceptance was not unanimous. On December 14, 1990, now eight years after Nancy's car accident, the trial court again ruled in favor of Nancy Cruzan's parents. We were at the state hospital within minutes of the public release of that ruling; a doctor there removed her feeding tube, and that afternoon the hospital transferred Nancy to their hospice wing.

Over the course of the next eleven-and-a-half days, the national discussion about the right to die began again in earnest. Protesters from around the country arrived in the hilly southern Missouri town of Mt. Vernon, with the satellite television trucks not far behind them. On the fourth morning, Joe Cruzan watched from Nancy's second floor window as a van with the sign "Abortion Kills Children" in its window and a blue school bus with the word "MIRACLE" written on it pulled up out front, and dozens of protesters emerged and began walking quickly or jogging toward the hospital wing. Joe was alarmed at how many there were and how quickly they were streaming into the building below him. He leaned against the door, and said later that he was ready to "knock out anyone" who tried to enter Nancy's room.

He need not have worried, because the dozens of police officers in the building had the situation under control, and they quickly thwarted the onslaught. Some protesters were arrested while others were sent back outside, where they milled around. Various groups and individuals also filed emergency appeals in the state and federal courts over that eleven days, seven appeals in all. The weather turned on a dime from unseasonably warm to a bitter, biting cold, with snow. Signs popped up on the lawn of the hospital that read "Missouri Euthanasia Center" and "Atrosity [sic] Torture Murder." On the day before Christmas a big new sign read "Nancy's Gift at Christmas from her Parents and Doctor—DEATH!"[10]

Randall Terry from Operation Rescue and the Reverend Pat Mahoney from Florida arrived and led protests and media outreach, as they would later in the *Schiavo* case. Inside the hospital the family huddled together, day after day, talking softly, holding Nancy's hands, and praying. The hospice people took care of Nancy and her family. And at 2:47 a.m. on December 26, 1990, Nancy Cruzan's breathing stopped and she died.

Two days later the Cruzans buried Nancy in the Carterville town cemetery, about a mile outside of town. Her favorite music played during her service; all of the songs were by now consigned to oldies stations. Respectful reporters and cameramen did not venture much closer than about a hundred yards from the graveside as the minister prayed and the family cried. Then the first Gulf War broke out in January of 1991, and like Terri Schiavo and the death of the Pope in the spring of 2005, the media moved on.

In the wake of the *Cruzan* case, the federal government passed a law called the Patient Self Determination Act, which provides that all hospitals in the U.S. must counsel entering patients about living wills and other health care planning. Many states also passed laws seeking to address the issues raised by the case. In Missouri, for example, the legislature in 1991 passed a durable power of attorney for health care. This law allows a competent adult to name another person to make health care decisions if they become unable to make such decisions.[11]

The public education from the *Cruzan* case caused significant changes in the public policy reflected in the new Missouri law. In 1985, when Missouri passed its living will law, that law had specified that feeding tubes were not medical treatment. In 1991, after *Cruzan*, the legislature reached the opposite conclusion. More importantly, the new law endorsed the weighing of quality of life factors in making decisions under the new law. The Missouri Supreme Court in *Cruzan* had rejected quality of life as an inappropriate factor for loved ones to consider. Other states, like Florida, adopted what some people call hierarchy laws.[12] These laws basically set up an order of preference of who will make decisions for a patient who cannot speak and who left no clear instructions such as a health care power of attorney or living will.

All of these legislative efforts were useful to an extent but, ultimately, were limited in their reach. Fifteen years after Nancy Cruzan's death, Terri Schiavo would help the American public understand that the law, though well-intentioned, has limited usefulness in the emotional terrain of making decisions about dying.

How We Die in America Today

THE POINT OF the first half of this book is that the hard questions raised by a case like Terri Schiavo's are blindingly new for humankind. They've come at society in a remarkable rush of technological change. They are enormously complex. And the black and white of the law is no place to find answers to such humanly nuanced, gray-area questions.

I often hear people in the field of bioethics claim that society has worked on the issues raised in a case like Terri Schiavo's for "a long time" without significant progress. My reaction is the opposite. It strikes me that the questions brought on by medical technology have come upon us in a relatively short time, and that society is at the beginning of even grasping their dimension and complexity, let alone coming up with satisfactory answers.

Consider the changes we've covered so far in this book. All of that technological progress has arrived in basically one generation, from Karen Ann Quinlan to Nancy Cruzan to Terri Schiavo. Karen Quinlan landed in an emergency room in New Jersey on April 15, 1975. To that point, medicine, law, and certainly the greater public had not really thought much at all about what to do when technology was able to "save" the stem of the brain that houses basic reflexes, but not the upper, thinking part. The question hadn't really come up. The 911 system to summon help to an accident scene more quickly had just been invented in 1968; the first school program in Miami to train ambulance attendants in CPR had held its first class in 1969; respirators for the injured in emergency rooms were still cumbersome and basic, with soldered wires that could come loose as they rolled clumsily over expansion joints in the hospital hallways.

Even a technology as seemingly simple as a feeding tube (discussed in Chapter 11) was far less sophisticated in 1975. Medicine had named the condition into which Karen Ann Quinlan had fallen—the persistent vegetative state—only three years earlier, in 1972. Informed, thoughtful discussion about any ethical issues raised by this newly named, newly created condition was years away.

THE LIMITED REACH OF THE LAW

The law had not been involved in the dying process in any real way before Karen Quinlan. Society had had no need. Sick or injured people who still had the capacity to make their own decisions were not really thinking about autonomy or informed consent at the time of *Quinlan*. The law had not begun to examine what the rules would be for a patient who might claim a newly recognized autonomy right to say "No" to medical treatment because the answer was nearly always "Yes."

The case of Karen Ann Quinlan presented an even more complicated and ethereal legal question: Did a permanently unconscious person somehow retain a "right" to "decide" about medical treatments that might be done to her? If so, how would the patient assert such a right? These issues were not even on the legal radar screen in the spring of 1975 when Karen Quinlan was rushed to the hospital. The law had not begun its awkward grappling with an idea like substituted judgment because this group of permanently unconscious people who needed the doctrine didn't exist yet. (By the time of our first trial in the *Cruzan* case in 1988, experts estimated that there were about 10,000 patients in United States with a diagnosis of persistent vegetative state at any one time.)[1] In the spring of 1975, living wills had quite recently at that point been a concept in one lawyer's head, and the experiment with that part of the law would start in earnest the following year when California passed the first state living will law in 1976.

The first hesitant steps of the law into the world of medical decision-making in the *Quinlan* case provided a glimpse of how limited the law's effectiveness might ultimately be. Eighteen days after the order of the New Jersey Supreme Court in *Quinlan*, the hospital still would not comply with the order, and the family and their lawyer found themselves across from doctors and administrators in a tense conference room. Sister Mary Urban, speaking on behalf of the Board of Trustees, told Mr. and Mrs. Quinlan that the Catholic hospital had not complied because to remove a respirator was "morally incorrect." After some wrangling she came to her point: "You have to understand our position, Mr. Quinlan. In this hospital we don't kill people."

"We're not asking you to kill anyone!" Joe Quinlan replied, leaping from his seat. "It should be obvious to anyone—to anyone—that the respirator is artificial. That's what this whole thing's about!" The ruling from the state's high court that an unconscious person still had rights didn't matter that much. The hospital was not going to remove the respirator, regardless of what the court decision said.[2]

Thirty years later, when the *Schiavo* case came into the public eye, the law had not grown significantly more effective at making end-of-life decisions. The law in Florida that should have applied in the *Schiavo* case is clear. It just didn't matter. In 1998 when Michael Schiavo went to court to seek removal of Terri Schiavo's feeding tube, before the real legal battling had even begun, Terri Schiavo had been diagnosed as being in a persistent vegetative state for nearly eight years.

Removing her feeding tube fit within the ethical guidelines of every major medical and religious group in the country, and by Florida law, Michael Schiavo—as Terri's husband and legal guardian—was the appropriate decision maker.[3] By that point in 1998, however, the fight with her parents had already festered for five years, and the Schindlers and Michael Schiavo had not spoken to one another that entire time. So they ended up fighting in the court system for seven more long years of their lives. The judges and the law ultimately decided the dispute, which is what courts do, but the law had no tools to repair the fractured relationships or the broken-down communication.[4]

I have talked with many judges who have faced cases like *Quinlan*, *Cruzan*, and *Schiavo*. All of those cases were less public than those three famous cases, of course, but the cases were still complex and emotionally charged for the families and judges involved. I have discussed these cases with judges who were active in the National Right to Life organization prior to ascending to the bench, and judges formerly active in the American Civil Liberties Union. I've never talked to any judge who claimed any special expertise in a right-to-die case. To the contrary, most said they would prefer that the rest of us in society would resolve the disputes without resort to the courts, because the judges have no special wisdom about dying.

Even when the law is involved through the more reflective, deliberative legislative process (that is, the passing of new laws), its ultimate effect is limited. Those involved in that legislative process typically enter with good will and high hopes. I talked with Missouri legislators in 1987 about the then-new Missouri living will law; they thought they were "solving" the Nancy Cruzan type of case when they had passed that law. In 1990 I provided comments and advice in the drafting of the bill that ultimately became the federal law applicable to the hospitals across the country, the Patient Self-Determination Act.[5] I know that Senator John Danforth and others who were intimately involved with this legislation had high expectations for its usefulness.

While these laws are useful to a point by providing structure, guidance, and rules, often the written law doesn't end up mattering much in decision-making around our dying and death. Medical providers all have stories about living wills or health care powers of attorney not working as intended. A father makes one copy of his living will, which he keeps in his safe deposit box at the bank, but he's now in a coma, and no one else has access to that box. Or a living will, patterned after a state law passed years ago, speaks mainly of life support and terminal condition. The doctor tells the family that the living will does not help in answering whether their now-frail and increasingly demented father would want aggressive antibiotic treatment for pneumonia. Or, very commonly, a clear power of attorney or living will may exist, but the adult children are in conflict about what is "right" for mom, as they've been in conflict on most topics for many years. Medical providers faced with warring relatives usually find that the piece of paper cannot bring resolution to either the broken relationships or the "war" over mom's care.

During such times of difficult decision-making, medical providers basically look for help wherever they can find it. They are trying to do what's right and don't have a lot of time or energy left to worry about the law. At a talk I gave in Chicago in the spring of 2005, a lawyer stood during the question and answer period and said he'd enjoyed the talk but worried about how my general advice might be interpreted for his state.

"In Illinois, for a living will to be effective, the language about refusing nutrition and hydration, by statute, must be in all capital letters," he said. We had a good discussion about the constitutional right to make decisions, which I believe would extend to the right to draft a reliable living will in your own words (and even, in my opinion, to exercise that right simply by expressing your wishes orally). Then we moved on. Afterward, a nurse came up and said quietly, "I didn't want to contradict the lawyer, but we take anything at our hospice: forms they get off the Internet, handwritten living wills, even what family members tell us they said. We're trying to get an idea of what the patient would want."

No doubt medical providers look for help wherever they can find it because the questions are so complicated. As technology has proliferated, the questions related to its proper use, quite logically, have grown more complex. Judges will decide disputes that technology creates, like the *Quinlan*, *Cruzan*, and *Schiavo* cases, and legislators will pass laws regulating living wills and other documents. But the law always will have a limited ability to guide families in deciding what is "right" when they face medical decisions for a seriously-ill loved one.

THE TIME OF "LETTING NATURE TAKE ITS COURSE" IS GONE

Each spring, lawyers and judges from Kansas City gather together in an Ozark mountain resort for a weekend of meetings and fellowship. I remember sitting at one of these meetings in the early 1990s on an outdoor terrace with a breathtaking view of an Ozark mountain lake far below, listening to a group of much more senior lawyers talk about when they thought the practice of law had "gone wrong." The obvious thread tying their complaints together was technology. The complaints moved back through time: computers that allowed cutting and pasting of documents had caused a flood of paper; all of it still had to be read. No, it started earlier, another said, with the IBM Selectric typewriter; no, Mag card machines; no, Dictaphones.

They were laughing, nostalgic about a simpler time. The oldest one there had been sipping his scotch and listening, and then he cleared his throat. "You guys want to know where it went wrong? And I'm serious. Air conditioning," he said. "Before they remodeled the courthouse in, when was it, 1965, 1960? Anyway, it was too hot to do much in the summer, so everybody took it easy. Summer had a nice, relaxing pace. We'd come in some days, others we'd play some golf. The damn air conditioning ruined the practice of law." They all sat there quietly, apparently thinking about the dark side of air conditioning.

It would be interesting to reconvene this group now in 2006, twelve or so years later, and see if e-mail, the Internet, BlackBerrys, document scanning, camera cell phones, and law books on CD had delivered to these men their technological promise of greater efficiency and more time with family—or if they have, perversely, tightened still further the technological bind of these lawyers to their offices. We live in a time when it's nearly impossible to fathom how deeply technology affects every part of our world, including medicine. This same discussion among the lawyers happens with doctors, too. A neurosurgeon who testified as an expert for me in the *Busalacchi* right-to-die case in St. Louis told me that there once was a time when he had a decent handle on most of medicine, not just neurology. By 1992 (the time of that trial) it had grown so complex that he could not even keep up with the reading of the two leading journals in his neurosurgical subspecialty, let alone the broader field of neurology—or even broader, medicine itself.

Dr. Lown was one doctor in Boston in November of 1959. Out of options, he came up with a radical idea when confronted with a dying heart patient: shock the heart of that conscious patient from the outside. Today, an entire industry exists of doctors and technicians and manufacturers of devices and drugs who carry on the work that began one cold morning in Boston at the bedside of Mr. C. Cardiologists receive specialized training to become electrophysiologists and arrhythmologists, spending their days focused solely on diagnosis and treatment of heart rhythm disorders. Specialized technicians called echocardiographers use high-frequency sound waves (ultrasound) to view all four chambers of the heart, the heart valves, the great blood vessels entering and leaving the heart, as well as the sac around the heart. Angioplastic surgeons have learned noninvasive procedures using long probes and balloons to repair damaged hearts.

Pharmaceutical companies invent new heart drugs constantly, such as Coreg and Tiazac and Dilacor. Medical device companies like Medtronic develop new devices, such as tiny ICDs, or implantable cardioverter-defibrillators (first approved by the FDA in 1985). These devices—known as pacemakers—are placed surgically below the skin near the collarbone. Tiny lead wires are threaded through a vein into the heart, and a computer chip in the ICD device tells it when to deliver the electrical shock to control a heart that is beating too fast, and to correct the dreaded V-fib. (At about the time Dr. Lown was shocking Mr. C in November of 1959, Medtronic was a fledgling company founded by two brothers-in-law in Minneapolis—a former electrical engineering student and a lumberyard worker—who operated out of a garage, repairing medical equipment like centrifuges. Medtronic today operates from about 250 manufacturing, sales and research facilities around the world.)[6] Walking down airport hallways across the country today, passengers see compact defibrillator paddles mounted on the wall, and airport personnel are trained in their use. The technology to save lives is now available in malls, high school gyms, churches, and many other public areas.

Cardiologists aren't the only medical professionals who have benefited from these technological advances; physicians specializing in other organs including the brain, skin, liver, kidneys, intestines, lymph nodes, uterus, pancreas, bladder, esophagus, intestines, lungs, and so on have benefited as well. Doctors today can treat a sick body from head to toe, part by part, with tools that were pure science fiction when Dr. Plum was naming the persistent vegetative state in 1972.

Advances in medical science have helped to create remarkable improvements in health and survival. In 1900 the average life expectancy was 41 years in the United States; by 2000 it had risen to an astounding 77 years, thus nearly doubling in 100 years.[7] Economist Julian Simon has described this development as "the greatest single achievement in history."[8] Today the elderly in the United States are getting knees replaced, hearts transplanted, arteries ballooned open, and not only living to tell about it, but also thriving. How could we not love technology?

Our doctors are equally subject to technology's allure. They learn in medical school to assess, treat, and cure. They then move into a hospital culture where a death, even among the aged, is seen as a failure. The young Dr. Lown in 1959 plied the silver paddles on the chest of a living human being for the first time, and saw a miracle: a racing, out-of-control heart instantly returned to normal heartbeat. The young Dr. Potter in 1963 compressed a chest and saved the hardware store owner, and the whole town knew it. Their tools were unbelievably basic compared to the arsenal available to a young doctor today, but the miracles are equally wonderful. How could we deny today's doctor such joy? Or today's patient? Why in the world would we want to?

In truth, we don't want to, and we shouldn't want to. We want the technology, and we want the cure. As I pointed out earlier, when surveyed, the majority of us say that when our dying comes, we hope to be at home, free from pain, surrounded by loved ones, and not hooked up to machines.[9] But I'm convinced that we also very much want our doctors to continue to use those machines right up to the very moment when the doctor is sure that those miraculous tools can't "fix" us. Trying to find that exact line is no easy business.

Often during the public wrangling over Terri Schiavo's fate I heard commentators or advocates argue that "we should let nature take its course." Interestingly, people from either side of the divide attempted to claim this ground to support their version of what was "right" for Terri Schiavo: leave the tube in, or take the tube out and let nature take its course. The dispute makes the point—the time of nature taking its course for the seriously ill in America is over.

It is frequently stated in the medical and social science literature that dying once took place in the home. It was common, and the "death bed" was familiar furniture. Infection spread quickly, medicine had no real tools to fight it, and death predictably came. By contrast, today most dying (around 80 percent by the reckoning of many groups) takes place in institutions, either a hospital or nursing home.[10] Over a course of years of living with and battling a chronic illness, dozens of decisions are made about the use of medicines and technologies to beat back an illness. Like a river altered for commerce by locks, dams, and channel dredging, nature's course is radically transformed in this technological world. The path is chosen and altered. But the river still ends up in the sea.

Most of the questions about dying and medical treatment today do not involve young, recently healthy patients like Karen Ann Quinlan, Nancy Cruzan or Terri Schiavo; they involve the elderly. But the ethical issues are in many ways the same. Dr. Joanne Lynn served as one of two assistant directors on the first President's Commission, in the late 1970s and into the early 1980s, and she has written and worked to improve end-of-life care ever since. She and I sat together at the PBS roundtable in December of 1989 following the oral argument in *Cruzan*. That same year she began work as co-director of the largest scientific study of the dying ever done in this country, the SUPPORT study, which I'll talk about in the next chapter. Dr. Lynn has long been a passionate voice in a world of advancing medical complexity.

I heard Lynn speak in November of 2005 at a briefing for legislative staffers on Capitol Hill in Washington. She started her talk with this bit of a party trick for the audience: "Let's say that everyone in this room can choose how you will die. How many of you would pick cancer?" Three hands went up, including mine. "How about heart and lung disease?" A few more hands. "Then the rest of you have chosen to die of old age and frailty, your body and mind dwindling over a period of several years."[11] She laughed then, and less confident laughter made its way around the room to join her.

Lynn had just described the three major paths to modern dying. About 2.5 million people die each year in the United States,[12] and a large percentage of those deaths, about 80 percent, follow three basic paths. The first group (the one I chose), includes about 20 percent of Americans, or 500,000 people annually. Cancer patients typically die after a long period of living with a fatal illness, sometimes years, during which they were able to stay fully, or mostly, engaged in life despite the illness. Death usually comes with a few weeks or months of rapid decline at the end.

The second group includes about 25 percent of the dying in America or 625,000 annual deaths. With chronic heart failure and emphysema, decline is slower and takes place over a longer time than with cancer. That decline is punctuated with acute episodes, hospitalizations and recovery, with overall function declining to some degree with each acute episode. At some point, an acute episode comes, and this time the patient has gone too far downhill to climb back up. Death comes then, within hours or days, or more often weeks, depending on the severity of the acute episode and the amount of the patient's residual function.

The final group is the largest, accounting for nearly 40 percent of all deaths in the United States today, or about one million deaths annually. These patients are the frail elderly, destined for years of declining function, both mentally and physically. About half of these patients have serious mental decline as part of their aging. As these patients lose function, they need increasing care and support, often from a family member or friend. Death ultimately comes at a point of significant physical frailty and as a result of a challenge that would have simply been an annoyance earlier in life to a stronger body—the flu, a broken hip, pneumonia, a urinary infection. The likelihood of a particular manner of death is proportionate to the age of the patient. The incidence of cancer peaks around age 70, and chronic heart and lung failure peaks around age 80. For those who make it past age 80, they are likely to experience health challenges related to frailty, or dementia, or both.[13]

What is the cause of death for those in the final group—the one million frail and demented elderly—who die each year? Is it truly an attack of pneumonia, or is the cause really old age? In the newest version of the International Classification of Diseases, a list that doctors use to indicate the cause of death on a death certificate, there are 113 possible choices. But "old age" is not one of them. That category was removed from the list long ago, in 1913. Scientists, doctors, and anthropologists today debate whether old age in technological America is a natural part of the dying process, or a disease to be attacked.[14]

Another end-of-life pioneer, Dr. Sherwin Nuland at Yale-New Haven Hospital in Connecticut, conducted some fascinating research in the 1970s. Dr. Nuland suspected that many of his elderly patients were in effect dying of old age (whether he was allowed to write that on their death certificates or not), that their bodies were declining and their systems shutting down across the board. Together with Dr. G.J. Walker Smith, the director of autopsy, Nuland studied the autopsies of twenty-three patients who died over a two-year period at Yale-New Haven. The subjects were old when they died, with an average age of 88, the oldest being 95. Twelve were men, eleven were women.

The results confirmed Nuland's intuition. All 23 autopsies revealed advanced atheromatous disease (thickening and calcification of arteries) in the vessels of either the heart or brain, and nearly all had it in both. Three who died of other causes had cancers that doctors had never known about. Three others had similarly undetected aneurysms, ready to explode if another organ had not failed first. Eleven brains that were studied microscopically showed old infarcts (strokes), even though only one of the eleven had a history of stroke. Several had urinary tract infections. Fourteen had atherosclerotic arteries leading to their kidneys. One man who died of stomach cancer had gangrene in his leg.

"An octogenarian who dies of myocardial infarction is not simply a weather-beaten senior citizen with heart disease," Dr. Nuland wrote about this research. "He is the victim of an insidious progression that involves all of him, and that progression is called aging."[15] And Drs. Nuland and Smith were looking at deaths from 1970 to 1972, long before our country began in earnest its technologically-supported aging.

Aging happens in human beings, like leaks developing in a dike. When technology plugs one hole here, a new leak springs open down there because the water continues its relentless pressure against the entire weakening wall. Joanne Lynn makes the point that the newspaper headlines shouting "New Drug Prevents Heart Disease in Elderly" could just as accurately read "New Drug Promises Major Increases in Dementia."[16] The Alzheimer's Association estimates that today there are 4.5 million Americans suffering from Alzheimer's disease, and that that number could climb to 16 million by the year 2050 unless a cure is found.[17] When a cure is found, pressure will build in another spot along the dike.

Likewise, the U.S. Census Bureau estimates that the population aged 85 and older will more than quadruple between now and 2050, from 4 million to 18 million. At present, one person in twenty after age 85 is fully mobile.[18] In the year 2000, only Florida had a population with at least 17 percent of the citizens age 65 or older. Twenty-five years from now, 44 states will look like Florida.[19] My parents retired to Naples, Florida in 1984, and we spent many great Christmas holidays on the beautiful Gulf Coast beaches. Parked at the beach one day, I saw a hot-rod Camaro with this bumper sticker: "When I Get Old I'm Going to Move North and Drive Real Slow." Changes are coming.

The impact of our aging society is only beginning to emerge. Indeed, it's hard to fathom the questions we will face in a world where technology is advancing so rapidly. And it's perhaps even harder to fathom how many of us will be asking these questions. Likely the idea of nature taking its course will be an ever more distant memory as the U.S. population ages. Decisions about the appropriate use of medical treatment will need to be made all of the time. The tension will no doubt grow. We will want the machines if the doctor believes she can return us to living life, and we will want a natural dying free from machines if the doctor can't help us. That line, elusive today, will likely grow harder to find as technology continues its march forward.

Yet, however elusive that line may be, we still eventually will step across it. Dying then will come to each of us, as it did to Dr. Lown's Mr. C in 1959, Dr. Potter's Mr. X in 1975, Nancy Cruzan in 1990, and Terri Schiavo in 2005. The machines and new medicines can delay our dying, but they can't stop it. And *that* ultimate fact, it turns out, is very hard to talk about—hard for patients, hard for families, hard for doctors, even hard for lawyers.

CHAPTER 8

Dying on the "Institutional Glide Path"

OVER A FOUR-YEAR PERIOD beginning in 1989, a group of researchers conducted the largest study of death and dying ever undertaken in this country.[1] Dr. Joanne Lynn was one of the two co-directors of this study, which is now called by its acronym, SUPPORT (The Study to Understand Prognoses and Preferences for Outcomes and Risks of Treatments). The research team enrolled 9,105 seriously ill patients in five teaching hospitals around the country. Approximately 5,000 of those patients died during the study. The initial goal of the project was to better understand how decisions were made for these seriously ill patients, to provide better information about what treatments could accomplish, and then to provide better support for whomever was making decisions. The study took place in two phases: an initial investigative phase and a second intervention phase.

The results of the initial investigative phase of SUPPORT are disquieting. Half of the conscious patients suffered pain that went untreated before they died. Written directives like a living will, when found, were vague. Doctors and family did not understand patient preferences. Often doctors had no idea whether their patients wanted a do-not-resuscitate (DNR) order in their charts. Patients frequently died after prolonged stays in ICUs.[2] (The Robert Wood Johnson Foundation, which funded the research, worried that publishing these findings would alarm the American public because the conclusions were so dismal.)

In the second, intervention phase of the study, conducted from 1992 to 1994, Dr. Lynn and colleagues sought remedies to these rather dismal results. They divided study participants into two groups. For the test group they hired specially trained nurses to communicate with families and their doctors about disease prognosis and treatment, and appropriate goal setting. Doctors received specialized training to deal with this seriously ill population. They devoted substantial time, effort, and money to improving end-of-life decision-making.

Remarkably, these significant interventions made no difference in how decisions were made in the two groups or the basic patterns of care.[3] Looking back, it wasn't that doctors refused to follow patients' wishes. The explanation for the failure of the intervention to change behaviors is more complicated than that, consisting of several layers, all produced in one way or another by medical technology.

First, is the difficulty in prognosis. "Doc, how much longer have I got?" comes the raspy, weather-beaten voice in the old Westerns. Those movies would have had a very different story line if the kindly, white-haired country doctor had shaken his head, chuckled, and said, "You know, cowboy, I don't have much idea at all." To me, a layperson, the most startling conclusion from the SUPPORT study is that doctors don't really know with any certainty how to predict when a very ill patient will die. Until I read SUPPORT, I thought about death as being predictable for doctors as it is on television today, as it was in the old Westerns. I thought doctors knew when "our time" would come.

They don't. As Dr. Lynn described it, most of the 9,105 seriously ill patients faced an uncertain future, their illness landing them in "the 'middle muddle' of prognoses, bad enough to be at risk of death but good enough to hope for longer survival with the appropriate treatment."[4] The day before they died, over 60 percent of the congestive heart failure patients in the SUPPORT study would have been estimated to have at least two months to live.[5] Even patients with lung cancer—a disease that is more predictable—had a similar optimistic prognosis. Over 40 percent of lung cancer patients had a prognosis of at least two months to live just six days before they died.[6]

Other studies have reached similar conclusions. Drs. Christakis and Lamont in a study of 468 terminally ill patients concluded that while doctors are often called upon to tell these patients "how long they've got," most felt uncomfortable making such a prognosis. Remarkably, when they did make the prognosis, only 20 percent did so with any reasonable accuracy. Overall, Christakis and Lamont concluded that doctors overestimate survival for critically ill patients by a factor of 5.3.[7] In other words, if the doctor says you have six months to live, you'd better plan on about a month. St. Louis University Law School professor Sandra Johnson recently wrote about a study of nursing home residents in which doctors estimated that 1.1 percent of the residents in a study would die within six months. At the end of that time frame, 71 percent of the group was dead.[8] Prognosticating about dying is difficult in today's technological world.

Second, medical technology has dramatically altered how doctors communicate with the seriously ill. When Dr. Plum named the persistent vegetative state in 1972, most doctors did not tell patients bad news, fearing that learning bad news would destroy the patient's hope.[9] Hippocrates taught doctors to "comfort with solicitude and attention, revealing nothing of the patient's present and future condition."[10] Before the 1970s, that's what doctors did. In one study conducted in 1961, 90 percent of doctors said that they would not tell their patients the truth about a cancer diagnosis. The same survey done again in 1978 found a changed medical society; 3 percent of the doctors then said that they would withhold the truth. The President's Commission for the Study of Ethical Problems in Medicine speculated in its 1983 report that advances in medical technology were a big reason for that change in doctors' behavior.[11] In 1961, the cancer diagnosis was "very nearly a death sentence"; by 1978, "remission and even cure" was possible, so they had to talk about all of the various treatments.

The idea of talking to patients openly and honestly is new in the medical world. Many in that culture are working to understand how to do the talk "right" in order to preserve real hope and at the same time avoid false hope. Some social workers bemoan doctors who are too blunt, what some call truth-dumping or false hopelessness. As a social worker at Memorial Sloan-Kettering Cancer Center said in a recent *New York Times* article, "Telling someone they have two years to live isn't useful knowledge. It's noise. Whether or not that prediction is true, they lose their ability to live well in the present."[12]

False hope, however, is equally debilitating. Many doctors avoid the reality of the dying, critically ill patient and look instead to the next piece of technology or clinical trial available, even if it offers little hope of recovery. The patient then simply moves from one technology to the next, ultimately dying in the ICU without the chance to understand that he is dying and find meaning in his remaining time.[13]

Third, if modern technology has made prognoses complex for doctors, and made navigating the discussions with patients significantly more difficult, it shouldn't be a surprise to realize that patients moving into this culture find it daunting. Much of the ethics discussion about medical decision-making revolves around the legal concept of autonomy—the "right" to make decisions about your own medical treatment. In law school (and medical school), autonomy is often treated as sacrosanct. In the day-to-day real world of modern-day hospitals where uncertain prognoses and complicated discussions are commonplace, the doctrine of autonomy is more nuanced.

Legal disputes like the *Cruzan* case shaped the doctrine of autonomy for medicine. And true enough, over the three and a half years from when I met the Cruzans until the court cases were finally over and Nancy died, the family and I had ample time—years, in fact—to sit together and discuss what Nancy would want, what the Cruzans wanted, and how to implement those decisions. Her medical condition, diagnosis, and prognosis, did not change over that time. She was permanently unconscious, in a persistent vegetative state, without hope of regaining consciousness. The medical reality was pretty clear.

For most medical decisions, the medical reality is far less clear. What's more, the moral issues are equally daunting. A friend of mine who is a hospice doctor believes that in the end-of-life discussions today we drastically underestimate the moral and spiritual responsibility that goes with making a life-or-death decision, no matter how the doctor tries to reframe that decision—"Your mother is dying from her disease, not from lack of life support." Many patients and families believe that they do not have the authority to make such decisions and are reluctant to try; they say it's "up to God." Doctors experience the same kind of internal conflict.[14]

Doctors also struggle with questions of how much of a role to take in decision-making. Few want to return to the days of medical paternalism, when doctors simply told patients what they should do. But "full autonomy," simply giving information and telling the patient that she must decide, abandons the duty the doctor has to counsel and to relieve some of the stress of decision-making. A doctor's recommendations can have influence, but so can making no recommendation at all. One approach is for the doctor to encourage a patient to talk out loud about his values before making a recommendation, so that the recommendation will reflect the patient's and not the doctor's values. And when making that recommendation, doctors can make it easy for the patient to pick a different path by telling the patient that many patients make decisions contrary to the doctor's recommendations, and they remain valued patients. Finding such a balance in a hospital filled with technological options is difficult.[15]

Unfortunately, these profound decisions often must be made without time for significant reflection. With the majority of deaths in this country—the 1,625,000 elderly patients dying each year from emphysema, chronic heart failure, frailty, dementia—the patients and their families do not have a similar extended period of reflection during which a hopeless medical condition remains unchanged. It is common to hear loved ones say, "If I'd only known Mom was dying, I would have come sooner, talked with her about this, helped get her affairs in order." Medical providers for the elderly hear words like these all of the time.[16] Even though Mom was in her eighties—with high blood pressure, pulmonary disease, and on oxygen—dying still came suddenly and as a surprise.

Most deaths among the elderly have end points that typically involve sudden onset with the final illness. The family does not have years to reflect on autonomy with prognosis bleak and unchanging as the Cruzans did. They find themselves thrust into the unfamiliar, stressful, emotional setting of a hospital, often nearly in a state of shock. Even if Mom has been ill for a couple of years, the family has likely been on the roller coaster of chronic illness, with some recovery, some illness, some decline in function, some improvement. Whether or not this "next" hospitalization is the final downturn is not clear; effectiveness of different treatments is muddled; and patient preferences are ambiguous, unknown, or changing. All are hard to discuss. Even families that have discussed the issues are often overwhelmed when the hypothetical turns real.

In that place and that emotional state, families and patients don't really want to talk or think or choose, so typically they don't. Instead, the standard hospital practice and culture "takes over" and governs the care that is given. In an acute care hospital, that treatment is often aggressive, what a friend of mine who works at an academic medical center calls the "full court press." Families, patients, and the medical team settle into the routine of providing that standard care—care which that hospital provides for the bulk of its patients, simply doing what they've always done. Dr. Lynn described this settling in as following an established "glide path" in the institution, the family taking comfort that they are good people, following the well-worn path that others have already been down.[17]

The second, intervention phase of SUPPORT (where specially trained nurses were brought in to counsel families and doctors received special education to communicate better), not only failed to improve communication, but also did not affect the default institutional glide path in any way. These glide paths were not the same at each of the five SUPPORT hospitals; in fact, they were quite different, with home vs. hospital deaths and use of supportive home visits and hospice care varying widely among the hospitals.[18] What did not vary was that once an institutional pattern of care was established, interventions intended to change that pattern for a particular patient had no effect.

Dr. Lynn concluded that her team's initial belief that they could change decision-making for the seriously ill was "naively optimistic."[19] I think she is being a little hard on the work of SUPPORT. As new and as complicated as these questions are, it's not a surprise that as a society we are still trying to figure out the best way to use this medical technology. In fact, the SUPPORT results confirm that we are really at the beginning of the venture of understanding how to make choices about the appropriate use of medical technology. Far from reflecting on autonomy and making considered choices, we step onto an institutional glide path heading for a landing, and take the treatment that happens as we descend.

Indeed, for many of the 9,105 patients, the only discussion that happened came when the patient became more difficult to arouse, signaling that the end could be near. At that point, family and care providers in some cases discussed entering a do-not-resuscitate order, or DNR, in the medical chart. Almost half of all DNR orders for SUPPORT patients were written in the last two days of life. The agreement by family to enter the DNR acted in some ways as more as an acknowledgement of physical decline than an actual decision.[20] In many of the 9,105 cases, even this limited discussion did not happen.

DO-NOT-RESUSCITATE ORDERS

As a teenager in the early 1970s, *M*A*S*H* was one of my favorite shows. I remember an episode where Hawkeye and Trapper John were huddled over a soldier and Hawkeye said something like, "We've got to cut him open!" Trapper put his hands on the boy's chest and started pumping, saying, "Wait, I read about this in a journal." They saved the soldier's life.

Dr. Lown's first defibrillation came in 1959. Mouth-to-mouth ventilation was reported in the medical literature the year before; closed-chest cardiac massage to manually restore circulation for victims of cardiac arrest was reported a year later.[21] These discoveries launched the modern era of CPR.[22] Initially, the technique was used primarily on otherwise healthy individuals who experienced cardiac or respiratory arrest during surgery or as a result of near-drowning.[23] As will be discussed in Chapter 11, the same progression happened with feeding tubes, which were initially used with otherwise healthy patients who needed a temporary medical bridge after illness or accident to recovery of their ability to eat. (The *M*A*S*H* writers apparently took some poetic license since CPR appeared in the medical journals after the Korean War.)

Today, of course, the use of CPR is dramatically expanded. When I was watching *M*A*S*H* in high school in 1972, few students had heard of CPR. Today most high school students learn to perform CPR as part of their basic health curriculum. Many in the general public attend classes to learn how to use CPR in an effort to manually circulate the blood until emergency medical technicians arrive. Those EMTs then can use more sophisticated medicine and tools, including intubation, mechanical breathing, and defibrillator paddles to restart the heart. When cardiac arrest occurs in a hospital, CPR is tried unless a doctor's order is in place to the contrary. The American Medical Association estimates that CPR is attempted in nearly one third of the two million deaths that occur in hospitals each year.[24] This number includes the frail elderly and other seriously ill patients.

All seriously ill patients in a hospital have a "code status." If the hard conversation has happened and the doctor has written the note in the chart, then the patient is a "DNR," or the medical chart might read "no code" or "no CPR" or "DNAR," for "do not attempt resuscitation." These patients might have a red dot above their bed or other marker to warn responders not to perform resuscitation. If the conversation has not happened, as is often the case, then by default in most hospitals the patient is a "full code."[25] The words "full code" are not written in the medical chart; the full code is simply a fact of hospital life.[26]

When the patient's heart stops, the call of "Code Blue" goes out over the hospital intercom, and action happens. In his bestselling 1995 book, *How We Die*, Dr. Sherwin Nuland described the drama that he acted in many times:

> As chaotic as they may appear, all resuscitations follow the same basic pattern. The patient, almost invariably unconscious because of inadequate blood flow to the brain, is quickly surrounded by a team whose mission is to pull him back from the edge by stopping his fibrillation or reversing his pulmonary edema, or both. A breathing tube is rapidly thrust through his mouth and down into his windpipe so that oxygen under pressure can be forced in to expand his rapidly flooding lungs. If he is in fibrillation, large metal paddles are placed on his chest and a blast of 200 joules is fired through his heart in an attempt to stop the impotent squirming, with the expectation that a regular beat will return, as it frequently does.
>
> If no effective beat appears, a member of the team begins a rhythmic compression of the heart by forcing the heel of his hand down into the lowest part of the breastbone at a rate of about one stroke per second. By squeezing the ventricles between the flatness of the yielding breastbone in front and the spinal column in back, blood is forced out into the circulatory system to keep the brain and other vital organs alive. When this form of external cardiac massage is effective, a pulse can be felt as far away as the neck and groin . . .
>
> By this point, IVs will have been inserted for the infusion of cardiac drugs, and wider plastic tubes called central lines are being expeditiously inserted into major veins. The various drugs injected into the IV tubing have assorted purposes: They help to control rhythm, decrease the irritability of the myocardium, strengthen the force of its contraction, and drive excess fluid out of the lungs, to be excreted by the kidney. Every resuscitation is different. Though the general pattern is similar, every sequence, every response to massage and drugs, every heart's willingness to come back—are all different. The only certainty, whether spoken or not, is that the doctors, nurses, and technicians are fighting not only death but their own uncertainties as well. In most resuscitations, those uncertainties can be narrowed down to two main questions: Are we doing the right things? And, should we be doing anything at all?[27]

On the Thursday night television show *ER*, resuscitation is dramatic, like the real-life description of Dr. Nuland. The difference is that on *ER*, resuscitation works far more often than in real life.[28] A review of

ER and two other medical shows found that short-term survival after resuscitation on these shows was 75 percent, and long-term survival 67 percent.[29] The reality is that a patient's chances of being resuscitated with CPR and surviving to be discharged from the hospital is much lower, about 15 percent.[30] For the seriously ill, dying patients, and the frail elderly, CPR almost never works.[31] The public, of course, believes *ER*. Remarkably, that includes those in the public with medical training who, when surveyed, rated the effectiveness of CPR at a whopping 75 percent.[32]

In 1970, at Bethany Medical Center in Kansas City, Kansas, a call of "Code Blue" over the intercom summoned every doctor in the hospital, according to Dr. Potter, and many of those who responded did not yet have much idea of what to do after they'd rushed to the room. Resuscitation was new, so the idea of a do-not-resuscitate order was still years away.

By the time the President's Commission for the Study of Ethical Problems in Medicine published its report in 1983, three state medical societies, in Alabama, Minnesota, and New York, had developed and published guidelines to establish standards of care for DNR orders.[33] Today, of course, many more guidelines exist in many institutions and medical societies, and we have significantly more experience with and understanding of CPR than we did in the early 1980s. But the medical world is still struggling with the questions of when resuscitation is appropriate and when it is not.

Why is "full code" the default? Why do we perform CPR on the frail elderly when the literature is clear that such treatment will not work? When I talk with groups of doctors who deal mainly with critically ill patients, I often ask them these questions. The first answer that comes back, typically, is fear of litigation. A doctor will say, "If I don't attempt resuscitation and do the full code, I'll be sued." As we work through that answer a bit, most agree that there is not really litigation to fear in this area. Doctors are not being sued for failure to perform painful, rib-breaking CPR for patients on whom they know it will not work.

That reality does not necessarily remove the fear. This fear in our litigious American society is real and understandable. Or perhaps doctors are remembering back to the formative years of DNR policies. In 1982, the state medical society in New York became one of the first three states to recommend DNR guidelines. That same year, *The New York Times* reported widely on a criminal investigation by the New York Attorney General's office of a hospital in Queens. The Attorney General was investigating whether doctors were committing a crime by writing DNR orders for elderly patients.[34]

Fear of litigation is part of the answer. The fuller answer, though, is that futile attempted resuscitations are performed far too often in the hospital because that's the practice that has evolved in those hospitals over the last thirty years. That treatment has become part of the institutional glide path. Those times when the discussion does happen, it comes near the end—and frequently with the family rather than with the patient, as the patient becomes more difficult to rouse. The family ultimately agrees to a DNR order as part of the acceptance of the inevitable course of the disease, with the DNR discussion acting as a powerful "symbol that death cannot be averted."[35]

Far too often the discussion does not happen, though, even with the family, and even near the end. Again, a part of the difficulty is in "knowing when the end is coming." Too often the patient's condition deteriorates suddenly and quickly, and the "right time" to discuss a DNR has passed.[36] Then a full code is called, and seriously ill patients spend their last days in an intensive care unit,[37] the result that the American public says it does not want.

The medical world is not satisfied with these outcomes, either. That world is filled with many smart, caring people who are working on a variety of creative projects to better understand, talk about, and follow patient wishes. Several of those projects have made excellent headway.

In Oregon in the early 1990s, doctors at Oregon Health & Sciences University and others convened a multi-disciplinary task force that met over a four-year period to address the issue of patients with serious illness and advanced frailty being transferred from the nursing home to the hospital for aggressive treatment. The result was the POLST program. POLST stands for "Physician Orders for Life-Sustaining Treatment." The key to the program's success is the POLST form, a bright-pink, one-sheet medical order that converts patient wishes into the language of medicine—a doctor's order. In 1996 the Oregon State Board of Medical Examiners redefined appropriate medical practice to make sure that the POLST form is honored by EMTs and by the physicians with whom those EMTs are communicating back at the ER.[38] A copy of the POLST form is in the Appendix.

Dr. Susan Tolle spearheaded the program and has studied the effect of POLST extensively. One clear outcome of her research is that the POLST program has forced people—patients, families, health care providers—to talk. That talk now happens well before crisis, and importantly it has meaning within "the system." EMTs and nursing homes recognize the bright pink form and know how to act when they see it. The medical culture is thinking and talking about the idea that sending the frail elderly to the ICU may not fit with the admonition, "First, do no harm." All concerned, especially patients and family, know that the bright pink form stays either on the patient's person or typically on the refrigerator in a pouch that is provided when the form is given to the patient.

Oregon has the lowest rate of in-hospital deaths in the country.[39] That result is likely because the people of Oregon have talked more about dying than people in the other states. In addition to the focus on POLST, Oregon also had an extensive public debate and heavily-funded legislative campaign lasting many years over the question of legalizing physician-assisted suicide, which is discussed in Chapter 14. Though refusing unwanted medical treatment with POLST and hastening death through physician-assisted suicide are significantly different acts to those who work in the end-of-life world, most of the public does not dwell on such distinctions. Talking about dying is talking about dying. And in Oregon, they've done more of that than in any other state. At least thirteen other states subsequently have developed versions of POLST.[40]

Other creative projects are underway as well. A program called "Respecting Choices," developed in La Crosse, Wisconsin, has succeeded in institutionalizing advance care planning. This program works from the top down, making sure the hospitals understand and place a high priority on this decision-making. Other groups such as

Five Wishes, from Florida; the Caring Conversations program and other community initiatives at the Center for Practical Bioethics in Kansas City; the new Caring Connections program of the National Hospice and Palliative Care Organization, which provides free information and state-specific documents to help with end-of-life planning; and many other groups have made inroads in improving planning. All of these efforts share the common denominator of a charismatic leader with a vision and the commitment to work hard for a long time to promote the importance of end-of-life planning and conversation.

Professional associations also are working on educational programs, including groups such as EPEC from the American Medical Association (Educating Physicians on End of Life Care) and ELNEC (End-of-Life Nursing Education Consortium) from the American Association of Colleges of Nursing.[41] Many states are investigating rules for out-of-hospital DNR orders, which can give guidance to emergency medical technicians about not performing CPR on a patient who does not want the intervention, if a family member or caregiver has nonetheless called 911. Some states have developed DNR bracelets for patients to wear, or have their own brightly-colored document.

All of these efforts represent a beginning. Most of the work of improving our dying in the modern technological world is still to come, and most of the rest of society is nowhere near as far along in understanding the issues as these visionary projects or groups. State legislatures, for example, are grappling with a smorgasbord of laws trying to make improvements: out-of-hospital DNR laws (which basically help assure EMTs that they do not need to perform CPR on the frail elderly when someone panics and calls 911); new guardianship statutes; better health care proxy laws; and more. Hospitals, hospices, nursing homes, professional societies of medical providers, chaplains, lawyers, community groups, and many others are discussing the question of improving end-of-life care. The National Association of Attorneys General adopted this issue as its lead initiative in 2003.

America is going to need all of the energy and vision of these efforts and more. Over the next twenty years, three forces moving together will bring significant urgency to this discussion. The first force is the huge demographic bulge of Baby Boomers entering old age (the current one million deaths per year of the frail elderly will seem minuscule). They will face the second force: an assortment of medical options that we cannot even conceive today, so quickly will the changes to technology come. Finally, they will almost certainly be confronted by limited resources to pay for this health care. Like it or not, American society soon will be talking frequently about the appropriate care of the seriously ill.

Will the change to better, more informed decision-making, and the thoughtful control over the conditions of our dying, need to come from the top down, from the medical institutions and doctors? Or can it come from the grassroots, from the people? In part in reaction to the SUPPORT results, Joanne Lynn and others have questioned whether it is possible to improve patient-level decision-making simply by providing more information for the patient.[42] And efforts like POLST illustrate that institutions can change, and that those top-down changes can contribute to improving end-of-life care.

I'm not ready, though, to give up on significant change coming from the grassroots, from the patients and their families. Obviously there's room for huge improvement in the public's understanding of end-of-life issues. From the thousands of people I've talked with over the last several years as I've traveled the country, I remain optimistic that society can make significant inroads working from the consumer side—your side, our side.

Medical providers, immersed in the day-to-day rhythms of their jobs, may well underestimate how foreign their world remains to the greater public. Most of us arrive like Dorothy landing in Oz when we enter a hospital. But after she'd been there awhile, Dorothy started to realize that the Wizard was well-meaning but not all-powerful, and she learned about the neighborhoods she should avoid.

As a society, we've only recently landed in our medical Oz. As our families begin to face and understand end-of-life decisions, we'll get better at them. Boomers as a group have been demanding as they've moved through their passages—from voting rights, to civil rights, to reproductive rights, and finally, to end-of-life rights. Don Schumacher, head of the National Hospice and Palliative Care Organization, jokes that we will be the group that asks for our own "personal death trainers."

I've seen the seeds of this change. Joyce Cruzan, who watched her daughter Nancy's death, and then watched Nancy's aunt go through agony with chemotherapy only to die in the ICU, simply told the doctor "No" when she learned that she, too, had lymphoma. She spent her last months at home, with family, supported by hospice.[43] I'm not advocating her choice nor supporting her doctor's objection to that choice. I'm simply saying that the first two experiences with technological dying for a family informed the choices made the next time around. When I speak at nursing homes that are active, vibrant places, where the residents meet and talk, I find they've usually tried to take an active role in the conditions of their dying.

At John Knox Village in Kansas City years ago, an elderly lady rose after I gave a luncheon talk and said, "I'm 87, my husband and all of my friends are dead. I've had a good life, but if a heart attack comes, I'm ready to go." Gray heads were nodding in agreement. "I read in the same chair every day, and have a cardboard tent sign that I made sitting on a table next to the chair, with a big 'DNR' written in red on it. I have my living will that says 'No CPR' lying right next to it. On the door to my room I taped a large sign that says 'DNR.' Whenever we get new staff, like orderlies or nurses' aides, I always instruct them how to keep me comfortable, and how NOT to call 911. Here's my question: Do you think I need to get a tattoo on my chest that says, 'DNR?'" This was a serious question.

I have not gone back to check, but my guess is that this woman did not die in the ICU. Or perhaps she is still alive, still instructing the new orderlies; she'd be about 100 today. As we gather experience through the aging and the technological dying of our families and friends, our decision-making at the end-of-life will be better informed, and it will improve.

The medical world, of course, is working in myriad ways to support this improvement as well, through pilot programs like those discussed above, through medical school and professional continuing education, and in other ways. Those in the health care field naturally want to help others, including helping society understand how to make better decisions at the end of life. This technology has come at them in a rush, however, as it has for the rest of us, and they're still learning, too.

A nurse in Maine wrote and performs a wonderful one-act play called B.O.A.T.I.N.G. (Before Offering Another Treatment Investigate New Goals). An ICU doctor in California asks, "Shouldn't we be asking, 'What is the long-term goal?' not what some monitor is saying about this 80-year-old man with problems in multiple organs?"[44] Ethics committees debate questions about the Terri Schiavo case.

Positive institutional change will come from within, and that is good. But should it really be solely up to the medical world for the rest of us to retain informed, thoughtful control over the conditions and decisions of our dying? Aren't these our lives and our families?

CHAPTER 9

In Terri Schiavo's Shoes

IN THE SOCIETAL DISCUSSION about our dying, the phrase "quality of life" has taken on a fascinating life of its own. With *Quinlan* in 1976 and *Cruzan* in 1990, the quality of life for each of the young adult women was often discussed as not only an appropriate factor for the parents to weigh in making decisions, but their main concern. As the discussion about Terri Schiavo spread through the country in the spring of 2005, the meaning of the phrase "quality of life" had shifted fairly significantly.

Advocates who argued that her feeding tube should remain in place would make statements like, "Michael Schiavo needs to respect Terri Schiavo's life, not make judgments about her *quality* of life." The reporter and others seated around the coffee table on the TV studio set would then nod in agreement, and the discussion would move on to new ground, the group appearing to believe that they had avoided a topic that was somehow inappropriate for discussion.

Three reports from different federal government commissions also treated the phrase differently. The 1983 President's Commission for the Study of Ethical Problems in Medicine report stated that when making decisions about medical treatment for a seriously ill loved one, the decision maker "must take into account such factors as the relief of suffering, the preservation or restoration of functioning, and the quality as well as the extent of life sustained. An accurate assessment will encompass consideration of the satisfaction of present desires, the opportunities for future satisfactions, and the possibility of developing or regaining the capacity for self-determination."[1] A 1987 report prepared for the federal Congress made a similar assessment of the importance of quality of life factors.[2]

In the fall of 2005, a new presidential commission weighed in, the President's Council on Bioethics. It appeared that in the twenty-two years since the publication of the last President's Commission report, the federal government's view of the role of quality of life had changed dramatically. On September 28, 2005, Dr. Leon Kass sent to President George W. Bush a 307-page report entitled, *Taking Care: Ethical Caregiving in Our Aging Society*.[3] That document stated:

> Public discussions today of end-of-life issues frequently speak of 'quality of life,' implying that certain 'poor' qualities of life might disqualify one from a claim to treatment or from further prolongation of life. Questions about the worthiness of expending time and resources treating the severely disabled or demented patient seem increasingly tied to tacit—or sometimes explicit—judgments about the worth of the life being cared for. Like it or not, alien or not, we must take up this topic, if only to be better equipped to deal with public arguments that traffic casually in these grave matters.[4]

In other places the report goes further, suggesting that those who might consider quality of life factors are making improper judgments about "life unworthy of life."[5] That phrase has historically been used to describe the Nazi doctors and their judgment of *ein lebensunwerten Leben*, a life unworthy of life.

One member of the President's Council dissented publicly from the report. Dr. Janet Rowley from the University of Chicago School of Medicine wrote a separate, two-page statement, which began, "For me, this report on the care of the demented aging is a scary document for a number of reasons." She objected to the use of "rigid ethical rules" that would make dying painful and draconian. Though she did not state this expressly, presumably one point she objected to was the dismissal by the Council of the quality-of-life standard that earlier government commissions had valued. Dr. Rowley called for a national commission "composed of members with very diverse views, not just the conservative right," and concluded with this caution: "These are very serious issues. The report of the President's Council on Bioethics provides answers from a very restricted perspective and thus it, unfortunately, cannot serve as an enlightened guide as we try to cope with these critical challenges."[6]

The advances in the world of medical technology have affected even the words we use. What exactly is "quality of life" and should it factor into decisions that are made about medical treatment? Or is quality of life a topic to avoid, or to discuss "only to be better equipped to deal with public arguments that traffic casually in these grave matters"?

The problem with avoiding the topic of quality of life is this: the main issue in the *Schiavo* case was Terri Schiavo's quality of life. Though not usually cast that way, that's what the whole debate of the case was about. More specifically, the issue is whether a medical intervention can restore function, relieve suffering, and provide sufficient quality to life so that the patient (or person speaking on her behalf) chooses to accept that medical treatment. Indeed, just the opposite of what the President's Council calls "trafficking casually," quality of life is what the serious public debate *should* be about.

If we avoid talking about the goals of medical treatment, the medical team can end up simply performing procedures on a patient because the technology exists, without anyone asking whether the patient is truly benefiting or *would want* the treatment. Ultimately, different sides in the argument may come down with different conclusions, as happened in the public debate over Terri Schiavo's feeding tube, and as often happens with hard societal questions. But the talk about whether a treatment can deliver sufficient quality of life must happen. At the heart of that talk is this question: What is the purpose of medicine?

The words of Hippocrates have guided philosophers and doctors for over 2,300 years. It seems unlikely, though, that when he wrote the often-quoted words "*Primum, non nocere*"—first, do no harm—that Hippocrates was contemplating the plight of using technology to sustain a patient in a permanently unconscious limbo for thirty years or more. (Life expectancy at birth in Hippocrates' Greece in 400 B.C. was about 25 years.) The struggle to understand what "do no harm" means in the world of technological medicine is a new one.

When the *Cruzan* case began in 1987, many medical and ethics groups were just beginning to wrestle with the questions the case raised. The guidelines of the American Academy of Neurology were submitted at trial in March of 1988 in draft form because they hadn't been finalized. Guidelines submitted to the court from an influential New York think tank called The Hastings Center were new that year. Guidelines from the American Medical Association were new as well.

In March of 1986, the Council on Ethical and Judicial Affairs of the American Medical Association published an ethical opinion titled "Withholding or Withdrawing Life-Prolonging Medical Treatment."[7] That opinion began, "The social commitment of the physician is to sustain life and relieve suffering. Where the performance of one duty conflicts with the other, the choice of the patient, or his family [or other spokesperson] should prevail."

That opinion went on to say that for a patient whose "coma is beyond doubt irreversible . . . it is not unethical" to stop all life-prolonging medical treatment, including tube feeding. In an earlier section of the document titled "Quality of Life," the AMA counseled that "quality of life" was a factor to be considered in decisions, and that "life should be cherished despite disabilities and handicaps, except when the prolongation would be inhumane and unconscionable."[8]

That all makes sense: the physician's duty is to sustain life, life should be cherished, and quality of life is a factor in decisions to stop medical treatment. But how does one apply these abstract phrases in the modern hospital? As with the phrase, "let nature take its course," it's easy to envision how either "side" in the Schiavo dispute would bend these phrases to their end.

The same is true for the principles that the 2005 President's Council reviewed, which have historically guided such decision-making in society. The Council cited four principles: "*autonomy*, where one's worth is manifested in one's power to choose and determined entirely by one's own judgment; *utility*, where one's worth depends entirely on one's usefulness to oneself or others; *quality*, where one's worth depends on possessing or exercising certain humanly fitting, admirable, or enjoyable traits and capacities; and *equality*, where every human being possesses an equal and intrinsic worth simply by being part of the human community."[9] The Council concluded that the greatest among these is equality. The Council also reviewed standards that have been used historically in making medical decisions—weighing the potential benefits of a proposed treatment against its burdens, and evaluating whether treatment is extraordinary (can be refused) or ordinary care (mandatory for all patients).

But all of these concepts—equality, benefits vs. burdens, quality, utility—are like "nature taking its course" or the AMA ethics statements: they can cut in exactly opposite directions depending on who is wielding them. What do these ethical opinions from the AMA or the guiding fundamental principles set out by the President's Council really *mean* if a person ends up in Terri Schiavo's medical state?

For me, whichever principle is chosen, the words mean that if I'm ever in Terri Schiavo's shoes, I want the feeding tube removed. Straightforward enough. I hold this opinion now, in 2006, because I believe that if accident or illness leaves me in a state of permanent unconsciousness, without hopes of regaining consciousness, then my quality of life would not be sufficient to accept continued medical treatment.

The AMA counsels that the physician owes the duty to "sustain life." To understand this duty, I believe that we have to answer the question, "What is life?" Again, for my own decision-making, the "life" in this ethical pronouncement is not a vitalistic, biological definition of existence; it means living on the terms I describe in the next paragraph. I believe that the purpose of medicine is to serve as a bridge to recovery so that I can *live* life. That is what my own doctor's duty to "sustain [my] life" means. If a treatment cannot help me live life, then I reject it. That rejection is completely supported by my understanding of the President's Council's fundamental principles of autonomy, utility, quality, and equality.

What does it mean for me to say I accept medical treatment if it can serve as a bridge to recovery so that I can *live* life? Answering that question requires looking at what's important to me about living. Like most people, I love my children—four of them—more than life itself. I try to cherish my time with them: playing catch, driving to events, working on homework, reading together, sorting through problems, even holding the vomit bucket when one of them has the flu. I want my children to believe that the world is a place where they can accomplish good if they put their minds to it. I want them to feel the safety of a father's arms around them whenever they need it. I try to show them by example how a husband loves his wife, honors his parents, siblings, and friends, and contributes to his community. And surely more mundane, but still important to me, I want to be able to mow the grass, ride my bike, and talk and laugh while having a beer with friends.

If medicine can do for me what it did for my dad and restore me to a place where I can *live* this life with my wife and children, then I want all of the scans, scalpels, stents, and shunts that my doctor with the duty to "sustain life" can bring to bear. I want it if I'm a heart patient like my dad, or if, like Nancy Cruzan I'm in an accident so severe that the injuries *might* ultimately leave me in a vegetative state. If the doctors aren't sure of the prognosis, and there's a realistic chance that I can live life in the way I described, I want the medical treatment.

On the other hand, engaging in life is the key to my assessment of my own quality of life. If all medicine can do is to sustain me in a vegetative state like Terri Schiavo or Nancy Cruzan, without hope of living life again, then I believe the medicine or technology should be stopped, and earlier rather than later. This is also my decision if the illness or accident has left me in a minimally conscious state, the state outside the vegetative state which some of the doctors in the *Schiavo* case claimed was Terri Schiavo's correct diagnosis. If my diagnosis is one of extremely limited consciousness and awareness, then I do not want continued aggressive medical treatment. To me such a decision-making process respects life—trying all means for recovery or cure, but stopping such intervention when I cannot live my life.

I also realize that at age 50 and in good health, this discussion is abstract and hypothetical. Though the landmark cases—*Quinlan*, *Cruzan*, *Schiavo*—all involved young people, statistically I won't face these issues until I'm older. Many people's views and values change as they age and get closer to the end of their lives. Mine may, too. My dad said on his 75th birthday that 80 didn't look so bad to him from that point of view. (He fell just one month shy of seeing for himself.) I have talked with my wife and sisters many times about the purpose of medical treatment and what living life means to me. I plan to talk with them many more times in the years to come and as my place in life changes. But for now they have a pretty good idea of my views and values.

Let me be clear, though. My purpose in expressing my opinions about living life and for having these repeated talks with my family has nothing to do with a desire that my own wishes be carried out, or my autonomy respected, or in achieving a death with dignity for myself. If I am in Terri Schiavo's shoes I do not care what happens to me. If I am unaware, without hope of regaining awareness, what will it matter to me what decisions are made then?

What will matter to me, and what I can have an effect on right now, is doing all I can to make sure that the family I will have left behind at that point feels as good as they can about any decision that my condition will force them to face. If I fall into Terri Schiavo's shoes, I know that that serious illness will leave big hole in the social fabric of the family I love. I want to do all I can now to arm my family to make decisions together and to support one another. I want to prepare them now so that the damage to my family is repaired as quickly and as well as it can be. Unlike trying to control how decisions are made, I care very much about doing this preparation thoroughly right now.

So my wife and sisters know from repeated, in-depth discussions we've had that if I am permanently unconscious in a persistent vegetative state, medicine would serve no purpose simply to keep me in that state. They know that I don't think they should consent on my behalf to treat any infections, or tube feed me, or give me medicine of any kind. They know that I hope that my kids get to remember me mainly as a thriving, aware person, not bedridden and unaware, and that the modest nest egg I worked to build goes to those kids, not to medical care that makes no sense. In the years ahead, as long as I have my wits about me, I will continue to reinforce these beliefs.

My family also knows, though, that if they come to that place and they take some comfort in caring for me in my demented state, that's okay, too. If they want to dress me up in my orange-and-black polyester East Moline High School letter sweater and sit me out in a chair each day on our front lawn in Kansas, I don't care. Give me over to the Kansas University Medical Center for experimentation, I don't care. All I want is for them to feel the greatest amount of comfort and confidence and the least amount of second guessing or guilt in any decision they make.

ALZHEIMER'S DISEASE AND QUALITY OF LIFE

These decisions are pretty clear cut for a large percentage of Americans when the topic is persistent vegetative state, that is, permanent unconsciousness. But what if I have some consciousness? What if it's Alzheimer's disease or some other dementia that confronts my family? The chances are much greater that my family will face exactly that scenario rather than a vegetative state. Of the 2.5 million deaths in the United States each year, very few of those patients are in a persistent vegetative state prior to death, but about half a million are elderly, frail, and demented. So, statistically, it's much more likely that my family will be discussing my advancing Alzheimer's disease or other dementia.

What then about my wishes? The AMA guidelines state that when a "coma is beyond doubt irreversible . . . it is not unethical" to discontinue life-prolonging medical treatment. The Academy of Neurology guidelines and others draw similar bright lines. At the time these guidelines were drawn up (and still today), many in the debate argued that the ethics of decision-making were the same whether the patient was permanently unconscious or not. An assessment still had to be made about the potential benefits of a treatment versus its burdens, and about how the physician's duty to sustain life applied. The guidelines, however, were written with the bright line of permanent unconsciousness, or irreversible coma. Sliding into Alzheimer's, I will not meet that standard, so the ethical opinions won't directly apply. What should the rules be?

This is not a simple question. For those who favored leaving Terri Schiavo's feeding tube in place, even the asking of this question raises the specter of the slippery slope, a society that devalues life, discriminates against the handicapped, and condones euthanasia. Those on the other side fear a slavish worshipping of medical technology and biological life, without anyone asking the important questions of the purpose or goal of using any particular medical treatment, and instead simply piling technology on top of technology to no sensible end.

A surprising number of doctors have asked me this question: "Can I write into my living will that if I suffer from Alzheimer's disease, I do not want to be force-fed by spoon? Can I tell people to simply set the food on my bedside table and if I eat, fine; if I don't, that's fine, too?" Perhaps these questions were triggered by these doctors having read in the *Journal of the American Medical Association* a thoughtful and artfully written essay by Dr. William Hensel titled "My Living Will."[10] In that one-page piece, Dr. Hensel traced the evolution of his own living will. His first document, written in 1986, directed that no "extraordinary means" be used if doctors determined that his condition was "terminal and incurable." His current living will is far more narrative and detailed. It talks about what the doctor values most in life and the lessons that he has learned from his own patients.

The baseline in Dr. Hensel's living will is being able to recognize his family. The doctor talks of the guilt he's seen families suffer when they put their loved one with dementia in a nursing home, and the ordeal and pain endured by those families through years of visiting that home.[11] He rejects that end for himself:

> So it is important that I make this clear: If I ever suffer irreversible central nervous system damage to the point that I do not recognize my family, I believe that it would be best for me to die. I want no active treatments that might prolong such an existence. Even more, if physician-assisted death is legal, that is what I choose. If not, do not place food or water in my mouth. Instead, place it on my bed table. If I feed myself, I live another day; if I do not, I will die and that is fine.[12]

Regardless of whether the doctors who have asked me the questions about their own living wills got the idea from Dr. Hensel, they take little comfort in my answer when they ask if such a document is legal and binding. "Of course you can write those words in your living will," I answer, "but whether you have some 'right' to what you ask for, and whether or not your family and doctor will carry out the wishes you express, that's not clear, and the law doesn't make it clear."

This question involves the fundamental issue of how we live with one another, and how and why we make rules for that society. Consider this basic question: "What exactly is the state?" The drastically oversimplified answer is that the state is all of us, living together, deciding the rules that we want to have govern those intertwined lives. Long ago, the Cruzans' pioneer ancestors decided to settle in the beautiful, fertile place that would later be named Missouri. The first group maybe sat around a fire and started talking about what the rules should be for their camp. That was part of the rudimentary beginning of the state. Those people kept talking, their numbers grew, and they ended up formalizing the process. In 1821 (the year Missouri was admitted to the union), they agreed on an initial state Constitution.

Laws regulating the relationships of people in the state began growing up through something called the common law. The common law basically is the body of law that judges made, which grew over time out of disputes between people within a state. One farmer's dog killed another farmer's sheep, and a judge decided how to resolve the dispute if the farmers couldn't work it out between themselves. Another farmer down the road built a fence to keep the killer dog out, but a third farmer thought that fence encroached on his land. Ranchers nearby complained that the fence invaded their range lands. As society grew more complicated, judges resolved disputes, and the common law expanded.

At the same time, the state legislature was formed and began to pass state statutes, laws that would govern the citizens. Legislatures typically focus on issues that are coming up frequently, causing problems within the society, the state. These laws can be criminal (defining when the state might put someone in jail), or civil, like laws defining how one person might pass property to another at death.

The law generally reflects how we want to live together. We value life, so we make murder one of our most serious crimes. But we also value freedom, so we put the highest burden of proof in place, the "beyond a reasonable doubt" standard, before we send someone to prison for a crime and take away that freedom. The time-honored cliché expressing that principle is that it's better for ten guilty men to go free than for one innocent man to go to jail.

No state legislature has yet said exactly what the rules will be for a living will like Dr. Hensel's. This question is new. As will be discussed later in a chapter on physician-assisted suicide, American society has long had laws prohibiting suicide and physician-assisted suicide. It's not clear, though, whether a living will that rejects spoon feeding would be prohibited under these laws, or whether the law might reach the opposite conclusion—that the right to autonomy would protect the making of such wishes.

Will state legislatures in the years ahead debate and pass new laws authorizing such clauses in state statutory living wills? Prohibiting such clauses? If a state passes such a prohibition, will some citizen like Dr. Hensel sue the state, claiming that the state law violates his federal constitutional right to liberty, which is a higher law than the state prohibition? For years to come, we will be encountering new bridges that neither the law, nor society, has yet crossed.

The 2005 President's Council spent a significant amount of energy contemplating such hard questions. To its credit, the council did not claim to resolve the questions. One of its recommendations calls on

President Bush to form a Presidential Commission on Aging, Dementia, and Long-Term Care to address the health care crisis that's coming as Boomers age. Perhaps that recommendation came largely from the difficulty the council had in analyzing the case of the Alzheimer's patient they called Margo.[13]

Margo was a cheerful Alzheimer's patient. Each day she listened to the same music, painted the same simple pastel shapes, randomly read from the same book. She had no memories of her earlier life or even what had happened earlier on any given day, and she could make no new memories. The council spent many pages debating the question posed by the doctor who treated her: "Who is Margo?"

When Margo first learned of her Alzheimer's diagnosis she filled out a living will making clear that if an infection came during her slide downhill into dementia, she did not want it treated. The President's Council pondered what it meant to honor such a request. If that 20-year-old request was honored, would that somehow deny to the pleasantly demented Margo, who seemed to be experiencing some kind of pleasure and who was here now, the right to change her mind? Did the demented Margo have the ability any longer to "change" her mind? If the clear living will was ignored, did that ignore the rights of the "original" Margo?

Near the end of its report, the council worked through a case study similar to Margo's story. The patient was an Alzheimer's patient with a similar seemingly cheery disposition. Nurses found blood in his stool and, following a battery of tests, doctors discovered a tumor in his colon. Doctors believed they could repair the blockage with surgery, but the surgery was contrary to the man's clear living will, written years before in anticipation of his advancing dementia. The man's daughter nonetheless requested the surgery for her father.

The council argued in favor of surgery. In its report, it reasoned "The primary moral obligation of caregivers is to serve the well-being of the patient now here, and to ask not only what the patient would have wanted but what we owe the person who lies before us."[14] Dr. Rowley (the council member who wrote the strong dissenting statement included at the end of the President's Council report) reacted to this resolution and what she saw as its cavalier disregard of the written wishes of the patient: "The clear message from this report is, if you feel strongly about not living in a decerebrate state, you better kill yourself while you have control over your fate!"[15]

I'm not sure the council goes quite so far, but I understand Dr. Rowley's point. I also understand the call from the council for significantly more study and societal discussion of such profoundly difficult issues. Until a lot more of that societal discussion happens, though, I don't have a good answer for these doctors when they ask me if their living wills will work when those living wills ask that food simply be set on the bedside table and not force-fed to them. The question goes to the very heart of what kind of society we want to live in, and the proper role of the state. Like the rest of the questions in this book, it is new, and brought to society by the advance of medical technology. We need to debate the question around our modern-day campfire.

The President's Council set up the example of Margo in a somewhat extreme fashion, likely in part to make its point. The council talked about how Margo of twenty years ago, when she filled out a living will, might not speak for the Margo of today. Suppose, though, that instead of Margo we have Dr. Hensel, who doesn't write his living will and put it in his desk. Instead, he keeps reaffirming his views and values—clearly, persuasively, publicly, passionately—right up to the very moment when he loses that ability to advocate. Will the rest of us, as the state, want to step in and overrule that request?

Maybe we will. If he asked in the document to be injected lethally, the rest of us have said, through our laws, that we do not want that behavior in our society. That's a line we've chosen not to cross (except in the case of capital punishment). Possibly we will say "no" again, and decide that someone will spoon the food into his mouth because we decide that that is the appropriate behavior in a caring culture. Possibly in the case of the President's Council hypothetical of the demented man, society will order the bowel obstruction surgery, ignoring the earlier living will to the contrary.

The President's Council argued the question this way: "Surely physical well-being is central to the obligation of best care, and so finding ways to ease suffering and treat physical ailments as they arise—broken hips, pneumonia, urinary tract infections—would have a strong moral claim."[16] A question society will face is whether such a moral claim of the state will outweigh an explicit living will refusing antibiotics in the event of pneumonia.

What if Margo or Dr. Hensel left no living will, but had a loving family who now declines surgery for removal of a bowel obstruction or refuse IV antibiotics when pneumonia sets in? Family has long been the bedrock in culture, and in the law, for all kinds of decision-making. The U.S. Supreme Court has described the bond within a family as "a relation as old and as fundamental as our entire civilization" and has ruled that there is a "private realm of family life which the state cannot enter."[17] Is my refusal of IV antibiotics for my elderly, demented mother within that protected realm, or will the state step in and overrule that decision in the interest of protecting life? What if Mom has a large estate, and the day I make this decision is the first time I have visited her in two years; does the state have some role in checking my motives?

What of the demented patient who has outlived family and friends, and the only one to speak for him is a government employee called the public guardian? In Kansas City, the public guardian has over 1,000 people for whom her office makes decisions. Such public guardians are fairly new government creatures, another result of advancing technology. If the decision maker is not family, but a government employee, does that employee apply different standards to make decisions? The President's Council intimated that in such cases, the default decision should be to provide medical treatment.[18] However, if we force citizens without family to receive treatment that we allow those with family to reject, are we trampling on the right to refuse treatment of the first group?

The President's Council is right: Our society needs to keep this discussion going. With 44 states poised to have the elderly demographic that now exists only in Florida, and with advances in medical technology rocketing forward (news in the fall of 2005 reported on the first face transplant in France!), our society will be talking about these questions frequently, and for a long time.

For now, though, when the doctors ask me about their own living wills and spoon feeding, the best I can do is tell them what I've done. Not that my resolution is the gold standard, but I am a lawyer, and I have thought about these questions for a while. The following chapter presents in greater detail the approach I've taken.

CHAPTER 10

My "Living Will"

I DO NOT HAVE A LIVING WILL. I don't believe I can anticipate all of the maladies that might befall me or the potential treatments that might or might not help. More importantly, a written living will cannot advocate for me. When the time comes for making hard decisions about my care, I want a breathing, reasoning advocate, one who understands everything I've said in the last chapter. A piece of paper can't really do that.

The President's Council reported that fewer than 25 percent of Americans have filled out a living will, and the report also cited studies showing that, of this small percentage, 16 percent of those documents made it into the patients' medical charts.[1] If those numbers are right, then only 4 percent of patients in hospitals have living wills in their medical charts. That sounds too low, and other studies indicate higher numbers. Whether the number is right or not may not matter. A survey of doctors published in the summer of 2004 in the *Archives of Internal Medicine* found that 65 percent of doctors said they would not follow a living will if the instructions conflicted with the doctor's own views about the patient's prognosis or expected quality of life.[2]

Not surprisingly, lawyers are the group most aghast when they hear of studies like this one. One of the smartest lawyers I know recently finished updating his own living will in the fall of 2005. When I talked about the possibility of his document not being followed, he said, "But I've taken care of this, the doctor will have nothing to say, my document controls." The idea that a clear, written, notarized document will not work is contrary to how lawyers think and live.

Though I don't have a living will, I do have a written document: a health care power of attorney. A "living will," as discussed earlier, is a document in which the writer attempts to spell out what medical treatments he would accept or reject if he can no longer communicate, with statements such as, "If I'm in a comatose state, I do not want a respirator." Often these documents have lists of conditions and treatments and boxes to check to indicate the writer's choices. The "health care power of attorney" is simpler, and usually much shorter. With this document the writer simply names a person to make decisions if he can no longer communicate. The person who is given the power is often called the "agent" or "health care agent."

For those who do complete these planning documents, some have both types of documents, some have only a living will, and others, like me, only have the health care power of attorney. While I have chosen that approach, I recognize that a living will can be useful for a person who has no family and no friend to speak for her, or when family members cannot agree. The living will can also provide comfort to a family in knowing that they are taking the path that their loved one would choose if, as so often happens, the family finds it hard to have "the talk." I've completed the health care power of attorney because I believe that is the best course for me and my family, as explained more fully, below.

In addition to health care documents, three other documents that sometimes cause confusion for people who are doing their health care planning are a living trust, a will, and a durable power of attorney. These are all financial planning documents. A "will" and a "living trust" are complex legal documents that allow a person to provide for distribution of their financial assets. A "durable power of attorney" allows a person to name another to manage financial affairs in the event of incapacity. A person needs a lawyer's advice to complete these financial documents. A lawyer is not needed to fill out a "living will" or a "health care power of attorney," although you may choose to consult one.

My own health care power of attorney (see Appendix) is quite simple; it's less than a page in length. Its function as a legal document is specific and narrow. The document names my wife as the person to speak for me if I can no longer make decisions. She is my health care agent. Additionally, the document strives to make sure that anyone who is reading it will understand that I want my wife, acting as my agent, to have as broad a power as the state is willing to grant, or as the federal Constitution grants, whichever is greater. The document also lists my sisters and then my best friend as alternate agents. My document has been witnessed by two people (because that is required in many states), and notarized. Notarization is required in three states—North Carolina, West Virginia, and Missouri.[3] I have had my document notarized because our house in Kansas is only about five blocks from the Missouri state line, and I also think it makes the paper look more "official."

My document does not follow exactly the form dictated by the statutes of Kansas, where we live, or the statutes of Missouri. Yet I'm confident that my document is legally valid in both states. In fact, I'm confident that it is binding in all fifty states—no disclaimers here. I think you could copy and use my document, and it will be "legal" in all states.

All Americans have a constitutional right to make decisions about their own medical treatment. That right was established by the U.S. Supreme Court in the *Cruzan* case, the case that drew me into this field in the first place. In *Cruzan*, the Court reasoned that the Fourteenth Amendment to our Constitution, which provides that no state shall "deprive any person of life, liberty, or property, without due process of law," includes a constitutionally-protected right to liberty for each citizen "in refusing unwanted medical treatment."[4]

That's the right I am exercising with my power of attorney naming my wife as my agent, not any right granted by a state statute. States can put safeguards in place to make certain that the right is exercised carefully, but they cannot unduly restrict that right. My document is notarized, witnessed, and is a very clear statement of how I choose to exercise my right. I only have one desire: to name the person I want to speak for me. For the few states that require "clear and convincing evidence" of a person's wishes to stop treatment (Missouri is no longer one, by the way), I believe my document complies. In fact, this document exceeds that standard because it provides evidence beyond a reasonable doubt of my wishes. I have one wish, and that is that my wife make decisions for me, without interference.

I've added language singling out feeding tubes as being within her decision-making power in my document because many state laws require a separate statement about tube feeding. I believe the document as an exercise of my federal constitutional rights would still control tube feeding if I did not have such language, but I add it out of abundance of caution.

Understand, though, that no court including the U.S. Supreme Court has yet declared the law to be exactly as I've described it. Someone no doubt will be the test case at some point. This interpretation of the reach of the *Cruzan* decision is a reasonable one, however, and I am confident we all have the federal constitutional rights as I've described them.

At the same time, I'm also convinced that all of this analysis of the law doesn't even begin to provide the full advice needed, legal or otherwise. We worry about a living will complying with state law requirements or whether a living will from one state might work in an adjoining state. Unfortunately, when 65 percent of doctors surveyed state that they wouldn't follow a clear living will if it conflicted with their own views of proper medical treatment, when the SUPPORT study concludes that doctors often find living wills vague, and when medical providers tell you that if the living, breathing family members

Nancy Cruzan in 1982, shortly before her accident (courtesy Cruzan family).

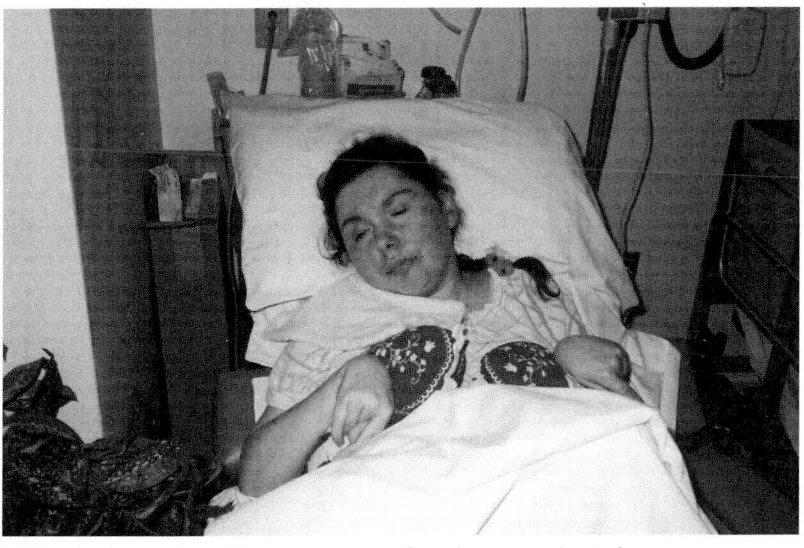

Nancy Cruzan in 1988, six years after her accident (courtesy Cruzan family).

Christine Busalacchi high school yearbook photo (courtesy Busalacchi family).

Christine Busalacchi and her father, Pete, in May 1990, shown on the cover of *Time*, three years after her accident (courtesy *Time* magazine).

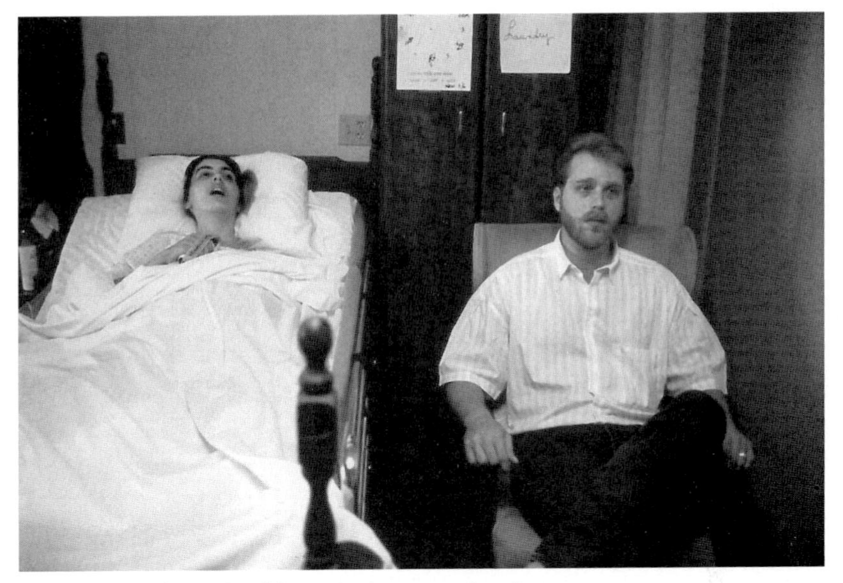

Michael and Terri Schiavo in her nursing home room on November 7, 1990 (World Picture News).

Bob and Mary Schindler outside the Hospice House Woodside (World Picture News).

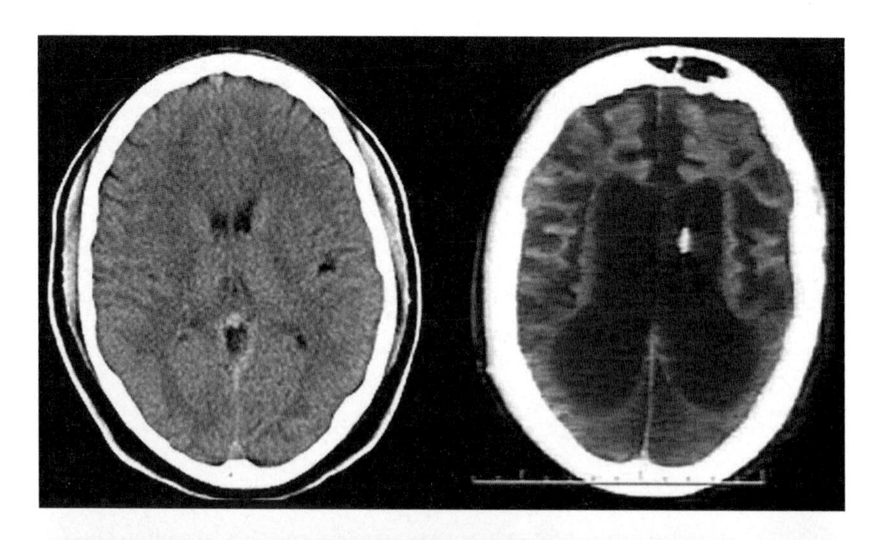

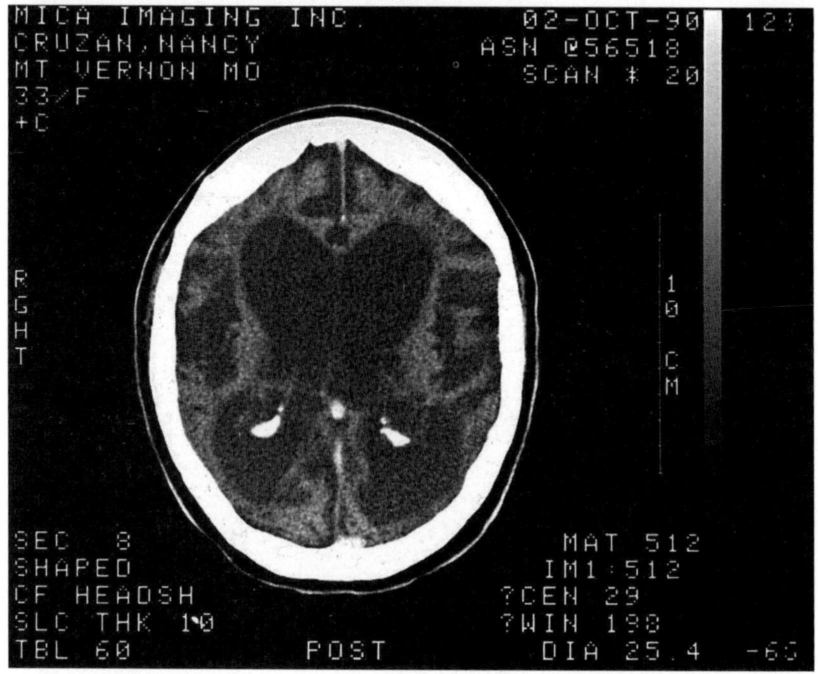

TOP: CT scan of the uninjured brain of a 25-year-old woman side-by-side with a scan of Terri Schiavo's brain, taken twelve years after her cardiac arrest. BOTTOM: A CT scan of Nancy Cruzan's brain taken seven years after her accident. The dark areas represent fluid, which has replaced damaged brain tissue. (Normal scan side-by-side with Terri Schiavo scan from the court file, courtesy Dr. Ronald Cranford).

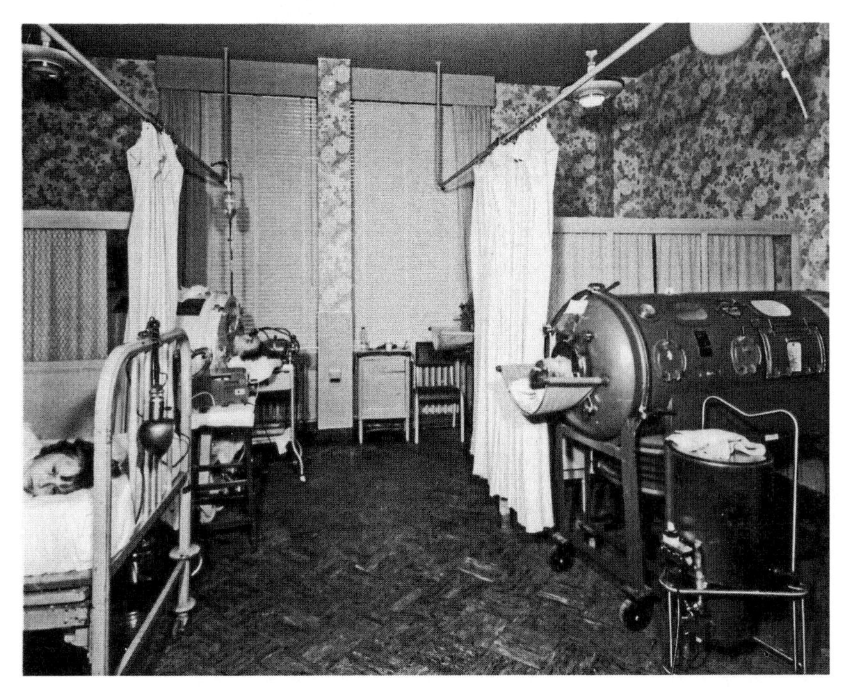

A polio ward with patients in "iron lungs" (courtesy National Library of Medicine).

Protesters outside Barnes Hospital in St. Louis in March, 1993, protesting the removal of Christine Busalacchi's feeding tube (courtesy *St. Louis Post-Dispatch*).

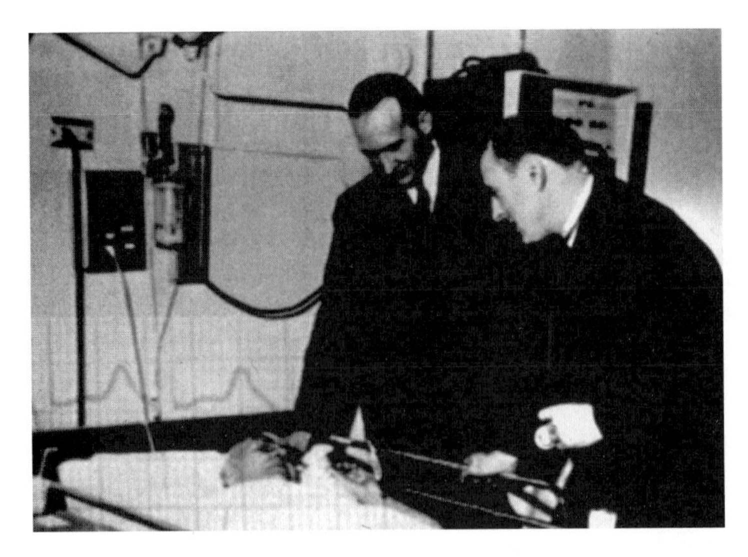

Dr. Bernard Lown visits with Dr. Hughes Day at Bethany Medical Center in Kansas City, Kansas, observing the first cardiac critical care unit (courtesy Dr. Robert Potter).

The device that Dr. Claude Beck used in first successful defibrillation of a 14-year-old boy in 1947 (courtesy Bakken Library, Minneapolis).

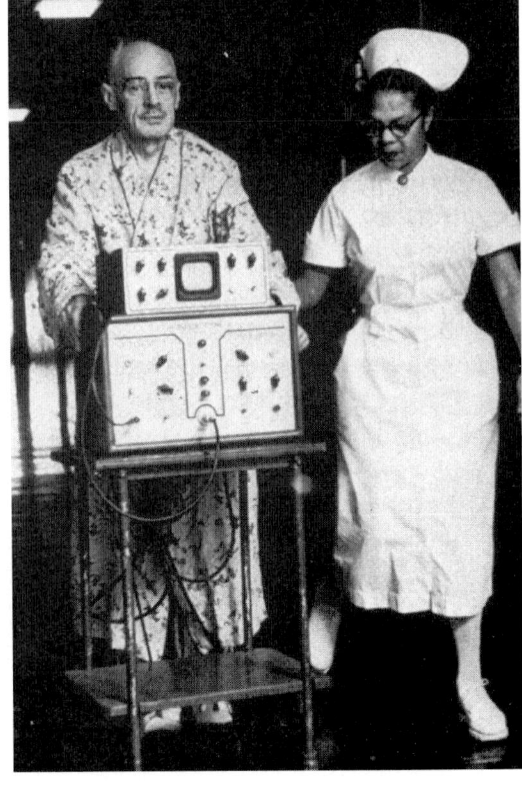

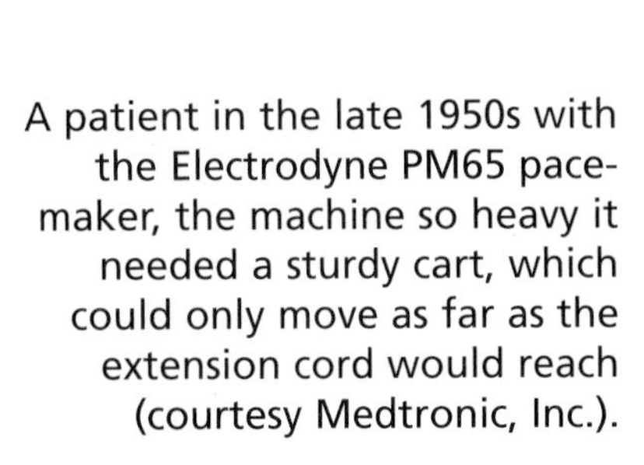

A patient in the late 1950s with the Electrodyne PM65 pacemaker, the machine so heavy it needed a sturdy cart, which could only move as far as the extension cord would reach (courtesy Medtronic, Inc.).

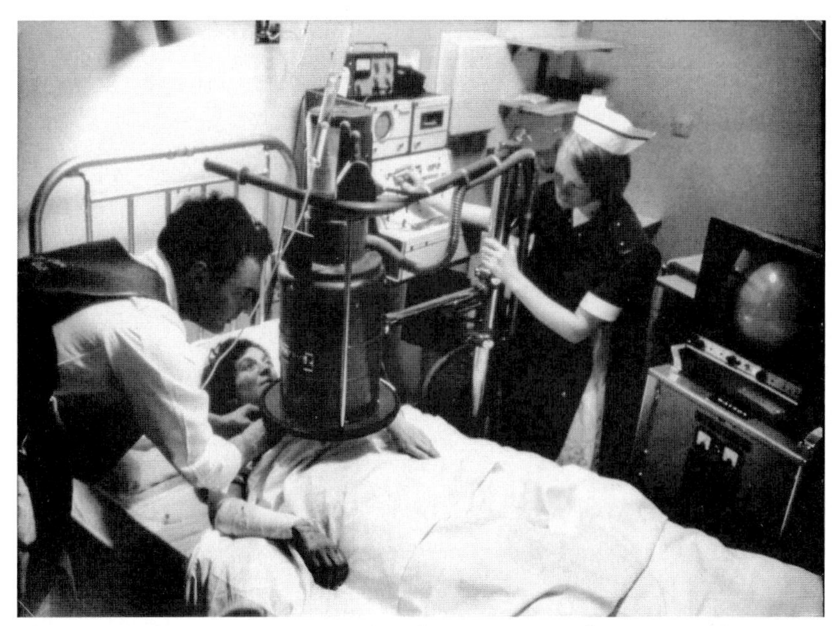

The connections to a pacemaker being inserted into a patient's heart (courtesy National Library of Medicine).

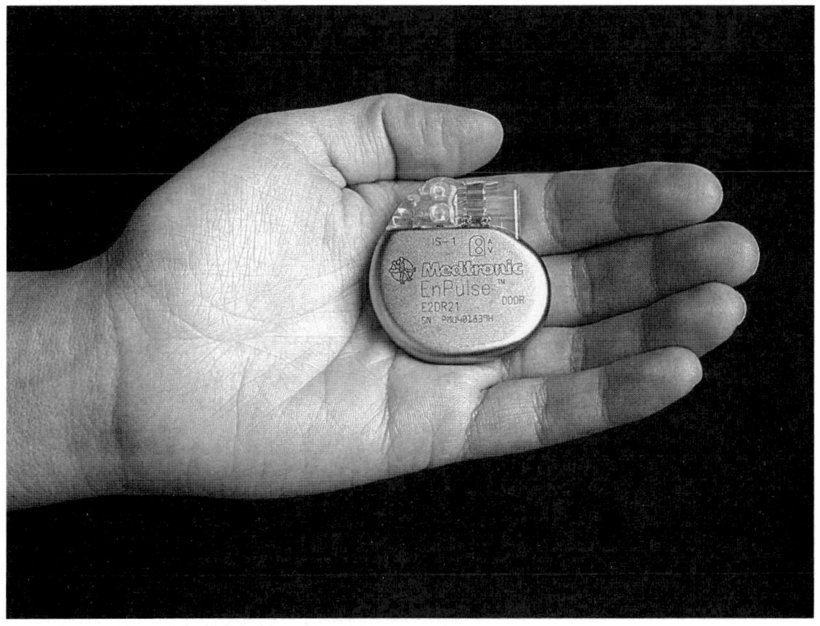

A modern implantable Medtronic pacemaker (courtesy Medtronic, Inc.).

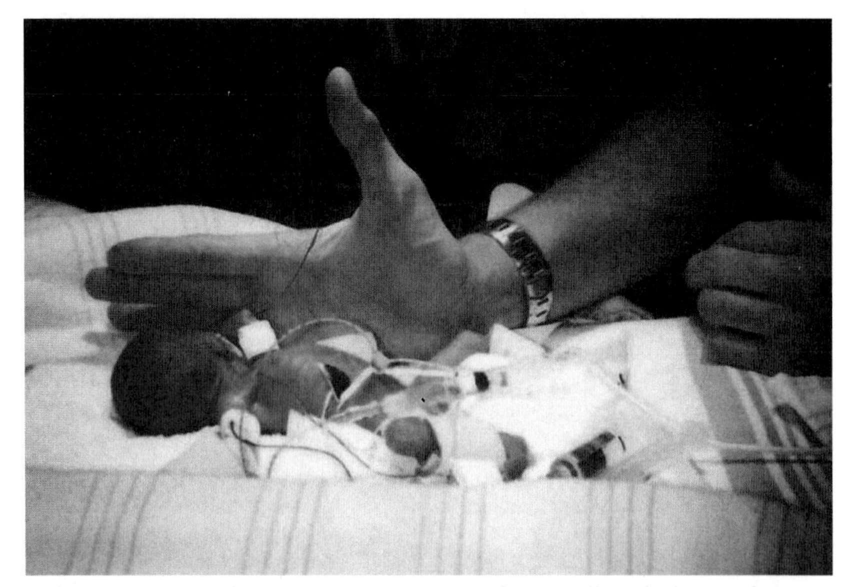

Baby Rumaisa Rahman, at 8.6 ounces, the smallest baby in the world (courtesy Oscar Izquierdo/Loyola University Medical Center).

"The Courtroom" by Elizabeth Layton, 1990, drawing inspired by the Cruzan case at the U.S. Supreme Court (From the collection of the Center for Practical Bioethics, Kansas City, gift of Don Lambert).

are in conflict, a living will is often ignored, those state-specific, requirements become almost irrelevant. On the other hand, remember my discussion last spring in Illinois in which the lawyer mentioned that state law required capital letters in a living will in order for it to be valid. The hospice nurse quietly told me afterward that medical personnel looked to any document that helped provide information.

The point is, if you want your document to *work*, you'd better do more than fill it out. I'm, of course, not saying that state law requirements should be ignored; I am simply suggesting that they're not all that need to be considered. I believe a clear, witnessed, reliable document is legal in every state. In fact, I believe that even an oral expression naming the person one wants to make the decisions, as long as that expression is reliable and witnessed by others, for example, is legally binding. I also know that other lawyers would argue that this statement reaches too far. For the document or the oral expression to be effective, however, we need to prepare our agents to act as our advocates. They need to know what we think of the stories—Terri Schiavo and Nancy Cruzan, and even more importantly, stories like Margo's, so that they have an idea of our views and can advocate. And we need to talk not only with the person to whom we've given decision-making power, but with everyone we think might be in that room when decisions are made.

I've done all that. My family knows my views. They have this entire book explaining those views. Even with all that, when the time comes to face life-and-death decisions, those decisions will not be simple, maybe not clear cut, and emotionally they'll be hard.

I picture the scene: a gleaming, high-tech hospital somewhere in the year 2037, when I'm 82. My wife will be 74, and my kids, 45, 42, 40 and 37 then. With luck, I will be one of the smiling Alzheimer's patients, not one of those yelling obscenities at my family when they enter my room, screaming that they are stealing my things. For the first two to four years, the first phase of the disease, I will have lived at home while suffering increasing lapses of recent memory. These lapses will have started with repeating questions over and over ("Is Tom coming for Christmas?"), and progressed to mild disorientation (not remembering how to get to the grocery store).

In the second phase, maybe two to three years in length, my family likely will have moved me into a nursing home. Caring for me in my own home will have become too difficult, as my communication and dressing, eating, and personal skills collapse. At some point in this phase, I likely will stop recognizing my loved ones. In stage three, lasting a year or two, I will have become bedridden, paralyzed, incontinent, and eventually unaware of the world. Aspiration pneumonia (food gagged into the lungs because I've forgotten how to eat) or some other infection will afflict me.

I hope and believe that all four of my then-adult children and their spouses will be by my wife's side. I hope my two sisters will be there with her. Let's say a young doctor is talking to my family about a feeding tube because I'm becoming malnourished. Or maybe by 2037, a simple feeding patch will be required. It would be applied once a week to the skin, with no side effects; it would be nearly a noninvasive procedure he will tell them.

Maybe they'll have a caring, supportive doctor, and they'll talk through the issues. Maybe the hospital chaplain will be there, too, and it will be a reverent family time befitting the solemn occasion. Maybe the latest version of the federal President's Council will have a one-page think sheet that they will work through. Or maybe the doctor, who will look like he's about ten years old to my wife, will say to her when she says "No" to the feeding patch, "Mrs. Colby, that would be starving your husband to death, I can't do that."

At that point, my family might say "okay" to the patch because they aren't ready to let me go, or because they are too distraught to think clearly, or to debate with the doctor. As I said, what is critically important to me now, and I will continue to affirm this between now and then, is that those decisions are okay by me if it helps them. And it's okay if that's the only decision they can make.

Chances are, though, given my views and a lifetime of writing and talking about end-of-life issues, my family will step off the institutional glide path sooner rather than later. My wife likely will turn to the doctor and say, "Young man, first get your medicine right; dehydration comes long before starvation. I've been listening to him at cocktail parties for 49 years now talk about exactly this question. For him, the decision to refuse artificial nutrition and hydration that's not a bridge to living his life—tube or simple patch, it doesn't matter—is a life-affirming one. Your technology can't help him *live* life any more, so he is going to meet his Maker." If the doctor persists, I think he will run into the stone wall of my entire family and will ultimately leave the room.

They will then laugh, and cry, and feel alternately confident and distressed that they made the "right" decision. They will understand the doctor's responsibility to "first, do no harm," the doctor's duty to sustain life, and how to factor quality-of-life considerations into making decisions about medical technology. They will understand that with the doctrines of autonomy, utility, quality, equality, benefit vs. burden, extraordinary vs. ordinary, quality of life, that I'm not exactly sure which of them applies to my own wishes, but that I know, and more importantly they know, what those wishes were.

They'll understand that I believe that I am on my way to Heaven, and that there will be a great pickup basketball game going on all day long, and that I'll be able to run and jump again like I was 28 years old, and my own mom and dad will be watching from the bleachers (where the hardwood seats are comfortable), and that thought will make my family smile. And it will also make them cry, as it should, because life is our greatest, most precious gift, to be cherished, respected, honored, and used wisely, from birth to death, as best we can.

CHAPTER 11

Feeding Tubes—The Hardest Question

DINNERTIME AT OUR HOUSE is controlled chaos. The four kids, ages 13 and under, race in, sometimes from soccer or baseball or the neighborhood, usually trailing dirt behind them. Milk gets poured, the table set. Sometimes grace is said, and when led by the 5-year-old, he ends the prayer with a sung "Alleluia, amen." Food is eaten, laughter comes often. If anyone wrinkles a nose and says, "What's this?" when they look down at their plate, they're in trouble with Mom. Later that night, cold cereal at the island is a snack. The two little ones sip water from cups with lids in their bed, listening to a parent or older sibling read a book. In the morning, we do it all again. And that is why feeding tubes are the hardest question.

Feeding evokes emotion, and the questions around feeding tubes obviously reach deep emotional places in our society. Consider the language of protest itself: When doctors remove a dialysis machine, those opposed don't speak of poisoning; when a doctor turns off the respirator, opponents don't cry suffocation. The rhetoric around feeding tubes and their removal is unique among medical treatments. Legal briefs in the *Cruzan* case likened the Cruzans' decision to the Holocaust. Opponents in the public debate painted the stereotypical picture of a dying man crawling across the desert, tongue cracked, mouth parched, skin burnt red.

In the last days, the signs held aloft by protesters in *Cruzan*—"Please Feed Nancy!"—looked like the signs seen outside Terri Schiavo's hospice in the spring of 2005, and outside Christine Busalacchi's St. Louis hospital in 1993. Randall Terry, the anti-abortion protester to whom Bob and Mary Schindler gave "carte blanche to put Terri's fight in front of the American people" in the spring of 2005, also spoke to reporters in December of 1990 on the steps of Nancy Cruzan's hospital: "If we don't work quickly, Nancy will be dead. The issue is that a woman is being starved to death. Isn't there one judge with the moral integrity to save this woman?"[1]

Whichever side you came down on in the *Cruzan* or *Schiavo* cases, the feeding tube raised emotional issues. I can close my eyes and see the picture of Joe Cruzan sitting in front of Nancy in his tan construction overalls, trying to spoon food into her mouth, placing it onto the back of her tongue, trying to stop her teeth from clamping down reflexively on the spoon, trying to coax her to eat. "C'mon Nancy, you can do this. All you have to do is swallow a little banana, you love banana."

He'd spend an hour or more and would succeed in some food moving down her esophagus headed for her stomach, propelled by a gag or swallow reflex (those reflexes housed in the brainstem), not by conscious swallowing. Most of the pureed food would end up on Joe and Nancy, though. Joe would clean his daughter up, and then run down the hospital hallway hurrying to work, food splattered on his coveralls, his jaw set, ready to try again the next day. (The gastrostomy tube stayed in place from the time of the surgery in January of 1983 until

Nancy's death in December of 1990, and provided the nutrition and hydration that sustained her, the efforts at spoon feeding simply a part of her attempted therapy.)[2]

Joe was my age then, his life undone. Of all the pictures I might conjure up from the case, this one sends a knot into my chest as much as any. Perhaps that's because, in hindsight, I can see the pain and the utter futility of that effort, a father trying to retrain his daughter's mind to eat when that mind was completely gone, the gray matter slowly, inexorably shrinking and fluid filling the vacuum.

Does a feeding tube provide the same nurturing and loving that my wife and I do with our four kids, a basic caring that we could not conceive of denying to another human, let alone our own flesh and blood? Or is it something wholly different—an FDA-regulated nutrient being pumped by an FDA-regulated device into a body that has permanently lost the ability to eat?

These are hard questions, for sure, and like the rest of the issues in this book, essentially brand new questions for humankind. To a layperson, the idea of a feeding tube sounds simpler than a machine like a respirator or dialysis machine. But as a question of emerging technology, there is little difference. One of the groups that filed a brief in support of the Cruzan family at the U.S. Supreme Court in the fall of 1989 was A.S.P.E.N., the American Society for Parenteral and Enteral Nutrition, an association of 5,300 health professionals with expertise in feeding tubes.

A.S.P.E.N. told the Court that the nutrient formulas and tube delivery systems had grown sophisticated enough to maintain someone in a severely compromised medical state for an extended period of time only since the mid-1970s.[3] Like respirators and dialysis machines and new heart drugs and internal defibrillators and many other technologies, feeding tubes were new technology, bringing with them new questions.

Tube feeding is delivered to patients by different methods, depending on their needs. "Parenteral" means that the formula enters the body through the bloodstream, in a large vein; "enteral" means that it comes directly into the stomach or intestine, the gastrointestinal tract. The most common short-term method of tube feeding is the nasogastric tube, or NG tube, for which surgery is not required. A soft, pliable tube is threaded through the nose, down the esophagus, into the stomach. Conscious patients are instructed to sit up and attempt to swallow water as the tube is being placed. Patients can gag with this process. Confused patients sometimes are restrained if they are frightened. Inserting the tube in an unconscious patient requires considerable medical skill.[4]

When longer-term feeding is required, a tube is placed surgically. In the late 1970s and into the 1980s, such a device, called a gastrostomy tube or G-tube, was inserted through a hole surgically cut into the stomach. If injury or illness required bypassing the stomach, the tube could be inserted into the jejunum, or small intestine, a J-tube. A seriously injured or ill patient could also receive total parenteral nutrition (TPN) directly into the bloodstream, bypassing the gastrointestinal tract through a catheter that was surgically inserted into a large vein beneath the collarbone. The surgical placement of a gastrostomy feeding tube into the stomach involved major surgery, typically a laparotomy (surgical incision of the abdominal wall) with the attendant risks of anesthesia, infection, and organ rupture.[5]

In 1979, concerned with the risks that such surgery posed to children, two doctors in Cleveland experimented with a new technique that they named the percutaneous endoscopic gastrostomy, or PEG tube. The late 1970s saw the development of a whole new kind of minimally invasive surgery using a device called an endoscope, a small, flexible tube with a light and a camera lens at the end.[6] If a football player in 1980 had said to his teammates, "I'm getting my knee scoped," they would have looked at him like he was from Mars. Today, they just nod; all football players know about "scoping" knees.

Dr. Michael Gauderer, a pediatrician, and Dr. Jeffrey Ponsky, a new kind of doctor called an endoscopist, performed the PEG tube procedure for the first time on a human being, a four-month-old boy, on June 12, 1979. They first inserted a tiny, hollow tube through the skin into the baby's stomach, and threaded a strand of surgical thread through the tube. Then they moved up to his mouth, and snaked the endoscope with its tiny light and camera into the mouth, down the esophagus, into the stomach. Once in the stomach, the endoscope located the thread, and pulled it back out through the mouth. Outside of the mouth they tied an enteral feeding tube to the end of the thread, then pulled on the other end of the thread to draw that tube down into the stomach and out through the hole in the stomach wall and skin. The result was a fully functioning feeding tube, without the invasive surgery.[7]

But on January 11, 1983, the night Nancy Cruzan's car went off the road, the PEG tube was still an emerging technology and had not yet made its way to rural Missouri. Nancy Cruzan had a surgically placed gastrostomy or G-tube. Even by 1989 when A.S.P.E.N. filed its brief at the U.S. Supreme Court in *Cruzan*, that brief did not mention PEG tubes, the procedure still too new to be part of the formal, ethical discussion.

That single-car accident in January of 1983 set in motion the chain of events that would ultimately draw the entire nation into a new ethical, legal and moral debate: What exactly is a feeding tube? And can a family request doctors to remove such a tube once that tube is in place?

NANCY CRUZAN'S FEEDING TUBE

Nancy Cruzan's feeding tube surgery did not happen the night of her accident. In the emergency room that first night, the doctors worked simply to save Nancy's life. As part of their work, the medical team placed three tubes: an IV in one arm, a larger central line in the vein under Nancy Cruzan's collarbone, and a stiff tube down her nose into her stomach. Through the three tubes, she received medicine, blood, and large volumes of water in an effort to stabilize her fluids. For the first three days in the hospital, she received no nutrition through these tubes; her liver fresh from surgery and her bruised stomach weren't ready to work. On day three she started receiving Aminosyn 3.5%, a nutritional solution high in glucose and amino acids, through the central line into her vein. Eight days after the accident, doctors replaced the stiff tube in her nose with a flexible NG tube, and Nancy began to receive a more potent nutritional formula, Traumaide.[8]

However, it would be nearly a month later, as the picture grew clearer that any recovery for Nancy was going to take months, not weeks, that doctors began to talk about how to provide nutritional support for that longer-term recovery. The surgery to insert a gastrostomy tube directly through the wall of her stomach took place 27 days after the accident. The medical records contain this description:

> Pre-operative diagnosis, head injury. Malnutrition. Post-operative Diagnosis, Same. Name of Operation, Insertion of a #20 t-tube feeding gastrostomy. Operative Procedure: The abdominal area was prepped and draped. A previous upper midline incision was anesthetized with 1 percent plain Xylocaine anesthesia, IV sedation, Pryor group. The incision was opened. Bleeders were electrocoagulated. The peritoneal cavity was entered. The stomach was delivered and in the dependent portion, a 3-0 purse-string was inserted. A #20 short-arm T-tube was inserted and the purse-string tied. The stomach was secured to the under side of the peritoneum with interrupted 4-0 silk. The fascia and peritoneum were closed with interrupted 0 Ethibond. Skin and subcutaneous tissue were closed with skin clips. The patient was taken to the recovery room in a stable condition. Dictated: 2-7-83. Transcribed: 2-7-83. Signed: R.L. Willcoxon, M.D.[9]

Once that G-tube was in place, the NG tube in her nose, the IVs in each arm (a second had been added two nights after the accident), and the central line under her collarbone could all come out. One G-tube, under the blanket, would provide her body's nutritional and medicinal needs.

Four-and-a-half years later on October 21, 1987, when I walked into Nancy Cruzan's hospital room in Mt. Vernon, Missouri for the first time, I knew none of this. When I asked in a hesitant voice, "Is it possible to see the tube?" her father, Joe Cruzan, said, "Sure," and gently pulled Nancy's covers back. I felt like a kid watching the door to a cage being opened, worried about what might jump out. As with my education about the persistent vegetative state, my education about feeding tubes began that day, too.

Did the Cruzans make a "wrong" decision 27 days after Nancy's accident when Joe Cruzan signed the hospital consent form agreeing to the surgery to insert the gastrostomy tube? Did he even really "make" a decision that day, or was he simply caught on the institutional glide path, agreeing to do what the doctor's told him came next?

At that point this family had lived for nearly a month with their lives utterly upside-down. Many nights they slept in the hospital; they were physically and emotionally drained. They were waiting for word on whether the rehabilitation hospital was going to accept Nancy or whether doctors there would conclude that her brain was too damaged to attempt rehabilitation. They were talking to social workers about whether they might take Nancy home or where else they might treat her if the rehabilitation hospital said no. They had no real idea of what was ahead of them. Yet they still had hope that "their Nancy" would come back. In that state, did Joe and Joyce Cruzan simply nod, glassy-eyed, and do what the doctors said?

By contrast, the family decision to remove Nancy's feeding tube four years after they had agreed to its insertion was one based on extended deliberation and discussion. Joe and the rest of the Cruzans had no doubt that removing the feeding tube after years of Nancy being unconscious in a persistent vegetative state was the right decision. They had tried everything for recovery, and it had not happened. None of the medical treatment, including the tube feeding, had delivered what the family so desperately hoped and prayed for: Nancy's recovery, her return to "being Nancy." So the Cruzan family made the decision that it was time to "turn her loose." The national debate about whether the Cruzans' decision was the right one began soon after that family decision.

By the time the case ended, the clear consensus reached through that debate (with a vocal minority dissent) was that a gastrostomy tube was a medical treatment. The technology had taken the place of a natural function that had been lost, and such technology was typically intended to serve as a bridge to recovery of that function. The American Medical Association in its 1986 ethical opinion, "Withholding or Withdrawing Life-Prolonging Medical Treatment," stated the rule quite simply: "Life-prolonging medical treatment includes medication and artificially or technologically supplied respiration, nutrition or hydration."[10]

When the U.S. Supreme Court's opinion in *Cruzan* came down in June of 1990, five of the nine justices recognized explicitly that artificial nutrition and hydration is medical treatment, and the remaining four recognized that fact implicitly.[11] Justice Sandra Day O'Connor in her separate, concurring opinion wrote, "Artificial feeding cannot readily be distinguished from other forms of medical treatment." She went on to describe the different types of feeding tubes, like Nancy's gastrostomy tube, an NG tube, and a J-tube. Her opinion did not mention the new PEG tube technology. Justice O'Connor described the applicable law for such medical treatments: "Requiring a competent adult to endure such procedures against her will burdens the patient's liberty, dignity, and freedom to determine the course of her own treatment. Accordingly, the liberty guaranteed by the Due Process Clause must protect, if it protects anything, an individual's deeply personal decision to reject medical treatment, including the artificial delivery of food and water."[12]

Nancy Cruzan died on December 26, 1990, eleven and a half days after her doctor removed her feeding tube. As in the *Schiavo* case, national public attention was riveted on the Cruzan family during Nancy's dying. But the public discussion in 1990 was in many ways unsophisticated, resembling the discussion in 1976 around the *Quinlan* case. In *Quinlan*, society took its first unsteady baby steps into understanding modern medical technology. We looked at Karen Ann's still black-and-white high school photo and tried to grasp the idea that medical technology could keep a person forever in a state of permanent unconsciousness, tried to picture what that state looked like and meant. No longer, perhaps, did we simply want our doctors to "do everything."

With *Cruzan* in 1990, society began thinking and learning about "feeding tubes." It took most of the energy that society could muster to understand that something named a "feeding tube" was probably not the same as feeding our children. For the first time, we had pictures and video, stark images to help our understanding.

While a consensus emerged that feeding tubes were medical treatment, many in society understood that they also remained somehow different, probably because of the special emotions attached to the idea of feeding. State legislatures that passed laws in reaction to the *Cruzan* case often treated tube feeding differently than other medical treatments. For example, a law would allow an adult to name a health care agent, but that adult had to write specifically in the document that the agent's power extended to refusing or removing a feeding tube.[13]

The national debate about feeding tubes began with the case of Nancy Cruzan in 1990. Fifteen years later, in 2005, American society returned to that debate in earnest with the case of Terri Schiavo. Technology, however, had not stood idly by in those fifteen years. To the contrary, it had continued its relentless advance, and by the time society had returned to the questions first raised in *Cruzan*, the questions themselves had changed.

PEG TUBES AND THE ELDERLY

In the spring of 2005, Drs. Ponsky and Gauderer, the inventors of modern-day PEG tube, found themselves and their invention in the news as a result of the *Schiavo* case. The doctors said that they did not envision in 1979 that the procedure they invented to facilitate recovery in a pediatric population would be used for end-of-life care. And it "never entered our minds this would produce such a massive ethical dilemma," Dr. Ponsky said.[14]

But it did. Though the doctors might not have envisioned the minimally invasive PEG tube procedure being used in end-of-life care, they did quickly see its potential for patients other than their pediatric population. In the early 1980s, they began tinkering with and adapting the PEG device for use in adults, first with stroke victims, and soon after that for terminal cancer patients and the demented elderly.[15]

This invention, coupled with improved development of complex nutritional formula, made long-term tube feeding simple. Prior to the PEG tube, use of feeding tubes for the long term required major surgery like Nancy Cruzan's. Doctors typically only performed such surgery on patients who had the chance to recover. In 1983, at the time of Nancy Cruzan's accident, virtually no elderly patients with dementia had a feeding tube surgically inserted. A 1999 survey by Dr. Susan Mitchell in Boston concluded that nearly 34 percent of severely demented patients in nursing homes already had PEG tubes in place. In 2005, Dr. Gauderer estimated that doctors now insert about 300,000 new PEG tubes a year, and that roughly 225,000 of these new PEG tubes are for patients 65 and older.[16]

This pervasive use of PEG tube feeding has changed the question for society. In *Cruzan*, the debate centered on a small population of brain-injured patients who had tubes inserted when their prognosis was unclear but who tragically never recovered consciousness. By 2005, although the debate took place in the context of a similarly young, brain-injured patient, Terri Schiavo, the broader debate stretched to a huge, completely new population—millions of elderly, demented patients with PEG tubes.

In fifteen years, a once-complicated medical procedure had grown simple, and the relative ease of implanting the PEG tube moved tube feeding for the elderly directly onto the institutional glide path. As the procedure grows even more refined in the years ahead, the default option of PEG tube surgery for the elderly will grow more entrenched on that glide path. It will be important as that happens for society to spend time discussing exactly what is the goal of such medical treatment.

Some doctors are beginning to ask this question already. A recent *Wall Street Journal* article told the story of one such doctor. In the summer of 2005, Dr. Richard K.C. Wong at the University Hospitals in Cleveland, the place where Drs. Gauderer and Ponsky invented PEG tube feeding, received a referral to insert a PEG tube in a recent stroke victim who could no longer eat. She also had pneumonia. Her name was Lucy McGowan. Ms. McGowan was 100 years old. Dr. Wong, a 43-year-old gastroenterologist, had been a high school student when Ponsky and Gauderer did the first PEG tube on a child on June 12, 1979. Dr. Wong thought Ms. McGowan was nearing death. He wondered about the proposed surgery, "Why is she here?"

The internist who referred the woman for the PEG tube surgery had an answer. Before her stroke "she'd been fully functional," he said. "Granted, she was 100. But she was a young 100." Ms. McGowan's 51-year-old grandson agreed to the PEG tube surgery, the family not able to envision life without her. "She had to have a way of being able to eat," he said.

Dr. Wong decided to wait a day before seeing Ms. McGowan. "The woman had an active infection," he said. "A feeding tube is not an emergency procedure."[17]

When he checked in on her the next day, he discovered that she had died in the night. Like Dr. Nuland's autopsied elderly patients, Ms. McGowan had multiple complications: a stroke, pneumonia, and brain disease causing delirium. An autopsy would have no doubt revealed problems in other organs. What was "right" for Ms. McGowan?

Without question feeding tubes provoke emotional debate. Emotional or not, most religious, medical, ethics, and legal groups have concluded that the ethical analysis for tube feeding should work as it does for a respirator, or dialysis, or IV antibiotics, or any other medical intervention. One notable recent exception to this consensus came in a speech by Pope John Paul II in the spring of 2004, about a year prior to his death, which I'll discuss in more detail in the next chapter. Concluding that a feeding tube is a medical treatment does not make the questions any easier, however. The patient and his family still have to address the difficult questions of whether the treatment is providing a benefit, providing an acceptable quality of life.

In the summer of 2005, Dr. Wong in Cleveland estimated that of the thousands of PEG tubes other doctors had requested him to surgically insert, two-thirds of the time those requests had made sense, medically and ethically. He gave as an example the case of a 225-pound teenager named Isaac Hardges. Mr. Hardges was shot in the back, lost the use of his legs, lost his appetite, and saw his weight drop to 85 pounds before doctors inserted a feeding tube a year after the shooting. That tube saved Hardges' life. Years later in the summer of 2005, Mr. Hardges dislodged the tube, and he came to University Hospitals where Dr. Wong surgically inserted a new PEG tube. Mr. Hardges, by that point 28 years old, called the device "a miracle. I use nutrient shakes, put vegetables in a blender, take a big syringe and I'm able to feed myself." Dr. Wong described Mr. Hardges' case as the "reason why this device is necessary."[18]

But what of the other one-third, the thousands of PEG tubes that Dr. Wong had "qualms or doubts about?" What of those patients of Dr. Wong's who will never recover any function? Are these patients simply moving onto the institutional glide paths at hospitals around the country, with no one asking what the goal of this treatment is? What of Ms. McGowan?

MS. MCGOWAN'S SHOES AND TIME-LIMITED TRIALS

When Ms. McGowan's internist called her a "young 100," he likely was saying that she had the functioning of a younger person. I took his statement differently when I read it. The idea of a "young 100" takes me back to my dad saying that 80 didn't look so old to him anymore, looking at it from the vantage point of his 75th birthday. If I'm at the hospital at age 100, I don't think my family will automatically say "No PEG tube" just because I'm 100.

I hope my doctor will not be pointing to some monitor, telling my family what that beeping means about the status of one of my many aging organs. I hope instead that he is talking to them about the goals of my care. In this talk, feeding tubes, respirators, blood pressure medicines, any interventions, will all carry the same weight, and my family will know my main question: Can the technology help me to *live* life again on my terms, as I've defined those terms at age 100?

If I am 100 years old and in Terri Schiavo's shoes, or Margo's shoes (the smiling Alzheimer's patient from the 2005 President's Council report), I believe my family will say "No" to the PEG tube surgery. That answer does not depend on my age; it depends on my prospects for recovery. I think it would be the same if I were 70 or 55. If I'm 100 and in Ms. McGowan's shoes, however, the answer is less clear-cut and the discussion likely will be more complicated. If I am a "young 100" prior to a very minor stroke, with a mild pneumonia, and I'm still active, then my family may choose to insert the PEG. On the other hand, if the doctor says that his best guess is that the stroke has started me down a road where I will be bed-ridden and partly aware, my family may say, "Let the pneumonia run its course."

I hope and believe that the discussion will dig well below the surface on several levels, because Ms. McGowan's case demands such digging. One topic my family will certainly raise with the doctor is something called a "time-limited trial." For many years the medical ethics literature has compared two acts: 1) initially withholding a medical treatment, and 2) withdrawing treatment once begun. The 1983 President's Commission report, "Deciding to Forego Life-Sustaining Treatment," concluded that ethically it should be no more difficult to try a treatment and then later withdraw that treatment than it was not to start the treatment in the first place.

The Commission argued that, in fact, the better approach was to try a treatment to see if it might benefit a patient and then withdraw the treatment if that benefit was not realized. The Commission stated that a "troubling wrong occurs when a treatment that might save life or improve health is not started because the health care personnel are afraid that they will find it very difficult to stop the treatment if, as is fairly likely, it proves to be of little benefit and greatly burdens the patient."[19] The 2005 President's Council report essentially agreed with this ethical approach.[20] This question is not an abstract one. The director of ethics at Dr. Wong's Cleveland hospital said, when interviewed in 2005 by the *Wall Street Journal*, that "it's easier to put the PEG in than it is to sit down with the family" and have hard conversations about aging, dying, and the goals of medicine. And Dr. Ponsky acknowledged in that article, "Once they're in, it's so emotionally difficult to take it out and let someone die."[21]

In 1990, when the *Cruzan* case was in the national news, I received a frantic phone call from the mother of a 16-year-old boy. On the day of his birthday, the day he'd gotten his driver's license, the boy had crashed not far from Nancy Cruzan's hometown. Now a month later, he was still unconscious, though his eyes had opened, and he was becoming malnourished. Doctors told the mom that they needed to insert a gastrostomy feeding tube. They also told her that while they thought he had a chance to recover, they weren't hopeful. And they told her that if she consented to the surgery, she could never withdraw that consent; once the tube was in, it was in. Sobbing on the phone she said to me, "I want my son to live, but not like Nancy Cruzan." I agreed to represent her, and after she and I hung up, I called and set up a phone meeting for the next day with the hospital lawyer. Perhaps to spare his mother, the boy died during the night.

Nearly all ethics books say that there's no essential difference between withholding treatment and starting treatment but later withdrawing it. The reality is that doctors find it far easier not to insert the feeding tube in the first place than to insert it as a trial and then remove it. That is understandable human nature, but it will not work with my family. I'm fairly sure that in talking with the doctor about my PEG tube surgery, my family will have a clear discussion about the goal of the PEG tube, and about using this medical technology for a limited time to see if that goal can be reached. They will make certain that the doctor understands that if the goal is not reached, then the tube needs to come out as easily as it went in.

They'll make sure he knows that trying the treatment to see if it might "work" is the better ethical course. To say no to a treatment that has some chance at a benefit because the doctor fears he will not have the moral strength to stop that treatment if the goal is not reached is not an acceptable way to practice medicine. How long will they try the PEG tube? That's hard to figure out in advance. They'll do the best they can when the time comes, as families do.

I also believe my family will quiz the doctor about the benefits of the treatment. Some medical research, fairly new in 2005 and likely to be much more definitive fifty years from now if I reach 100, suggests that PEG tube feeding doesn't really extend life expectancy over spoon feeding for the demented elderly, and that it doesn't make feeding any easier or stop the risk of aspiration pneumonia.[22]

No doubt there will be other issues, too. The one thing my family will know unequivocally is that whatever they decide, I am okay with that decision. They will know that there is no perfect, or easy, decision-making at that point. It's likely that if I've reached 100 years, they will have heard about my views constantly for the last 68 years. So those I love will be prepared to act.

They will also understand that while I believe a PEG tube is a medical treatment, I also recognize that feeding is somehow different, too. Dr. Hensel's living will is not talking about stopping a medical treatment; it is asking his family to love him enough not to spoon feed him. Some ethicists contend that even spoon feeding of the profoundly demented is medical treatment, requiring considerable training and skill to avoid choking and aspirating.[23] I've thought about these issues for a long time, but I don't know yet how I feel about such an argument, or about Dr. Hensel's request, for me. I'm pretty certain that I don't want to live in a society where a medical culture would grant such a request easily, or without careful reflection. Dr. Hensel has reflected deeply and eloquently—that's not the point. I would want the rest of us, the state, to keep a close eye on how such decisions are made.

My fervent hope is that when my family faces these questions, they're able to talk with the doctor about the goal of the treatment and make a decision for me that makes sense for them. I hope they don't set their expectations too high, and just do the best they can because they love me.

■ ■ ■

The Bible tells us, in Matthew 14:19 (and in many other places), to feed the hungry. The meaning of these words is fairly clear to me for feeding my children. It's also pretty clear when I think about organizations like Second Harvest, the nation's food bank network, which helps provide for the 38 million Americans who are living with hunger or on the brink of hunger.[24] It's pretty clear in the question of inserting a PEG tube into the gunshot victim in Cleveland, Mr. Hardges. I have the sense, though, that if we could somehow have Matthew back with us for a moment, and ask him how that scripture admonition he wrote about 2,000 years ago should be applied to Terri Schiavo, Margo, and Ms. McGowan, he might tell us that it's not exactly clear what Jesus would do. He might tell us that we'd better keep talking amongst ourselves, people of good will and a variety of views, in an effort to figure that question out.

CHAPTER 12

But I Believe in the Right to Life!

"Thou shalt not kill."

—Exodus 20:13

"Lord, now lettest thou thy servant depart in peace, for mine eyes have seen thy salvation."

—Luke 2: 29–30

ON THE BITTERLY FRIGID DAY of December 22, 1990, I drove down to southern Missouri to say goodbye to Nancy Cruzan and her family. Writing today, fifteen years later, the picture remains clear in my mind. The tension and chaos outside—satellite television trucks, protesters huddled together against the cold, and the police at the door. And inside Nancy's room, with the family gathered together around their dying loved one, the strange mix of emotions that such a room can create—peacefulness together with the heart-knotting pain of a dying daughter, sister, and aunt. The room felt sacred.

One of the things Joe Cruzan did that day was show me some of the boxes of mail they had received (over a thousand letters by the time the case finished). One letter was from one of the leaders of the protest outside, Operation Rescue's Randall Terry. Handwritten on the stationery found in the desks of the nearby Bel-Aire Motor Inn in Mt. Vernon where the protesters had set up camp, the letter pleaded, "I *beg* you, in God's name, to reconsider your decision." Joe also showed me a letter he'd received from the U.S. Senator from Missouri, John Danforth: "I hope this Christmas season will be a time of hope for you and your family. May God bless you." Joe said to me, "I guess this God can cut both ways."[1]

Indeed He can. Though the word of the Bible may be old, the question about how we should apply our religious beliefs to decision-making in the era of modern, technological medicine is new, like all of the other questions in this book. Religion swirled around the public debate over Terri Schiavo, both figuratively and actually, with the parents of Terri Schiavo often framed in the television footage with the two brown-frocked friars, or a Catholic priest, or in the last days even the Reverend Jesse Jackson. Hundreds of religious leaders from all walks of life commented publicly on the *Schiavo* case. Consider a few of these statements, from leaders in various faith groups:

> "We've all been diminished by this slow agonizing killing of a woman who had done absolutely nothing to deserve such cruelty." *Dr. James Dobson, evangelical Christian psychologist with daily radio show Focus on the Family*[2]

> "Let's stop with the euphemisms—they killed her. Food and hydration are never considered medicine." *Catholic Cardinal Javier Lozano Barragan, President of the Vatican's Pontifical Council for Health Care*[3]

> "I'm not a liberal, I'm far from a liberal. But I can attest from a theological point of view that what Governor [Jeb Bush] and others are doing to

Terri is not doing any good for her . . . For Christians, it is a blasphemy to keep people alive as if you were doing them a favor, to keep people alive in that condition as if it benefits them. It doesn't benefit them. I know it is wrapped up in the pro-life, antiabortion activity, and while I am antiabortion, I also know there is eternal life and that we should not confuse or equate the antiabortion effort with the notion of withdrawing life support from dying people." *Catholic Priest Kevin O'Rourke, Loyola University (Chicago) Neiswanger Institute for Bioethics and Health Policy*[4]

"This is where blacks and whites find common ground. Conservatives and liberals. We watch her struggle. We see her on TV. She is now part of our lives. We are all potentially Terris. . . . Nobody should be left behind." *Rev. Jesse Jackson, a Baptist minister, twice a presidential candidate, speaking outside Terri Schiavo's hospice*[5]

"We believe life begins at conception and ends at natural death. God gives life, and God only can take life." *Rev. Ed Martin, Protestant minister protesting outside Terri Schiavo's hospice*[6]

"[Terri Schiavo's] autopsy report removed all doubt that the withdrawal of the feeding tube, far from being an act of euthanasia or even outright murder, was entirely consistent with traditional Catholic moral principles. Terri Schiavo, for her part, was re-born into eternal life." *Catholic Priest Richard P. McBrien, Professor of Theology at the University of Notre Dame*[7]

"As a Christian community, we must pray that all will come to recognize God as the sole proprietor of life and that he alone has the right to call us home to his kingdom in his own time." *Bishop Joseph McFadden, leading a Catholic mass for 1,200 students in March 2005 at Archbishop Wood High School in Warminster, Pennsylvania, where Terri Schindler Schiavo was once a student*[8]

"Jewish tradition [allows letting] nature take its course . . . Should there be a present factor that hinders the departure of one's soul—for example, if the sound of a woodchopper can be heard close by the house, or if there is salt on the dying person's tongue—it is permitted to remove this noise or the salt. Neither of these actions would be considered a positive

> act (*ma'aseh*) towards death, but rather the removal of an impediment (*Yoreh De'ah 339:1*) . . . Some observers question whether we can draw any useful comparisons between the world of our texts, which speaks of woodchoppers and salt on the tongue, and the sophisticated technology of contemporary medicine." *Rabbi Mark Washofsky, Professor of Rabbinics at Hebrew Union College-Jewish Institute of Religion in Cincinnati*[9]

> "[The dictate to leave the feeding tube in place is] straightforward from a Jewish perspective: The most important point from a *halachic* standpoint is that a compromised life is still a life." *Rabbi Avi Shafran of Agudath Israel of America*[10]

> "Any definition of 'brain death' is irrelevant to God . . . He gives us death, a biological marker, which says to us, 'A transition takes place and you relate to me now in a different way.'" *Rev. Kevin Fitzgerald, Georgetown University Center for Clinical Bioethics*[11]

> "One whose heart still beats still lives; despite the irreversible cessation of brain function; and it would be an act of murder to disconnect such an individual from a respirator." *Lawyer David Zweibel, not commenting on Schiavo, but arguing for a religious exemption to the definition of brain death under New Jersey law*[12]

> "These are the arguments of an advanced, free society. There are no such discussions in Egypt or Iran. There's no general public debate over death and dying. That's for the elite." *Prof. Abdulaziz Sachedina, Islamic bioethicist, University of Virginia*[13]

Our religious leaders have no magic words. The questions raised by medical technology are new for our religious leaders as they are for our doctors, lawyers, ethicists, and all the rest of society. Like doctors, lawyers, and ethicists, different religious leaders arrive at different conclusions about what was right for Terri Schiavo, and all are working like the rest of us simply to keep up with the rush of issues raised by advancing medical technology.

THE CATHOLIC CHURCH POSITION STATEMENTS

The Catholic Church has championed the sacredness and protection of life on a number of fronts—opposing the death penalty, opposing abortion, caring for the oppressed, feeding the hungry. While all religions have debated the issues raised by medical technology at the end of life, no church has played as prominent a role in those societal discussions as the Catholic Church. Examining that history provides a window into the role of religion in understanding the right to die.

Many courts in the United States in early right-to-die cases drew a distinction between extraordinary care (which is optional) and ordinary care (which the patient must accept and others provide). That distinction originally came from the Catholic Church. "Extraordinary" care is also sometimes described as "artificial" or "heroic" care or means.[14] Writers within the Church discussed these distinctions as long ago as the 1500s, examining which medicines subjects bound by religious obedience could be required to take. They concluded that extraordinary means weren't required, but that the subjects must preserve life by accepting "nourishment and clothing common to all [and] medicine common to all."[15]

The "modern" discussion of this doctrine is usually traced to a 1957 speech by Pope Pius XII to the International Congress of Anesthesiologists. Pope Pius XII was talking with the doctors about the emerging world of resuscitation and respirators and the doctor's responsibility to provide and the patient's "duty in the case of serious illness to take the necessary treatment for the preservation of life and health."[16] This was two years before Dr. Lown shocked Mr. C at Peter Bent Brigham Hospital in Boston, and a few years after Dr. Plum at New York Hospital had taken part in developing one of the first ICUs to combat serious polio cases. Changes were coming quickly to medicine. Three years earlier, in 1954, doctors at Peter Bent Brigham had performed the first successful human kidney transplant.[17] Pope Pius XII drew this distinction between ordinary vs. extraordinary means for the doctors: "Normally one is held to use only ordinary means—according to circumstances of persons, places, times, and culture—means that do not involve any grave burden for oneself or one another."

As medical technology began its advance in the 1970s, however, pinning down exactly how this ordinary-extraordinary distinction should apply proved as elusive as defining what letting "nature take its course" involved. For example, the President's Commission for the Study of Ethical Problems in Medicine heard testimony in 1981 at a field hearing in Florida. Both the doctor and the judge who had been involved in an early Florida case testified at the field hearing. The Florida case had addressed whether a 76-year-old man dying from amyotrophic lateral sclerosis (ALS or "Lou Gehrig's disease") had the right to request removal of a respirator so that he could die.

The judge told the President's Commission that he had conducted a bedside hearing in the case in the man's hospital room. The man, Mr. Perlmutter, told the judge that he was "miserable" and that his condition without the respirator couldn't "be worse than what I'm going through now."[18] The doctor, who had objected to Mr. Perlmutter's request, told the Commission, "I deal with respirators every day of my life. To me, this is not heroic. This is standard procedure." The judge in response said, "Certainly there is no question legally that putting a hole in a man's trachea and inserting a mechanical respirator is extraordinary life-preserving means."[19] In this case, the judge had ruled that Mr. Perlmutter had the right to have the respirator turned off.

Regardless of the evolving discussion about the ordinary-extraordinary distinction, leaders of the Catholic Church remained wary of legislation that might cheapen life. The Florida Catholic Conference opposed efforts to pass living will laws in Florida in 1973. In 1977, as many states started to consider such laws in the wake of the *Quinlan* case, the National Conference of Catholic Bishops issued a directive to their state groups opposing such laws.[20] In the *Quinlan* case, whether the respirator breathing for Karen Ann Quinlan was extraordinary or ordinary did not really matter in the conference room at the hospital where Sister Mary Urban told Joe Quinlan that "in this hospital we don't kill people."[21]

By 1980, the difficulty in understanding when a treatment might be extraordinary or not led the Vatican to abandon this standard and put in its place the terms "proportionate" and "disproportionate" in the document, *Declaration on Euthanasia*. Using these terms, the patient weighed the proportionate burdens and benefits of any particular treatment—simple antibiotics in some conditions being burdensome and disproportionate, and a respirator or other technology in some cases worth enduring due to the expected benefits.[22]

At about that point, roughly 1980 (soon after doctors in Cleveland had invented the PEG tube surgery), the feeding tube debate began. As the Catholic Health Association (CHA) recognized recently, "since the 1980 Vatican *Declaration on Euthanasia*, a debate has ensued within the Church regarding how to consider artificial nutrition and hydration."[23] The CHA is the trade association for 2,000 Catholic hospitals and related institutions in the United States.

In 1986, when the American Medical Association adopted its formal policy that artificial nutrition and hydration could be stopped for a patient in an irreversible coma, then-Archbishop of New Orleans Philip Hanna said, "The Church strongly condemns this position." Other influential Catholics like Father Richard McCormick at Notre Dame reacted differently: "With all due respect [to the archbishop], I believe that is just plain wrong. In my view, those who take such a position have departed from the substance of the Catholic tradition on this matter. That tradition never counted mere vegetative life a patient benefit."[24]

That debate inside the Church picked up steam with *Cruzan*. At the Missouri Supreme Court level in 1988, a joint brief filed by the Sisters of St. Mary Health Care System (the largest provider of health care in Missouri) and the Center for Health Care Ethics at St. Louis University Medical Center supported the Cruzans. That brief drew a formal letter to the Missouri Supreme Court from the lawyer for Catholic Bishops of Missouri and Missouri Catholic Conference, suggesting to the court that the St. Louis brief supporting the Cruzans did not represent the official Catholic Church position, and stating that the Vatican was studying the *Cruzan* case:

> In the Catholic Church the official teaching authority (Magisterium) at the local level is vested in the Bishops (not in individual theologians or theological scholars). Neither the Bishops of Missouri nor of the United States have issued an authoritative statement on the application of Catholic ethical and theological principles to the question of withdrawal of sustenance from persons in situations similar to Nancy Beth Cruzan. The issue is now pending under study before a Committee of the Catholic Bishops of the United States, headed by Joseph Cardinal Bernardin of

> Chicago, and also before a congregation (department) of the Vatican at Rome.
>
> If an authoritative statement is made by either the committee of U.S. Bishops or the Vatican while the instant legal case is pending, we shall share that document with this honorable Court.[25]

The next year, 1989, the U.S. Conference of Catholic Bishops filed an *amicus* or friend-of-the-court brief opposing the Cruzans in the U.S. Supreme Court. That brief counseled that "the law should establish a strong presumption in favor of" the use of feeding tubes because "food and water are necessities of life for all human beings, and can generally be provided without the risks and burdens of more aggressive means of sustaining life."[26]

Most of the brief, however, was devoted to legal arguments to curb any extension of the constitutional right to privacy established in the abortion case, *Roe v. Wade*. Richard Doerflinger, a spokesman for the U.S. Conference of Catholic Bishops, had emerged from a meeting in August where they discussed the *Cruzan* case and spoke to reporters. He said that the brief from the Bishops in *Cruzan* would urge the U.S. Supreme Court not to "constitutionalize" the right to die, as the right to abortion had been constitutionalized sixteen years earlier in *Roe v. Wade*, leaving "no room for the Catholic point of view."[27]

The National Right to Life Committee (NRLC) was incorporated in May of 1973, four months after that Supreme Court decision in *Roe v. Wade*. Though a separate entity from the Catholic Church, the Church provided the committee with funding, organization, and people. The Executive Director of the NRLC in 1975, Roy White, is quoted as having said, "The only reason we have a pro-life movement in this country is because of the Catholic people and the Catholic Church."[28] Abortion was the fundamental issue that linked the groups, but early on their joint efforts also extended to the right to die.

Joe Cruzan could never understand the link between the two issues. Any chance he had, he would explain his theories to right-to-life advocates. Joe said in an interview in 1989, as he waited to hear if the U.S. Supreme Court would take his case, "I think a lot of pro-lifers try to interweave our situation with the abortion law, but they're mixing apples and oranges. The fetus has potential for a life but our daughter hasn't. I just can't understand why they criticize us, and I don't know why they see things in black and white. None of the questions in Nancy's situation can be answered in black and white."[29]

After the *Cruzan* decision in 1990, the NRLC and state Catholic Conferences worked on the state level to limit the reach of laws passed in the wake of *Cruzan*. Typically their efforts were aimed at lobbying for language in health-care power-of-attorney laws, which required that people filling out such a document had to specify if they were giving their agent the power to refuse artificial nutrition and hydration. For Catholic hospitals throughout the 1990s, the formal ethical policy from the Bishops' Ethical and Religious Directives remained that artificial nutrition and hydration could be withdrawn if it provided no benefit, though there should be a presumption in favor of feeding, even tube feeding, as long as the benefit outweighed the burden.[30]

The case of Terri Schiavo called this policy into question. In the spring of 2004, at a conference in Rome named "The International Congress on Life-Sustaining Treatments and Vegetative State: Scientific Advances and Ethical Dilemmas," Pope John Paul II delivered a seven-page allocution, or speech. In that speech, the Pope said, "The administration of water and food, even when provided by artificial means, always represents a natural means of preserving life and not a medical act. Its use, furthermore, should be considered, in principle, ordinary and proportionate, and as such morally obligatory."[31] Some interpreted this allocution to mean that any person in a vegetative state must be given tube feeding. The Catholic Health Association in a press release after the speech said basically that the Church would need to "carefully consider" the implications of the speech, and that as "that dialogue commences" the historical policy (artificial nutrition and hydration could be withdrawn if it provided no benefit) would remain intact. In the wake of the publicity from the *Schiavo* case, the public discussion goes on.

The National Right to Life Committee has drafted for state legislators sample legislation, called the "Starvation and Dehydration of Persons with Disabilities Prevention Act," which would require feeding tubes in all cases where they had not been specifically refused in advance.[32] In my own state, Kansas, a bill proposed last session required a jury trial with a unanimous verdict and proof beyond a reasonable doubt before a feeding tube could be removed.[33] (The bill did not become law.) The National Right to Life Committee has championed its Will to Live Project, which encourages those filling out a living will to specify that they want tube feeding; "food and water are not medical treatment but basic necessities" is the language recommended.[34]

Amazingly, this debate, which has been picking up steam since the 1970s, is really only beginning as society looks out on the mass of aging Baby Boomers and the meteoric advance of technological options they will have. The main point of this section on religion is to show that our religious leaders have the same breadth and variety of opinion that our medical, legal, and political leaders do. Even within the Catholic Church, which has worked and studied more in this area than any other religion, that conclusion remains true. Religious leaders have no special power to answer these questions. To the contrary, they are like the rest of us, trying to figure out answers to new and complex questions.

CHAPTER 13

Special Concerns of the Disabled Community

THE RIGHT-TO-DIE CASES like *Cruzan* and *Schiavo* have generated new and unusual alliances, for example, liberal, pro-choice Baptist minister Jesse Jackson standing next to anti-abortion activist Randall Terry. When Jackson arrived in the spring of 2005 outside of the hospice where Terri Schiavo was dying, the crowd chanted, "Pray with us!" Jackson first met with the family privately. When he emerged from that meeting, before walking back to his limousine, he moved to the crowd, lifted his arms and said a few soft words of prayer. When one of the members of the group rushed to Jackson and pressed a "Pro-Life" sticker in his hand and asked him to wear it, Jackson took a look at the sticker, kept walking toward his limo, and folded the sticker in the palm of his hand.[1]

One of the most interesting alliances in the *Cruzan* and *Schiavo* cases was that of the disability rights community with the pro-life forces. When I give talks around the country, attendees are sometimes met by people in wheelchairs, handing out flyers. Those flyers warn that those attending the talk are about to hear from the lawyer (me) who created the constitutional right to starve a disabled woman, Nancy Cruzan, to death. I invite the protesters to come hear the talk because I'm fairly confident that's not what I did, but to date they have not come in.

Joe Cruzan endured a lot of name-calling during the public debate over Nancy Cruzan—Hitler, Nazi, Murderer, Devil. Most of it rolled off his back fairly quickly. But in the summer of 1988, the brief from the Missouri Citizens for Life sent him to the edge. The Missouri right-to-life brief claimed that Joe was guilty of abusing his daughter under state law that made abuse and neglect a crime. Joe thought about that charge all the time. He told me that he wanted to talk face to face with the lawyer who wrote those words, the man who said he was neglecting his daughter. He wanted to talk to him, convince him how absurd that claim was, and then punch him in the nose, Joe said to me.[2]

The next brief that came in the mail in the summer, from a group called the Nursing Home Action Group (NHAG), made him even angrier, if that was possible. NHAG is a not-for-profit organization composed of members with physical and mental disabilities. This new brief accused him of discriminating against the handicapped. "She is not disabled, for Christ's sake," Joe said. "What do they think, with some wheelchair access ramps she'll be back in the marching band?"

I understand Joe's frustration. But I also understand the concern of the disability community about discrimination. One of the groups often seen on television during the *Schiavo* protesting was named "Not Dead Yet." This group formed in the spring of 1996, founded by a lawyer in Chicago named Diane Coleman, a person with significant disabilities who has used a motorized wheelchair since she was eleven. The group formed shortly after the acquittal of Dr. Jack Kevorkian in

Michigan in, according to Not Dead Yet, "the assisted suicides of two women with non-terminal disabilities."[3] Their name is taken from a running gag in the film *Monty Python and the Holy Grail:* "No, no, not quite dead yet, feeling much better, thank you."[4]

In 2003, their work expanded beyond opposing physician-assisted suicide when the Terri Schiavo case made its way onto the front page. Joined by 25 other national disability groups, Not Dead Yet entered the Schiavo fray in 2003 to oppose "her guardian's right to starve and dehydrate her to death."[5] After Terri Schiavo's death, Diane Coleman was one of the people invited to testify in April of 2005 before a House subcommittee investigating the *Schiavo* case. In a single paragraph, she illustrated to the federal congressional subcommittee how she was beholden to neither political side, but to her disabled constituents:

> Here's how I'm beginning to look at things. The far right wants to kill us slowly and painfully by cutting the things we need to live, health care, public housing and transportation, etc. The far left wants to kill us quickly and call it compassion, while also saving money for others perhaps deemed more worthy.[6]

Unfortunately, the history of both the law and medicine gives disability advocates like Diane Coleman reason for concern. In 1927, the Supreme Court approved the state-ordered sterilization of "mental defectives," in this case a "feeble-minded white woman" named Carrie Buck who was the "daughter of a feeble-minded mother in the same institution, and the mother of an illegitimate feeble-minded child." The famous Justice Oliver Wendell Holmes, for an 8-1 majority of the Court, wrote these infamous words: "Three generations of imbeciles are enough."[7] Holmes's logic: "It is better for all the world, if instead of waiting to execute degenerate offspring for crime, or to let them starve for their imbecility, society can prevent those who are manifestly unfit from continuing their kind."[8]

In a 2000 book denouncing Justice Holmes as a eugenicist and a "cold, savage, and brutal man," University of Chicago law professor Albert Alschuler noted that as a result of Holmes's 1927 opinion upholding the Virginia law, eventually more than 18,000 "imbeciles" in 30 states were sterilized, "many of whom were hardly mentally disabled."[9] Alschuler quoted from private correspondence in which Holmes talked of "restricting propagation by the undesirables and putting to death infants that didn't pass the examination, etc., etc."[10]

Fifty-three years later, in 1980, Dr. K. Ray Nelson, then-director of the Lynchburg Hospital where doctors had sterilized Carrie Buck, began digging into his institutional records. He found that 4,000 state sterilizations had been performed there, as recently as 1972. He also found Carrie Buck herself, now living near Charlottesville with her sister, Doris. Doris had also been sterilized by the state under the mandatory sterilization law, but state officials had lied to her, telling her that the operation was for appendicitis.[11] Doris was bitter in her old age to learn the truth because she had desperately wanted a child in life and had never known why she could not conceive.

Professor Paul Lombardo from the University of Virginia School of Law also met Carrie Buck later in life as part of his research on the case. He concluded that though she was not sophisticated, she read the paper, did crosswords, and by no measure would be judged mentally ill or retarded.[12] His modern-day research revealed that Carrie Buck was committed to the institution for the feeble-minded, it appears, because she was raped by a relative of her foster parents and the foster parents wanted to hide her away. They had her sent to the same Virginia home for the feeble-minded where her mother lived.

We likely never would have heard of Carrie Buck if the state of Virginia had not passed a compulsory sterilization law in 1924. Carrie Buck was the first person selected for state sterilization. When Christian groups challenged the law and it grew clear that Carrie Buck's case would become a public issue, an organization called the Eugenics Records Office sent a field worker to test her. Using the Stanford-Binet test of IQ, the worker determined that Carrie scored a mental age of nine. The worker also tested her mother, who scored under eight. Mental health categories at the time labeled those who tested in age ranges from 6-9 on the test as "imbeciles;" "idiots" were lower on the scale, "morons" higher. A social worker examined Carrie Buck's six-month-old daughter, and testified at the trial challenging the law that "it seems to me not quite a normal baby."[13]

On that basis, Justice Holmes had his "three generations" in the trial record. The baby, Vivian, died at age 8 of colitis. Professor Lombardo years later unearthed Vivian's school report cards, which showed that she had received perfect scores in deportment, and good scores in all other areas—basically, a normal student. Ultimately, Professor Lombardo concluded that there were no imbeciles among the three generations of the Bucks, whatever Justice Holmes might have concluded.[14]

For those who might dismiss concerns of a disabled person about *Buck v. Bell* as old history (despite the fairly recent 1972 sterilization at Lynchburg), the Baby Doe stories from the 1980s provide a more modern-day cautionary tale. Baby Doe was born on April 9, 1982, in Bloomington, Indiana, with Down Syndrome. ("Baby Doe" is the name given by courts to protect the privacy of identity, like "Jane Roe" of *Roe v. Wade*.) Bassinets with signs reading "NOTHNG BY MOUTH" for Down Syndrome or other handicapped babies were not uncommon in the late 1970s, when parents had made the decision that they did not want a mentally retarded baby. Uneasiness had been bubbling up both in the medical community and in society generally over this mistreatment of the handicapped, and it boiled over with the Indiana Baby Doe.

The baby's esophagus was not connected to his stomach, and he needed a fairly simple surgery to repair the problem, but his parents refused consent.[15] The hospital went to court to overturn the parents' decision, but failed at the trial court level and at the Indiana Supreme Court. Their lawyers were on their way to Washington to seek emergency relief from the U.S. Supreme Court when Baby Doe died.

The issue, however, had finally moved from quiet discomfort in the hospital to a dawning public awareness. *The New York Times* quoted Dr. J.C. Willke, president of the National Right to Life Committee: "This is a direct killing. Since when do we allow people to be killed just because they are handicapped?"[16] The public outcry drew the attention of Washington. Congress held hearings, and the Health and Human Services Department of the newly elected Reagan administration looked for ways to address the questions.

In a statement delivered in the fall of 1982 to a federal House hearing on handicapped newborns, newly appointed Surgeon General

C. Everett Koop, also one of the first pediatric surgeons,[17] gave the congressmen an initial glimpse at the problems they were addressing:

> Medicine may *never* have all the solutions to all the problems that occur at birth. I personally foresee no medical solution to a cephalodymus or an anencephalic child. The first is a one-headed twin; the second, a child with virtually no functioning brain at all. In these cases the prognosis is an early and merciful death by natural causes. There are no so-called 'heroic measures' possible and intervention would merely prolong the patient's process of dying. Some of nature's errors are extraordinary and frightening . . . but nature also has the kindness to take them away. For such infants, neither medicine nor law can be of any help. And neither medicine nor law should prolong these infants' process of dying.[18]

Dr. Koop testified that Baby Doe was in a completely different category.[19] Six months later, the Secretary of Health and Human Services promulgated emergency regulations under a 1974 law that prohibited any entity that received federal funds from discriminating against the handicapped. The regulations authorized what became known as "Baby Doe squads" to police hospital treatment of seriously ill newborns, creating outrage in the medical community. Ultimately, after a couple of years of wrangling in the public policy arena and the courts over proposed Baby Doe laws, all involved compromised on a federal law called the Child Abuse Amendments of 1984.[20] Like most of the other language in the debate spawned by advancing medical technology, the standard in the new child abuse law—that doctors should provide treatment unless it was "virtually futile" or "inhumane"—would prove elusive.

The report of the President's Commission for the Study of Ethical Problems in Medicine went to President Reagan on March 21, 1983, the same month that the Secretary of Health and Human Services issued his emergency Baby Doe regulations. The President's Commission recognized in a chapter titled "Seriously Ill Newborns" that, like the rest of the issues in the report, the questions affecting newborns were novel ones for society. The first neonatal intensive care units (commonly called the NICU, pronounced "nick′–you") began to appear in the 1960s in the United States. The prominence of NICUs expanded with passage during the 1970s, in most states, of legislation requiring private insurers to pay for NICU treatment, and with the advent of the first neonatology certification examinations by the American Board of Pediatrics in 1975. By 1983 the Board had certified over 1,000 neonatologists.[21]

The Commission began the chapter on newborns like this: "Remarkable advances in neonatal care now make it possible to sustain the lives of many newborn infants who only" a decade ago would have died.[22] The writers of those words in 1983 likely would have been astounded to see the NICU less than a decade later, in the early 1990s. At the NICU in Westchester County Medical Center in Valhalla, New York, each tiny bed required support from 13 electrical outlets and three separate gas lines for oxygen and suctioning secretions. Laboratories there could perform a biochemical test on a few drops of blood, tests that five years earlier would have required an entire vial, or one-twentieth of the baby's blood volume. New drugs introduced in 1991 called artificial surfactants improved breathing capacity for tiny, stiff lungs.[23]

By the early 1990s, the definition of what treatment might count as "virtually futile" under the 1984 Baby Doe laws grew more elusive as NICUs were able to "save" smaller and smaller babies. A societal consensus had developed around the case that had spurred the 1984 law—a baby with mild Down Syndrome should receive fairly simple surgery. Technology quickly overtook that consensus on other questions, however, as the NICU of the early 1990s grew able to keep more and more tiny babies alive.

Infants who weighed less than 750 grams (1 pound, 10 ounces) faced weeks and months in the NICU, with doctors admitting that the chances that the survivors would be "normal" were less than 1 in 4. The remainder suffered brain damage, and doctors were hard pressed to predict which baby would fall into which group.[24] The discussion in the President's Commission report in 1983 dealt largely with low birth weight babies (below 2500 grams, or 5 pounds, 5 ounces) and very low birth weight babies (below 1500 grams, or 3 pounds, 5 ounces).[25] In the early 1990s, the popular press was discussing the recurrent ethical issues raised by babies *half* that weight. And in September of 2004, a woman in Chicago gave birth to baby Rumaisa Rahman, weighing only 244 grams, or 8.6 ounces. She was small enough to curl up inside a toddler's slipper. Rumaisa left Loyola University Medical Center five months later weighing 5 pounds, 8 ounces—almost ten times her birth weight; on her first birthday, she weighed 18 pounds, and according to her neonatologist, John Muraskas, is developing normally.[26]

Under what circumstances will the state allow parents to say "no" to a medical intervention for a low birth weight infant with a prognosis of severe disability? When will doctors be allowed to determine that treatment in the NICU is "virtually futile"? What treatments will the government pay for? Hard questions all, and it's understandable that they would raise concern in the disability community.

In addition to the Baby Doe cases in the mid-1980s, language in court decisions relating to handicapped adults also caused uneasiness in the disability community. One case that has become a lightning rod for their activism involved a California woman named Elizabeth Bouvia. Bouvia was a wheelchair-bound quadriplegic from birth, and later suffered from debilitating arthritis. She was also college-educated and married. After suffering a miscarriage and the breakup of her marriage, she tried to commit suicide but wasn't successful. She ended up in a county hospital, became malnourished, and doctors there inserted a feeding tube against her wish. She went to court.

The California Court of Appeals ultimately ruled that she had a constitutional right to refuse the feeding tube. The court cited the then-new President's Commission report and ethical statement from the American Medical Association in support. One judge wrote, "Fate has dealt this young woman a terrible hand. Can anyone blame her if she wants to fold her cards and say 'I am out'?"[27]

After the court ruled in her favor, Elizabeth Bouvia decided not to have the tube removed. She is still alive today. In the disability community, far from finding the *Bouvia* ruling as one upholding rights, many read it as simply reinforcing stereotypes and prejudices. According to this view, rather than treat Elizabeth Bouvia as a person who had suffered a miscarriage and marriage breakup, the able-bodied judges rushed to help her die because no one would want to live that way. As Diane Coleman said, "The court, the press and the public are so prejudiced against disabled people that they ignored the factors that might make anyone feel suicidal [miscarriage and marriage breakup], and only focused on [Elizabeth Bouvia's] disability."[28]

From Carrie Buck to Baby Doe to Elizabeth Bouvia, the concerns of the disability community today are understandable. And no issue raises these concerns about deeply ingrained societal prejudices more starkly than the societal discussion of physician-assisted suicide.

CHAPTER 14

Oregon v. Ashcroft/Gonzales and Physician-Assisted Suicide

"But we must be wary of those who are too willing to end the lives of the elderly and the ill. If we ever decide that a poor quality of life justifies ending that life, we have taken a step down a slippery slope that places all of us in danger. There is a difference between allowing nature to take its course and actively assisting death. The call for euthanasia surfaces in our society periodically, as it is doing now under the guise of 'death with dignity' or assisted suicide . . . I believe euthanasia lies outside the commonly held life-centered values of the West and cannot be allowed without incurring great social and personal tragedy. This is not merely an intellectual conundrum. This issue involves actual human beings at risk."

—*Former Surgeon General Dr. C. Everett Koop* (writing in 1991)[1]

DURING THE FIRST WEEK of October in 2005, new Chief Justice John Roberts on his third day at work tackled the thorny question of physician-assisted suicide. The dispute grew out of a 1997 Oregon law that allows a doctor in Oregon to prescribe drugs to a terminally ill patient which that patient can use to hasten his own death. Oregon is the only state that has passed a law legalizing physician-assisted suicide.

In this debate (in Oregon and elsewhere), two key terms are often muddled together. "Physician-assisted suicide" is usually understood as a doctor providing the means for a patient to hasten death, typically through a prescription of sleeping pills or other barbiturate. The patient is in charge of the timing of taking the pills. "Euthanasia" is the active administration by a doctor of a drug, typically by injection, to hasten death and end suffering.

Though the case of *Oregon v. Gonzales* involved a challenge by the federal government to the Oregon law, the oral argument that Chief Justice Roberts heard on October 5, 2005 had little to do with the distinction between euthanasia and physician-assisted suicide, or even the question of the place of physician-assisted suicide in a civilized society. Instead, the Court focused on much more technical questions of the relationship between the federal government and the states and interpretation of federal statutes. Specifically, the Court examined whether a federal law intended to combat drug trafficking, the Controlled Substances Act, should be stretched to regulate the prescribing of drugs by Oregon doctors under the physician-assisted suicide law.

The Court handed down its 6-3 decision on January 17, 2006. The ruling was as technical as the argument had been, concluding basically that the power of the federal Justice Department did not in fact stretch as far as the Bush administration had urged. Justice Anthony Kennedy wrote for the majority that such a position would "effect a radical shift of authority from the States to the Federal Government to define general standards of medical practice in every locality."[2] The case prompted the first dissent in the Supreme Court career of the new Chief Justice. He did not write separately, but joined in an opinion by Justice Antonin Scalia, who wrote, "If the term 'legitimate medical purpose' has any meaning, it surely excludes the prescription of drugs to produce death."[3]

Federal congressmen, state legislators, different medical societies, bar associations, religious groups, and many others, are discussing in earnest the broader issue raised by the Oregon law of whether we want to live in a society that allows physician-assisted suicide. That discussion promises to continue in the years ahead. Like the refusal-of-treatment cases—*Quinlan*, *Cruzan*, *Schiavo*—the questions of that broader debate are relatively new in society and have been brought forward by advancing medical technology.

PHYSICIAN-ASSISTED SUICIDE AND THE LAW

Suicide, of course, is not new. Throughout history, societies have had laws governing suicide. Early laws against suicide were harsh, requiring forfeiture of possessions to the state, and in some places forfeit of land, too, and a dishonored burial. The legislators of the Providence Plantations, present-day Rhode Island, passed this declaration in 1647: "Self-murder is by all agreed to be the most unnatural, and it is by this present Assembly declared, to be that, wherein he that doth it, kills himself out of a premeditated hatred against his own life or other humor . . . his goods and chattels are the king's custom, but not his debts nor lands; but in case he be an infant, a lunatic, mad or distracted man, he forfeits nothing."[4] Over time, states eased these penalties, but only to ease the punishment of the family left behind by the suicide; courts still widely condemned suicide as an abhorrent act.

The assisting of a suicide met with equal condemnation in early courts and legislatures. New York was the first state to outlaw assisted suicide, in 1828.[5] The New York Code made it a crime for "furnishing another person with any deadly weapon or poisonous drug, knowing that such person intends to use such weapon or drug in taking his own life." By the time the states had ratified the Fourteenth Amendment to the Constitution in 1868, most states had passed laws criminalizing assisting suicide. (That amendment, specifying that no State shall "deprive any person of life, liberty, or property, without due process of law," is the part of the Constitution that we used to argue that Nancy Cruzan retained a constitutional right to refuse medical treatment. Proponents of physician-assisted suicide often look to the Fourteenth Amendment for their own claim of constitutional right.)

Since 1990, however, the advance of medical technology has caused states to take a fresh look at these long-standing social rules. Four states—California, Hawaii, Oregon, and Vermont—have seriously considered laws that would legalize physician-assisted suicide. To date, only Oregon has passed such a law. That enactment has led to the remarkable situation where a doctor in Oregon is allowed by law to prescribe drugs to aid a terminally ill patient in hastening his death while just one footstep away, across the state line in Washington, that exact same action is a criminal felony, punishable by five years in prison and a $10,000 fine.[6] I can see the law school exam question now, with a doctor standing with legs apart, straddling the Oregon-Washington state line as he writes the prescription. ("Is the prescribing doctor right- or left-handed, professor?")

American society discussed physician-assisted suicide extensively throughout the 1990s. Most of that discussion did not come from the deliberative state legislative process, however; it came from the actions of one man, Dr. Jack Kevorkian. On June 6, 1990, nineteen days before the U.S. Supreme Court would issue its opinion in the *Cruzan* case, *The New York Times* did a story about "a doctor in a suburb of Detroit" under the headline, "Doctor Tells of First Death Using His Suicide Device."[7] The article described a doctor sitting in the back of an old Volkswagen van with a 54-year-old woman from Portland, Oregon, Janet Adkins, who was in the early stages of Alzheimer's disease.

Dr. Kevorkian's first assisted suicide was hardly glitch-free. Janet Adkins, her husband, and her best friend stayed in the Red Roof Inn in Madison Heights, Michigan, a Detroit suburb on Sunday, June 3, 1990. That night the three of them went to dinner with Dr. Kevorkian and his two sisters. The next morning Kevorkian's two sisters picked Janet Adkins up at the hotel about nine. She said goodbye to her husband and her best friend, and then rode for an hour in the car with the sisters to a remote campsite with electrical hookup, where Dr. Kevorkian and his van were waiting.

Once they arrived, Kevorkian went into the van alone, to test the machine. But he knocked over the vial of thiopental while reaching for pliers, so the four of them drove the two hours round-trip back to Kevorkian's sister's house for more drugs. It was noon before they finally got back to the park. Kevorkian did some more test runs while his two sisters and Janet Adkins waited in the car. Finally he was ready. Kevorkian told Janet to lie down on a makeshift bed in the rusted out, 13-year-old van. His first four attempts to find a vein failed, until finally, the IV needle held. The needle was hooked up to a contraption that looked like a junior-high school shop class experiment. Kevorkian gave the instructions and Janet Adkins pressed a button three times, sending the drug thiopental into her system, which would cause unconsciousness.

"Thank you," whispered Adkins, according to Kevorkian.

"Have a nice trip," Kevorkian replied. Her head fell back, and her skin turned gray. Then, after about a minute, the machine switched automatically to potassium chloride, which stopped her heart.[8] The *Times* article the next day said that news of Dr. Kevorkian's first assisted suicide "alarmed many experts in medical ethics and confused many legal experts."[9]

Eight-and-a-half years later, on November 26, 1998, the *Times* told the story of Dr. Kevorkian facing murder charges for a death viewed in more than 15 million U.S. households on the CBS News program *60 Minutes*.[10] Between the story of the first assisted suicide in 1990 and the 1998 article, the *Times* had published 471 stories that talked about Kevorkian.[11] By 1998, Kevorkian had presided over more than 120 assisted suicides. But on *60 Minutes*, for the first time, Kevorkian participated directly. In that video he is seen injecting Thomas Youk, a 52-year-old man suffering from ALS, with syringes containing seconal to induce unconsciousness, a muscle relaxant to stop breathing, and potassium chloride to stop his heart.[12] Prosecutors convicted Kevorkian of second-degree murder, and he went to prison. In late 2005, a Michigan parole board denied a request for parole or pardon for the 77-year-old Kevorkian, who suffers from high blood pressure, arthritis, cataracts, osteoporosis, and hepatitis C. Kevorkian is eligible for parole in 2007, though his lawyer says he may not survive until that time.[13]

Most of the national medical community expressed outrage at Dr. Kevorkian. The American Medical Association condemned Kevorkian as "a self-admitted zealot killing another human being to advance his own interests and ego-driven urge to martyrdom."[14] But that reaction was not universal throughout society. When I spoke to different groups during the 1990s about the issues of death and dying, I often asked a series of questions as part of the lead-in to the talk, to try to get people to think about the issues in perhaps a different way. One question was this: "Dr. Jack Kevorkian, hero or madman? You must pick one or the other, you have no other choices." When asked of professional audiences, like doctors and nurses at hospital grand rounds (hospital education programs for staff) for example, overwhelmingly the hands shot up to vote for "madman."

When talking with seniors, the response was almost always the opposite. At a luncheon talk to about 250 residents at a large retirement community, I remember only a few hands going up to vote for madman, and they belonged largely to the men in the room (a distinct minority at any talk to the elderly). The hands lowered slowly as the stares of women turned on them. The medical professionals at the grand rounds were typically surprised when I told them about the very different answer to the question that I received when I spoke to the elderly. Extreme or not, Dr. Kevorkian was forcing us in the 1990s to talk about our dying.

Not all doctors disagreed with Kevorkian. Or, more accurately, they supported the idea of physician-assisted suicide, though they disagreed with his methods. These doctors sought to change the law by working within confines of society's rules. In the early 1990s, small groups of doctors in two states—New York and Washington—sued their state officials. The lawsuits claimed that laws in those states that made assisting suicide a crime violated the federal constitutional rights of citizens to control how they die. In both cases, terminally ill patients joined the doctors in making the claims.

The two cases—*Washington v. Glucksberg* and *Vacco v. Quill*—eventually came together to the United States Supreme Court in 1997. That Court, in two unanimous decisions, found that state laws on assisted suicide did not violate the federal Constitution.[15] Much of the reasoning of the doctors' pleas to the Court was drawn from language in the Court's ruling seven years earlier in *Cruzan*. But the Court saw little connection between *Cruzan* and physician-assisted suicide. The constitutional right recognized in *Cruzan* was based on a long history in this country of the right to refuse unwanted medical treatment and let the underlying disease or accident run its course. The Court found such an act wholly different in kind from requesting assistance in suicide. The historical treatment in American culture of those two acts was far different, and the intent of the two acts—an important consideration in the application of law—was likewise different.

The Court concluded its opinion by recognizing the important role of the states in this ongoing debate: "Throughout the Nation, Americans are engaged in an earnest and profound debate about the morality, legality, and practicality of physician-assisted suicide. Our holding permits this debate to continue, as it should in a democratic society."[16]

THE OREGON EXPERIENCE

Nowhere was that democratic debate taking place more actively than in the state of Oregon. In November of 1994, the Oregon Death With Dignity Act, which came to the ballot through a citizen initiative petition, passed with 51 percent of the vote.[17] That vote came at the end of a spirited and heavily financed campaign on both sides of the question. After voter approval, opponents immediately challenged the law in federal court, delaying its implementation.

While that challenge made its way through the courts, the Oregon legislature looked at revising the law. Ultimately the legislature did not tinker with it, but sent it back to the voters as originally written for reconsideration on the November 1997 ballot. This time voters reaffirmed their earlier vote by a 61 percent approval margin.[18] The state legal challenge failed also, and the law went into effect in November of 1997. A later federal challenge also failed when the Supreme Court issued its opinion in *Oregon v. Gonzales* in January of 2006. The Death with Dignity Act remains the law of Oregon today.

The legislature included many attempted safeguards in drafting the law: the patient must be an adult; must have proof of Oregon residency; and must be diagnosed with a terminal condition that will lead to death within six months. A patient meeting these criteria can request a prescription from a licensed Oregon doctor. The process to obtain that prescription is bound up with several additional safeguards:

- The patient has to make two separate oral requests to his doctor, separated by at least 15 days.
- The patient must also make the request in writing.
- This writing must be signed by two witnesses, and they can't be family members or care providers.
- The patient can rescind the request at any time.
- The diagnosis and prognosis of the prescribing doctor must be confirmed by a second doctor.
- Both doctors must confirm that the patient is able to make the decision, and that his judgment is not impaired.
- The prescribing doctor must tell the patient about alternatives, including hospice and palliative (comfort) care, and pain management options.
- The prescribing doctor must request that the patient notify his next of kin about the physician-assisted suicide request.
- The prescription must be self-administered.[19]

In the two heavily financed public debates over the law, opponents raised a parade of horrible potential outcomes that would befall Oregon if the law passed: dying people would migrate to Oregon in droves; physician-assisted suicide death tolls would skyrocket; and pressure would be brought to bear by society on the handicapped and the poor to end their lives, among other things.[20] The seven-year experience (mandatory state reports cover 1998–2004) with the law has not seen those fears come true.

Virtually all of the deaths under the law have been those of long-term Oregonians, and the demographic of those using the law has skewed toward younger, better-educated, white, cancer patients.[21] Most telling about the Oregon experience, however, is how seldom the law has been used. Over the first seven years, 208 patients have used the law to hasten their dying, or about 30 patients a year. During that same time, roughly 200,000 Oregonians died, or about 30,000 per year. So about one-tenth of one percent (208 out of 200,000) of the deaths in the state resulted from physician-assisted suicide. Most of the 208 deaths—164 of them—were patients with cancer. During that same seven-year period, 42,717 Oregonians with cancer died without resort to assisted suicide.[22]

And that experience likely suggests why the debate over physician-assisted suicide, though heated at times and in places, in reality is not a major social issue. It turns out that most patients find they want to live their last few weeks, rather than hasten death, even when that living is in a significantly compromised state, at times bedridden and in pain.

We are human; we cling to life. Early experience with the law suggests that what patients fear more than pain, more than cost, is loss of control. Proponents suggest that the law has given control to those few who have used it, and a sense of control and comfort to many more, knowing that physician-assisted suicide is available. But significant use of the physician-assisted suicide law has not happened.

This law has had a significantly more far-reaching effect, however, than providing control for 208 dying Oregonians. The extensive public debate has improved the care of the other 200,000 Oregonians who died. Because the people in Oregon have talked about dying more than people in any other state, they know more about dying, and are better at it—patients, health care providers, chaplains, everyone. As former Governor Barbara Roberts said in testimony in Sacramento in the spring of 2005, where the California legislature was considering a law similar to Oregon's:

> Let me give you a quick look at what happened in Oregon over the last decade. First came the two heavily financed campaigns—debates, television and radio ads, newspaper articles and speeches. Oregon voters became the best informed Americans in any of our 50 states on the subjects of dying, pain medication, heroic medical procedures, advance directives and hospice care. Dying was discussed over dinner, in bowling alleys, at hair salons and barber shops, in gyms, classrooms, and churches. Once families had opened those discussions, they couldn't put the toothpaste back in the tube.[23]

Interestingly, Governor Roberts, who championed the physician-assisted suicide law, is a lifelong disability advocate. She began her career in politics in 1971 as a citizen advocate in the Oregon legislature, trying to gain access to a public school education for her autistic son. Her husband, Oregon senator Frank Roberts, was wheelchair-bound until his death in 1993. She told the California legislators, "Let me state emphatically, I would never support a law that was harmful to individuals with disabilities."[24]

Oregon is the case study for a vitally important point: talking about dying improves how we die. Most Americans when surveyed say they prefer to die at home rather than in a hospital, and Oregon has the lowest rate of in-hospital deaths in the country at 31 percent.[25] Oregon doctors have been on the cutting edge of education about advance care planning, creating the POLST program (the program discussed in Chapter 8 which has turned patients' wishes into doctors' orders and institutionalized their completion). Under the program, more than 170,000 of the bright pink forms had been distributed throughout the state by the year 2000. Oregon has increased hospice usage dramatically; figures for pain treatment and appropriate morphine use are among the best in the nation; and the state's only medical school has 14 hours of education in end-of-life care in its first-year curriculum (a topic many medical schools do not cover).[26]

Advocates for the physician-assisted suicide law did not necessarily plan that the public debate would improve dying across the board; that improvement was a side effect, though certainly a welcome one. The actual practice of physician-assisted suicide, though legal for seven years and seldom used, "remains highly controversial" according to the annual report of the Oregon Department of Human Services in the spring of 2005.[27] Even advocates of physician-assisted suicide speak in favor of eradicating the practice: "In what can only be considered a win-win competition, both proponents and opponents of the law are working to make assisted suicide rare by promoting the aggressive treatment of the symptoms of dying."[28]

Why, with all of the positive news about improvements in dying in Oregon, does some part of us still wince at the notion of a doctor assisting a suicide?

THE SLIPPERY SLOPE

For many, physician-assisted suicide simply crosses a line that they do not want society to cross. The American Medical Association (AMA), which supported the Cruzan family throughout their case, has drawn a clear line in opposition to physician-assisted suicide. In its brief to the Supreme Court in the 1997 cases, the AMA explained the difference between *Cruzan* and assisted suicide:

> The right to control one's medical treatment is among the most important rights that the law affords each person. [We] strongly support the recognition and enforcement of that right. Health care professionals are committed to their ethical and legal obligations to honor patient request to withhold or withdraw unwanted life-prolonging treatment and to provide patients with all medication necessary to alleviate physical pain, even in circumstances where such medication might hasten death. Through these means, patients can avoid entrapment in a prolonged, painful, or overly medicalized dying process . . . [However,] the power to assist in intentionally taking the life of a patient is antithetical to the central mission of healing that guides both medicine and nursing. It is a power that most health care professionals do not want and could not control.[29]

To illustrate this inability to control, the AMA, like many opponents of physician-assisted suicide, cited the example of the Netherlands.

Doctors in the Netherlands have long practiced physician-assisted suicide and euthanasia, and in 1986 the Dutch Medical Association published "euthanasia guidelines" which the Dutch government and courts approved. In 2001, the Dutch government passed a law outlining the procedures for euthanasia and physician-assisted suicide in the country.[30] Proponents of the Dutch experience argue that it is carefully regulated, and what the people want. Opponents portray a society out of control. Both sides try to use statistics to support their claims.

Wherever the exact truth lies, without question euthanasia is deeply ingrained in Dutch culture by now. Government statistics suggest, for example, that in 1995, of 135,675 deaths in the Netherlands, 3,600 came from active euthanasia by a doctor, 238 from physician-assisted suicide, and 902 from "active involuntary euthanasia," that is, a lethal dose given to a competent patient who has the ability to request euthanasia but whom the doctor does not ask.[31]

Dr. Leon Kass, the chairman of the President's Council on Bioethics that issued the 2005 report "Taking Care: Ethical Caregiving in Our Aging Society," decried the Dutch practice in his 2002 book, *Life, Liberty and the Defense of Dignity*. Dr. Kass portrays a slippery slope turned into a steep, well-greased slide—nearly 5 percent of all deaths in the Netherlands caused by doctors; 59 percent of Dutch doctors claiming that they do not report their acts of euthanasia; and 25 percent admitting that they had ended a patient's life without the patient's consent.[32]

Reading such assessment from a respected national medical leader, it's hard not to relate to the slippery slope concern voiced by Stephen Drake of Not Dead Yet during the *Schiavo* case: "Thousands of people with disabilities across the United States are watching the case anxiously . . . Obviously, we want to know how all those commenting in this case feel about the lives of people with Down's Syndrome, autism, Alzheimer's, and other disabilities."[33] The concern is certainly real, and given the history of discrimination against the handicapped, legitimate. It's not hard to imagine the reaction of Not Dead Yet members to the more than 10,000 Dutch citizens who one advocacy group claims all carry "Do Not Euthanize Me" cards in case they are admitted to a hospital unexpectedly.[34]

The United States is not the Netherlands. Our people and culture are vastly different; not better or worse, just different. Contrary to the Dutch Medical Association, the American Medical Association strongly opposes euthanasia and physician-assisted suicide (as do virtually all medical and nursing associations in the United States); our Supreme Court has found no right to such practices; and in the one state allowing such assisted suicides, the practice has been exceedingly rare.

To me, the more important question is this: Does all of the "side effect" good in the care of the dying that has come about in Oregon as a result of the debate outweigh any risks to society from crossing a line that many do not want society to cross?

Those opposing the Oregon law cite cases like Michael Freeland, an Oregon cancer sufferer, who was depressed and in pain. Rather than treat these symptoms, according to advocates, an assisted-suicide doctor simply gave Freeland the lethal prescription and sent him on his way, even though Freeland did not meet the requirements of the Oregon law. Another doctor found Freeland in his home confused, in pain, ready to take the lethal drugs. That doctor encouraged Freeland to let him treat the pain. According to the advocates, Freeland opted for pain treatment, his symptoms were relieved, he reconciled with an estranged daughter, and he died naturally from his cancer, with his pain and depression controlled, two weeks later.[35]

Supporters of the law dispute the account of Mr. Freeland's death, and instead cite stories like Ray Frank, who had kidney cancer that had spread to his lungs, causing shortness of breath. He asked his cancer doctors about physician-assisted suicide and they told him they would not participate. So Frank asked a friend to bring him a shotgun on the day of his hospital discharge so that he could kill himself that day. The friend instead called the Oregon advocacy group Compassion in Dying, who paired Mr. Frank with a doctor who treated his symptoms aggressively, and began procedures under the Act to obtain a prescription. Ray Frank, his anxiety relieved, did not talk of suicide again, and died of natural causes a couple of weeks later.[36]

Proponents of the Oregon law argue that physician-assisted suicide actually happens four times as often in the other 49 states, where it is illegal, but that it occurs quietly and privately between patient and doctor. They argue that the increased regulation and public scrutiny in Oregon has actually reduced the occurrence there. Opponents question these statistics.[37]

Proponents argue that physician-assisted suicide is little different from so-called "double effect" (which the AMA supports), where a patient receives medicine to treat his pain, but the medicine has a secondary effect of hastening death. Opponents say that intent is everything, and that virtually all pain can be controlled without the need of sedation that hastens death. Those on both sides recognize that some patients simply choose to stop eating and drinking, an option that is legal in all states.[38]

Not many of us want a society where Dr. Kevorkians flourish, though several chose his van and machine. The Oregon experience suggests that few seek physician-assisted suicide either; it is our nature to cling to life. The AMA counsels against a culture where doctors are hastening death, and in favor of a culture where doctors "aggressively respond to the needs of patients at the end of life."[39] Better emotional support, better pain control, better communication, better comfort care. Though their cases are held up by the competing sides, Mr. Frank and Mr. Freeland in Oregon arguably benefited from the same things: better emotional support, pain control, comfort care, and especially, better communication.

I'm a firm believer in states rights, didn't agree with the decision of the federal government to become involved in *Oregon v. Ashcroft* (later renamed *Gonzales*), and believe efforts by the federal congress in 2006 to overturn the Oregon law would be inappropriate. I also believe the social experiment with physician-assisted suicide in Oregon has been conducted thoughtfully and with careful oversight.

That said, my sense is that physician-assisted suicide presents a line that society does not need to and should not cross. As most who work in this area recognize, there is significant room for improvement in how the medical world responds to the needs of patients at the end of life. That is where our societal focus should be. Moreover, if the AMA concludes that "the power to assist in intentionally taking the life of a patient is antithetical to the central mission of healing," it strikes me that we should heed those words.

Roughly 7,000 people die each day in the United States. We die in many ways. There is no exact road map of how we can make that dying go down the path we might choose in this complex world of medical technology. There's no single answer to what we might want if we find ourselves in Terri Schiavo's shoes. Crude as his methods were, Dr. Kevorkian helped us navigate the social discussion by forcing that discussion to happen. The tragedies of Nancy Cruzan and Terri Schiavo have done that, too, as has the spirited societal debate in Oregon. Society is moving toward better care of the dying. The debate will and should continue. And as we move in that direction, as has happened in Oregon, hospice care will be a major part of the solution.

CHAPTER 15

Hospice: The Hidden Jewel

"I took care of the dying before there was a Cicely Saunders and before there were hospices, and people died badly."

—Dr. Eric Cassell of the New York Hospital talking about Dame Cicely Saunders from England, the founder of the modern hospice movement[1]

I'VE ALWAYS BELIEVED THE AXIOM that the cure to bad speech is more speech, not censorship. The public discussion of Terri Schiavo's case is a perfect case study. Many smart, caring people were disturbed at the extreme claims and theories raised as the debate grew more heated in the last months of Terri Schiavo's life. My sense, then and now, is that all of the discussion—even the factually inaccurate parts—was beneficial to society as a whole.

It's unrealistic to expect that our society, or our media, could understand quickly, easily, or seamlessly, the complexities of dying today. Two different President's Commissions, a committee of the Harvard Medical School, the U.S. Supreme Court, state courts, legislatures, and many other bodies have struggled over months and years to understand the persistent vegetative state, brain death, medical technology, and how the law and Constitution should apply in a family dispute involving these concepts. The issues are complicated, personal, and fundamental. All of the discussion around the *Schiavo* case helped move our education as a society forward, even if the discussion at times strayed far from the facts.

No group needed more speech to cure bad speech during the final months of the *Schiavo* case than hospice. Or, more particularly, the hospice house where Terri Schiavo lived her last five years, and where she died. The hospice that cared for Terri Schiavo is where you'd want your own mother to die when the time comes. The workers there are talented, committed, caring, selfless, and professional. They are part of the gift to society that hospice is. The people at Hospice House Woodside, which is part of a large hospice called The Hospice of the Florida Suncoast, had no axe to grind in the debate. To the best of their ability, the staff took care of Michael Schiavo, they took care of Bob and Mary Schindler, Bobby Schindler and Suzanne Vitadamo (Terri's brother and sister), and they took care of Terri. That truth was largely lost in the din.

Protesters screamed "Murderers!" at hospice workers as they came to work in the morning, like they did to the hospital workers in the *Cruzan* and *Busalacchi* cases. They held up signs like "Hospice Auschwitz." If they'd had it right, the signs might have read instead, "We Know You Take Beautiful Loving Care of Thousands of Dying People and Their Families!" Or "This Hospice Is Caught in the Middle of the *Schiavo* Case Because It Volunteered to Care for Terri!" Or "Thank You Hospice House Woodside for Your Unwavering Commitment to the People of Florida!" Those signs probably would not have been quite as newsworthy.

The morning that Terri Schiavo died in March 2005, the scene outside of Hospice House Woodside in Pinellas Park, Florida changed quickly. The protesters, satellite trucks, and police left, and most of the signs like "Hospice Auschwitz" came down. Even the juggler in the bright orange tie, who had showed up out front and entertained the protesters because "God told" him to come, took his silver juggling pins and headed home.[2]

Inside, the work that had gone on in the days and years before Terri's death simply continued. Volunteers bathed patients, the chaplain held the hand of a distraught father as they prayed together, a social worker counseled family members in a quiet room, an aide helped a man take a walk into the garden out back, a doctor with expertise in pain management treated the symptoms of her dying patient or gently told family members what to expect next.

And a nurse provided comfort care to a patient who had had artificial nutrition and hydration discontinued by placing ice chips on the tongue and using wet sponge swabs on the patient's dry mouth. The nurse also explained to the patient's family that cessation of eating and drinking has always been part of the end phase of an illness, that as a human body shuts down we do not crave or need food. The nurse told the family that their loved one had no hunger, and that this lack of hunger was a natural part of dying. In fact, medical research suggested that discontinuing tube feeding lessened fluid buildup in the lungs and throat, making it easier to breathe and reducing the amount of suctioning of secretions required. She told them that the research even suggested that removal of artificial nutrition and hydration caused the body to increase its release of natural hormones, lessening pain.[3]

The people of The Hospice of the Florida Suncoast have cared for thousands of patients in this devoted way for years. At Hospice House Woodside alone, in the 60 days after Terri died, 129 new patients entered the hospice house and 88 patients died.[4] The circle of caring, and of life, continued.

At this point in this book, you will not be surprised by the next statement: Hospice is new in our society, another by-product of modern medical technology. Modern hospice began as a grassroots movement in the 1970s, growing originally from the dissatisfaction of the families and some caregivers of cancer patients with their care and dying. It has experienced meteoric growth over the last twenty years. Hospice, simply, is a philosophy of respecting and valuing people who are dying, and a system of care to put that philosophy into practice. As Baby Boomers age, and as technology advances, hospice will play an ever-increasing role in how we die.

THE BIRTH OF THE HOSPICE MOVEMENT

The word hospice comes from the Latin "hospis," which means host. Hospitality, hospital, hotel all come from the same root.[5] In the Middle Ages, weary and sick travelers returning from the Crusades were given shelter and comfort in hospice houses set up by the Catholic Church.

The modern hospice movement is universally traced to one woman—Dame Cicely Saunders—and the place she founded, St. Christopher's Hospice in Sydenham, England, outside of London.[6] After World War II, Cicely Saunders was employed as a 30-year-old social worker in a hospital ward. In the course of that work, she cared for two months for a 40-year-old Polish Jew named David Tasma, who was dying of cancer. She saw that his physical pain was not being managed well, and also that he was suffering great emotional pain. Cicely Saunders later said that the experience with David Tasma was how she "came to be thinking of a place that would be so much more suitable for him to make sense of the end of his life, dying at the age of 40, and feeling he'd made no impact on the world whatsoever, and that nothing would make any difference when he died."[7]

Cicely Saunders was also a registered nurse, so she began volunteering in the evenings at one of the early homes for dying patients. These homes were sometimes called "almshouses" and were places where the poor and those without family were taken to die; those with family died in their own homes.[8] Cicely Saunders saw at this home that through the use of oral morphine given regularly, pain could be controlled better than by giving an injection after pain had escalated and the morphine "earned" as they did in the hospital. After three years of volunteering, she took one of the doctors she worked with at her day job as a social worker on one of her volunteer evenings. He encouraged her to go to medical school to pursue her vision, which she did, at the age of 33.

In 1957, Cicely Saunders finished medical school and began to do research. Over the course of several years, she investigated pain and its causes. Part of her research included making tape recordings of people talking about their pain. (The first portable tape recorders became available in the 1950s). Dr. Saunders years later recalled a particular interview she conducted in 1963 with a woman who had breast cancer that had metastasized, or spread. Dr. Saunders said to her, "Tell me about your pain."

The woman responded, "Well, Doctor, it began in my back, but now it seems that all of me is wrong." She described physical pain, but also social, spiritual, and financial pain, like worrying about her husband losing money by having to care for her. Cicely Saunders said about this patient, "She gave me the idea of a 'total pain', which I started writing about in 1964."[9]

Three years later, in 1967, Dr. Saunders opened St. Christopher's Hospice outside of London. One of her first staff nurses was Florence Wald, dean of the Yale University Nursing School. In 1966, Dean Wald had invited Cicely Saunders to Connecticut to give a lecture to Yale nursing students. Soon after St. Christopher's opened, Wald took a sabbatical and went to England to spend several weeks working at the hospice. Back in the States, Florence Wald devoted her work to the care of the dying, and in 1974, she helped to open the first hospice in the United States, the Connecticut Hospice in Branford, Connecticut.[10] Unlike St. Christopher's, the Connecticut Hospice did not have an in-patient facility; they had people and a philosophy, and they treated patients mainly in their own homes.

In 1973 in Canada, Dr. Balfour Mount, a surgeon at McGill University in Montreal, was asked to give a talk at a local church on death and dying. He recalled that lecture request years later: "Elisabeth Kübler-Ross had written her book [*On Death and Dying*] and it was an 'in' topic. I assumed that being a doctor I must know about death and dying. It didn't occur to me that I didn't know a thing about death and dying," he said, laughing.[11] As he read Kübler-Ross's book, he looked at the references in the back, most of which involved the work of Dr. Saunders. Through the telephone operator, he tracked down Dr. Saunders in London and talked to her over the phone. Before long, Balfour Mount found himself spending a week observing and working at St. Christopher's as Florence Wald had done.

Back home in Canada, Dr. Mount soon set up the first Canadian hospice in Montreal. Unlike St. Christopher's with its separate building, or the Connecticut Hospice which worked in people's homes, the first Canadian hospice was inside of the large teaching hospital, Royal Victoria, at McGill University. He also could not name what he planned to do "hospice," since the French root of that word described the almshouses.

Dr. Mount said that while shaving one morning he'd thought, "We have coronary care units and transplantation units and intensive care units. Why not have a palliative care unit. We'll call it the 'palliative care service.' And I looked up the etymology of 'palliative' and it was perfect because though initially back in Roman times it meant to conceal or to hide, in subsequent centuries it took on the meaning 'to improve the quality of.' That's what we were about."[12]

Eventually, over 50,000 others—doctors, nurses, students—would come to St. Christopher's Hospice to study and learn, and the vision of Cicely Saunders spread.[13] Today, there are nearly 8,000 hospices in the world.

Dr. Saunders also took her vision to the students as well. In 1997, Balfour Mount invited Dr. (and now Dame) Cicely Saunders to McGill University to speak to medical students. Dr. Saunders told the students about David Tasma, the patient she'd cared for as a social worker almost fifty years earlier. She described the talks that she and David Tasma had had, including discussing how there could be a place better suited for dying than a busy hospital ward. Tasma left Cicely Saunders 500 British pounds, saying to her, "I will be a window in your home." She told the students, "David Tasma, who thought he'd made no impact on the world by his life, started a movement." She said that she put Tasma's window into St. Christopher's: "It took me nineteen years to build a home around that window."[14]

It would take many more years after that window went up in 1967 for hospice to gain acceptance in the mainstream medical community.[15] Remember, doctors in the late 1960s still typically weren't even disclosing to seriously ill patients their diagnosis, let alone talking openly about dying and death. In the medical world, like the rest of the world, however, the times were a-changin'.

Dr. Eric Cassell from New York, a prolific contributor to end-of-life medical literature, remembered that time: "The slogan was 'the personal is the political.' And the personal became public. Suffering used to be silent, nobody talked about death, even. I once gave a lecture on the care of the dying in 1972 and somebody stood up in the audience to say, 'This is outrageous. You have no right to talk about this. These are private matters.'"[16] In that time of Kent State and Watergate, the personal became public.

Part of the catalyst for change in the medical world came from the work of Elisabeth Kübler-Ross, a psychiatrist, who in 1969 wrote *On Death and Dying*. The book became a bestseller and social phenomenon. *Time* magazine in a review claimed that the book had "vanquished the conspiracy of silence that once shrouded the hospital's terminal wards. It has brought death out of the darkness."[17]

Elisabeth Kübler-Ross told medical school students in a 1975 lecture about the culture she confronted when she began her research on dying for the book. She explained the difficulty she had even getting permission from the hospital administration to talk with dying patients. Once she finally had that permission, she went out onto the hospital floor and was told that nobody was dying on that floor. "I was naïve and went to the next floor—same answer—until I covered the whole 600-bed hospital," Kübler-Ross said. "And then only did it dawn on me that maybe the staff had a problem. That proved very true."[18]

Though the medical culture was changing in its willingness to talk about dying, that change was slow. Moreover, the push for hospice did not come from any changes within that medical mainstream; it came from patients—mainly cancer patients—and their families, and some of their caregivers, like Florence Wald, Balfour Mount, and Eric Cassell. These patients were dissatisfied with the lack of information they were given about their diseases, and with the way in which they were dying. The world of cancer treatment was focused in the opposite direction, tackling the "war on cancer" that had been declared by President Richard Nixon.[19] And in the early 1970s, these doctors found themselves with a growing array of tools to take on this enemy. The chance to fight a disease that had until then been a "death sentence," with support of significant federal funding, caused most cancer doctors to focus on that war.

Not all, however, had that focus. The seed of hospice had been planted and word began to spread that there was a way for dying cancer patients to avoid dying badly. The efforts of those people illustrate what the term "grassroots" means. A long-time hospice doctor in Buffalo, New York, Robert Milch, told me about the early years of the hospice in Buffalo. "At first, there was no reimbursement for hospital services. We would read the obituaries, hoping that the families of patients we cared for would list our hospice as the place for memorials," he said. Dr. Milch today is the full-time medical director of the Hospice Buffalo, but back then he had a busy surgical practice during the day. "I would make house calls on Saturday nights when my wife and I were on our way to the movies, while she waited in the car," he laughed. "Nearly all hospice medical directors and many of the nurses and others were volunteers. It was about service, what medicine and nursing were supposed to be about. At some gut level, we knew that medicine and the system would catch on and catch up, so we kept doing it," he said.[20]

THE GROWTH OF MODERN HOSPICE

After the establishment of the Connecticut Hospice in 1974, other hospices soon opened in Marin, California; Boonton, New Jersey; Boulder, Colorado; Buffalo, New York; and other places. These groups began sharing ideas, and in 1978, the National Hospice Organization (NHO) formed. In 1983, hospice care moved permanently into the mainstream when the federal Congress approved a Medicare payment for hospice. Medicare is the federal health insurance program for people 65 or older, or those with disabilities. Private insurers also began providing coverage for hospice around this time. In 1986, Congress established hospice care as an optional Medicaid benefit as well. Medicaid is the program that provides health care for the poor.[21]

With this funding support, hospice now had a payment stream. By 1985, there were 1,545 hospice programs in the country. The number grew to 2,470 by 1995 and reached 3,650 in 2004.[22] In 1985, hospice served 158,000 patients. In 2004, hospice served 1,060,000 patients. Of the 2.4 million people who died in the United States in 2004, about 750,000 were hospice patients.

Hospice today is a major health care field, with extensive government regulation and an entire industry built up around the care. The patients, once almost all cancer patients, now come to hospice with a variety of diseases. By 2004, cancer accounted for 46 percent of all hospice admissions.[23] Once exclusively provided by non-profit organizations, in 2004, 31 percent of hospices were for-profit entities and 6 percent were government-run, primarily services for low-income patients and war veterans.[24] Even with this rapid growth and the addition of bureaucracy, the basic philosophy of hospice remains essentially unchanged from its conception at the bedside of David Tasma. Hospice works to treat the emotional and physical pain and suffering of a seriously ill patient and the patient's family, helping patients "make sense of the ends" of their lives.

Modern hospices bring to that task an interdisciplinary team of doctors, nurses, aides, social workers, chaplains, volunteers, and others. The team works to provide professional services, help with daily living, spiritual counseling, and anything else the patient and her family need to maintain the highest quality of life for the life that remains.[25] As Dr. Balfour Mount has said, "A person is either 100 percent alive or 100 percent dead. While they're alive, then the issue is, what is the quality of life? And what is the way that that quality can be optimized and maximized and worked with and celebrated?"[26]

Sometimes hospice services are delivered in a hospice house, like St. Christopher's outside London, or Hospice House Woodside in Florida. Or they might be delivered in a bed or wing in a hospital that is designated for hospice care. Far more often, though, hospice care is brought to the patient living in the family home or a nursing home.

So while we think of a hospital as a *place*, a building, hospice is different. It can be a building, like a hospice house, but it's more a philosophy and a method of delivering health care at the end of life. And it's a philosophy that works. Interestingly, of the five teaching hospitals in which the 9,105 seriously ill patients of the SUPPORT study were followed, the one hospital that had the closest working relationship with a hospice reported a higher rate of patients dying at home rather than in the hospital—which is exactly what studies say almost all of us want.[27]

While hospice at the beginning of 2006 is much more a part of the medical culture in this country than it was even fifteen years ago, many doctors still do not really understand what hospice does beyond the idea that it's what people need when they're dying. The general public understands even less. I find that when I talk to community groups, many have a vague sense of hospice that it deals with the dying, and that it's a good thing, based on what others have told them. But they don't understand how important it can be in their lives, and perhaps, more importantly, how and when to ask for hospice. As we Baby Boomers age and technology keeps advancing, that understanding will grow.

Hospice care will no doubt grow, change, and improve, too. One obvious area for improvement is the number of people served. If 750,000 of the 2.5 million deaths in the United States last year had hospice care, then 1,750,000 did not. The number for hospice usage has risen steadily and dramatically over the last ten years. In 1993, 11 percent of the deaths in the United States had hospice care;[28] by 2004, that number had risen to 31 percent. Still, that's 1,750,000 people dying without hospice care. Some of those 1,750,000 deaths, of course, were accidents, homicides, and other sudden deaths where hospice could not have been used, but most were not.

Another clear challenge for hospice is that hospice care needs to reach dying patients sooner. For the 750,000 who died with hospice in 2004, the average length of stay was 57 days, and the median length of stay was only 22 days.[29] Yet many with chronic illnesses could benefit from the services and support of hospice for far longer than that time.

While hospice teams often can bring pain or other symptoms under control within days, the bigger mission of hospice—recognizing and affirming the life of the whole person—takes communication, building trust by the hospice team, and reflection from the patient.[30] To fully realize the benefit of hospice care, both the general medical community and the public need a better understanding of the full scope of hospice, understanding that hospice provides a far greater benefit to patients and their families than pain management for the dying.

That understanding will come. Hospice care is fairly new in our culture. The Medicare Benefit has been in place only since 1983.[31] Hospice usage began to increase significantly after the provision of that government funding, and it has grown exponentially in the last ten years. Awareness will continue to grow, and hospice usage will increase. Most hospice workers have received letters or had families say to them, "I wish we'd known about hospice sooner." As more families experience hospice, word will spread.

Education needs to happen in the medical world, too. The hospice benefit in 1983 was structured as care that came when curative care had "failed." Over the years hospice care has evolved so that it is provided alongside curative care. This change in how hospice care is viewed is depicted well in a chart developed by Dr. Joanne Lynn, reprinted in the Appendix. A nurse in Maine told me that it is her personal goal that no doctor will ever say again, "I'm sorry, there's nothing more that we can do." A referral to hospice is not "giving up" on the patient—a cancer patient can receive chemotherapy in the hospital and return home to have hospice workers deliver medicines, hospice doctors make a house call, and hospice social workers visit.

Different innovations in the medical world recognize this evolution. The emergence of palliative care programs within hospitals is an example. Different groups define "palliative care" in different ways, but basically it means providing comfort, treating the symptoms, at the same time that some disease-modifying or curative care is being given. In 1994, there were virtually no palliative care programs in U.S. hospitals. Today nearly one-fifth of community hospitals have programs, and nearly half of the roughly 400 major teaching hospitals already have or plan to implement such service.[32] According to the American Hospital Association, the number of such programs grew by 22 percent in the year 2002 alone.[33]

A thoughtful *New York Times Magazine* article in the fall of 2005 told the story of Dr. Diane Meier, a national leader in the palliative medicine field. One day in the mid-1990s, Dr. Meier looked into an open door in her hospital and saw a man, his arms and legs tied to the bed, writhing in pain. Shocked, she investigated, and learned that he was a cancer patient who had refused treatment, but his doctor had still inserted a feeding tube against his wishes. Even restrained, the semi-delirious man had been able to dislodge the tube seventeen times.

Dr. Meier asked the young intern why he had staff continue to insert the feeding tube when the man did not want it, and the doctor replied, "Because if we don't do this, he'll die." Dr. Meier called that her "light bulb moment." Seeing the young doctor's anguish as he spoke, she realized that he cared about his patient; he simply did not know what to do or where to turn. Not long after, Dr. Meier was running a palliative care service at the hospital, and she had helped organize and today is the director of the Center to Advance Palliative Care (CAPC), an initiative to increase hospital and nursing-home based palliative services.[34] Had that palliative service been in place in the mid-1990s when Dr. Meier saw the man tied to his bed, doctors might have offered alternatives like anti-anxiety medication, or removing the tube and offering foods by mouth in pureed form. There might have been other options for the patient and for the intern.[35]

It will be fascinating to watch the growth of hospice and palliative care in medicine in the years ahead. Some of the care that hospice and palliative medicine provides is technical and sophisticated, requiring an advanced understanding of complicated pain and symptom management using varying combinations of drugs, therapies, and devices. And some of hospice care is simply part of the comprehensive delivery of services, from a team, to address all sides of a disease, and honor a patient as a person.

A hospice doctor in Vermont told me about one rural family who were nearly at their wits' end before learning of hospice. The husband was driving fifty miles five times a week to the closest pharmacy for a whole variety of medicines for his wife who had advanced lung disease. When he wasn't driving, he was with her virtually around the clock, unable to work and losing sleep. She worried constantly about him. A pharmacist gave him the phone number for hospice and he called. Soon he had a hospice volunteer staying with his wife at times so that he could "get out of the house," which relieved her stress as much as his. Hospice had the medicines she needed delivered to the house so that he didn't have to drive fifty miles every day. Nurses, social workers, and aides came to the house.

Comprehensive care that changed stress to relief. People caring for others, affirming the value of their lives. It's no wonder that hospice has grown quickly, nor is it any stretch to imagine that hospice will be a major part of health care as we move forward.

THE PLACE WHERE TERRI SCHIAVO DIED

Which brings me back to Hospice House Woodside and its umbrella organization, The Hospice of the Florida Suncoast. The people of this hospice have a name for their time at work during the last few months of Terri Schiavo's life. They call it "The Siege."[36] Having been through the *Cruzan* and *Busalacchi* cases, I understand that reaction.

In the *Busalacchi* case in Missouri, the state government actively opposed family efforts to remove Christine Busalacchi's feeding tube. (The *Busalacchi* case is not as well known as *Cruzan*, but it went to the Missouri Supreme Court twice.) Chris lived in a state hospital. I did not talk with every health care institution in the state about taking Chris as a patient if we won the litigation, but I talked to several. Only one—Barnes Hospital in St. Louis (now Barnes-Jewish Hospital)—was willing to accept Chris. Barnes did this even though their administration knew that the decision would bring protests and problems.

The Hospice of the Florida Suncoast similarly had little incentive to take Terri as a patient in 2000; they did it because someone needed to care for her and her divided family. That decision required a deep commitment to the mission of health care as well as significant institutional resolve. Admirably, even now the staff and doctors at the hospice will talk little about their care of Terri Schiavo. The main statement they make is one of regret that, despite their best efforts, they could not bring the family together. Mary Labyak, the long-time CEO of the hospice, told a reporter that mediating family disputes "is a way of life for us." But she could not remember any other dispute so entrenched that the hospice workers were simply not able to reach any resolution of a family dispute before their loved one died.[37]

In the nearly thirty years of its operation before Terri Schiavo's death, The Hospice of the Florida Suncoast has cared for more than 75,000 people who have died. The Hospice started in 1977 in a garage with six people, grassroots organizers who were committed to make the lives of dying Floridians better. Today, it has over 1,000 employees and over 3,000 volunteers. In 2005 alone, The Hospice cared for about 8,000 dying patients in addition to Terri Schiavo. It also provided millions of dollars of charitable care to 129,000 people in the community who were in need of some type of service related to the end of life, such as grief counseling for the mothers of stillborn babies or decision-making help for families facing terminal illness.[38]

Each one of these thousands of patients was to one degree or another like Cicely Saunders' cancer patient, David Tasma, trying alone or with their loved ones to make some sense out of living and dying. Think about what hospice does. A hospice nurse comes into a patient's home as a stranger, sits down, and begins the hard work of building a trusting relationship in whatever time they have together. Aides come and bathe the patient, give haircuts, trim toenails. If the patient wants, a chaplain visits to talk about spiritual concerns. A volunteer drives to pick up groceries or sits with the patient so that family members can go for a long walk or out to a movie. The doctor comes and helps teach the patient about controlling her pain and what to expect in the days and weeks ahead. A social worker talks with the patient, the family, and anyone else who needs help with the emotions experienced by those facing the end of life.

As the patient grows sicker, nurses and aides help with basic feeding, and with toileting needs, and show families how to turn their loved one to avoid bed sores. If care at home becomes too much, the hospice helps move the patient to a hospice house or nursing home. The hospice workers soothe the fear that can happen if the patient starts telling his family that he sees long dead loved ones visiting in his room, telling the family that many dying patients have this exact experience, and no one knows exactly what is happening.[39] They sit with the family in the final hours, explain the death rattle to come, and tell them at the end, "I think she's gone now." After the death, hospice helps with planning, bereavement, and grief counseling.

That's what The Hospice of the Florida Suncoast has done for more than 75,000 dying patients and their families over 28 years. That's what they did for Terri Schiavo, and tried to do for both sides of her fractured family. Hospice is always ready to provide hugs, and inside Terri Schiavo's hospice those hugs from the hospice workers went to Michael, Bob, Mary, Susan, Bobby, and anyone else in the family, because they cared for them all.

As I said, I believe deeply that the cure for bad speech is more speech. I will defend always the right of the protester outside Hospice House Woodside to hold up the sign reading "Hospice Auschwitz." You will also understand by now that I believe that this protester had absolutely no clue about respecting life, or understanding death, or of the nature of hospice. I asked Mary Labyak almost a year after Terri Schiavo's death why her hospice agreed to accept Terri as a patient. "We made a covenant with this community that's now almost thirty years old," she said, "that we would be there when difficult end-of-life issues arose. I hope people saw that hospice doesn't abandon patients and their families if the going gets tough."[40] If anyone was watching at all, they should have at least seen that. They might also have seen that hospice workers understand, no doubt as well as those in any other sector of health care, what it truly means to care for another person.

Florence Wald, founder of the first hospice in the United States, said, "One of my dreams is that before medical students go to medical school and before nursing students go to nursing school that they would spend six weeks in a hospice. My feeling is that they then would have the experience of a patient and family coming first that would carry them into their respective schools."[41] Dean Wald's advice would work for the rest of us as well. Volunteers are a major part of hospice work, and most hospice volunteers I've spoken with say the same thing: "I take out far more than I put in with this experience." As Boomers and their parents age and we all look out the window and see ourselves approaching that institutional glide path, the more we know about hospice, the better our lives will be.

CHAPTER 16

Where Do We Go from Here?

WHEN I GIVE TALKS on this topic, I work hard to make the event energetic, engaging, and fast-paced. After all, I'm a lawyer talking about death and dying—not necessarily on anyone's top ten list of shows they need to Tivo this week. I have a pretty good sense that I've been able to accomplish this goal with my talks. But I also know that no matter how engaged an audience is, there comes a point in each evening when people have listened and talked about death and dying enough, and they want to go outside, breathe, and live.

So it is with this book. We've covered enough. Many topics I haven't covered at all or have touched upon lightly: guardianship, disparities in care for minorities, the "unbefriended patient," Jehovah's Witness cases, government regulation of pain medicine, grief, the funeral industry, stem cell research, medical futility, NAAG, HIPAA, AIDS, medical marijuana, Medicare Part D, 45 million uninsured Americans, news reports of alleged miracle recoveries, and more.

This will have to do for now. In fact, I feel a little sheepish that we've already passed 200 pages when my bottom line advice can be summed up in 71 words (though of course you will understand the advice much better if you've been through those pages):

> Fill out a health care power of attorney. Talk to the person you name as your agent about Terri Schiavo, Margo, and the other end-of-life stories that come up in your discussion. Tell your family and anyone else who might be in the room when health care decisions are made for you, about your conversation. Give copies of the document to your agent, other family members, and your doctor. Go live.

Lance Armstrong opens his book about recovering from cancer and going on to win the Tour de France bicycle race like this: "I want to die at a hundred years old with an American flag on my back and the star of Texas on my helmet, after screaming down an Alpine descent on a bicycle at 75 miles per hour. I want to cross one last finish line as my stud wife and my ten children applaud, and then I want to lie down in a field of those famous French sunflowers and gracefully expire, the perfect contradiction to my once-anticipated poignant early demise."[1]

Lance's way sounds a little scary, but I know what he means. Chances are, though, that given his lifetime of work to raise money to fight cancer, Lance knows hospice well now, he'll know it better then, and that's where he'll probably die. Given his VO2 max, that ending will likely come a long time from now. But of course, we can't know that, can we?

His sentiment is like a lot of popular writing about death and dying, like the number-one country hit in 2004 by Tim McGraw, "Live Like You Were Dying," a song written when his father was dying from cancer. One of the best books in this field was written by my friend Dr. Ira Byock, called *Dying Well: Peace and Possibilities at the End of Life*. In the introduction, Ira writes: "*Dying Well* is a book about living." The National Hospice and Palliative Care Organization's creative outreach campaign, Caring Connections, has the tag line, "It's About How You LIVE!"

I love the Tim McGraw song, and understand the intent of Dr.

Byock's words and the NHPCO campaign. I agree with the basic intent to think about how we live. But it's also about *how you die*. We owe it to everyone we love to think and talk about that.

The visiting nurses association in Burlington, Vermont put together a remarkable video that was released in 2005 called *The Pioneers of Hospice*. With this project they had the foresight and good fortune to videotape both Dame Cicely Saunders and Elisabeth Kübler-Ross before the deaths of each of these remarkable women in 2005. Florence Wald, Dr. Balfour Mount, Dr. Eric Cassell and others also appear. Part of the filming was done in the chapel at St. Christopher's outside London. Cicely Saunders and Florence Wald sat next to one another, discussing their lives, a fireside chat with two women who changed the world.

The film ends with the two talking about their own deaths. "I always know that there are going to be things that I haven't finished yet before I die," said Dean Wald.

"I'd love to tidy my desk," said Dame Saunders, smiling.

"Yes, me too," replied Wald, laughing. Then, she paused. "We won't."

"No," responded Saunders, as they looked at one another, and both started giggling.[2]

As I write in 2006, Florence Wald, now 88 years old, is still ministering to hospice patients, and also working on projects to establish hospices in prisons and to design new concepts for communities for the aging. Dame Cicely Saunders died peacefully on July 14, 2005, attended by devoted caregivers in the hospice house she built. No doubt the first thing she did when she arrived in the Heaven she so firmly believed in was look up David Tasma and tell him what he'd accomplished in those final conversations on Earth.

■ ■ ■

It's hard to imagine much better role models than Cicely Saunders and Florence Wald, so I think I'll take their advice. I'm going to try and tidy up my own desk right now; it's been covered with this book for a while. The rest of you, go and have a talk.

Godspeed.

APPENDIX

- Figure 1. Sample Oregon POLST form. (Courtesy Oregon Health & Science University.)
- Figure 2. Blank copy of author Bill Colby's personal Durable Power of Attorney for Health Care Decisions.
- Figure 3. Dr. Joanne Lynn's chart depicting appropriate care near the end of life. Joanne Lynn, *Sick to Death and Not Going to Take It Anymore!* (Berkeley: University of California Press, 2004), 38. (Chart courtesy and copyright of RAND Corporation.)

HIPAA PERMITS DISCLOSURE OF POLST TO OTHER HEALTH CARE PROFESSIONALS AS NECESSARY

Physician Orders
for Life-Sustaining Treatment (POLST)

First follow these orders, then contact physician or NP. This is a Physician Order Sheet based on the person's medical condition and wishes. Any section not completed implies full treatment for that section. Everyone shall be treated with dignity and respect.

Last Name

First Name/ Middle Initial

Date of Birth

A *Check One*

CARDIOPULMONARY RESUSCITATION (CPR): Person has no pulse and is not breathing.

☐ Resuscitate/CPR ☐ Do Not Attempt Resuscitation (DNR/no CPR)

When not in cardiopulmonary arrest, follow orders in **B**, **C** and **D**.

B *Check One*

MEDICAL INTERVENTIONS: Person has pulse and/or is breathing.

☐ **Comfort Measures Only** Use medication by any route, positioning, wound care and other measures to relieve pain and suffering. Use oxygen, suction and manual treatment of airway obstruction as needed for comfort. ***Do not transfer** to hospital for life-sustaining treatment.* ***Transfer** if comfort needs cannot be met in current location.*

☐ **Limited Additional Interventions** Includes care described above. Use medical treatment, IV fluids and cardiac monitor as indicated. Do not use intubation, advanced airway interventions, or mechanical ventilation. ***Transfer** to hospital if indicated. Avoid intensive care.*

☐ **Full Treatment** Includes care described above. Use intubation, advanced airway interventions, mechanical ventilation, and cardioversion as indicated. ***Transfer** to hospital if indicated. Includes intensive care.*

Additional Orders: ______________________

C *Check One*

ANTIBIOTICS

☐ No antibiotics. Use other measures to relieve symptoms.

☐ Determine use or limitation of antibiotics when infection occurs.

☐ Use antibiotics if life can be prolonged.

Additional Orders: ______________________

D *Check One*

ARTIFICIALLY ADMINISTERED NUTRITION: Always offer food by mouth if feasible.

☐ No artificial nutrition by tube.

☐ Defined trial period of artificial nutrition by tube.

☐ Long-term artificial nutrition by tube.

Additional Orders: ______________________

E

SUMMARY OF MEDICAL CONDITION AND SIGNATURES

Discussed with: ☐ Patient ☐ Parent of Minor ☐ Health Care Representative ☐ Court-Appointed Guardian ☐ Other: ________	**Summary of Medical Condition**	
Print Physician / Nurse Practitioner Name	MD/DO/NP Phone Number	Office Use Only
Physician / NP Signature (mandatory)	Date	

SEND FORM WITH PERSON WHENEVER TRANSFERRED OR DISCHARGED

Figure 1. Sample Oregon POLST form (front side of two-sided form).

HIPAA PERMITS DISCLOSURE OF POLST TO OTHER HEALTH CARE PROFESSIONALS AS NECESSARY

Signature of Person, Parent of Minor, or Guardian/Health Care Representative

Significant thought has been given to life-sustaining treatment. Preferences have been expressed to a physician and/or health care professional(s). This document reflects those treatment preferences.

(If signed by surrogate, preferences expressed must reflect patient's wishes as best understood by surrogate.)

Signature (optional)	Name (print)	Relationship (write "self" if patient)

Contact Information

Surrogate (optional)	Relationship	Phone Number	
Health Care Professional Preparing Form (optional)	Preparer Title	Phone Number	Date Prepared

Directions for Health Care Professionals

Completing POLST

Must be completed by a health care professional based on patient preferences and medical indications.

POLST must be signed by a physician or nurse practitioner to be valid. Verbal orders are acceptable with follow-up signature by physician or nurse practitioner in accordance with facility/community policy.

Use of original form is strongly encouraged. Photocopies and FAXes of signed POLST forms are legal and valid.

Using POLST

Any incomplete section of POLST implies full treatment for that section.

No defibrillator (including AEDs) should be used on a person who has chosen "Do Not Attempt Resuscitation."

Oral fluids and nutrition must always be offered if medically feasible.

When comfort cannot be achieved in the current setting, the person, including someone with "Comfort Measures Only," should be transferred to a setting able to provide comfort (e.g., treatment of a hip fracture).

IV medication to enhance comfort may be appropriate for a person who has chosen "Comfort Measures Only."

Treatment of dehydration is a measure which prolongs life. A person who desires IV fluids should indicate "Limited Interventions" or "Full Treatment."

A person with capacity, or the surrogate of a person without capacity, can request alternative treatment.

Reviewing POLST

This POLST should be reviewed periodically and if:

(1) The person is transferred from one care setting or care level to another, or

(2) There is a substantial change in the person's health status, or

(3) The person's treatment preferences change.

Draw line through sections A through E and write "VOID" in large letters if POLST is replaced or becomes invalid.

The Oregon POLST Task Force

The POLST program was developed by the Oregon POLST Task Force. The POLST program is administratively housed at Oregon Health & Science University's Center for Ethics in Health Care. Research about the safety and effectiveness of the POLST program is available online at <**www.polst.org**> or by contacting the Task Force at <**polst@ohsu.edu**>.

SEND FORM WITH PERSON WHENEVER TRANSFERRED OR DISCHARGED

 Form developed in conformance with Oregon Revised Statute 127.505 et seq September 2004

Figure 1. Sample Oregon POLST form (back side of two-sided form).

DURABLE POWER OF ATTORNEY FOR HEALTH CARE DECISIONS

I, ______________________, SS#______________________, appoint the person(s) named below as my agent to make health care decisions for me when I cannot communicate what I want done. I want my agent to have the broadest power possible to make all health-care decisions for me. If federal law provides broader power than state law, then I choose that federal law apply. I want my agent to have the power to make *any* decision she chooses, just as if I was making the decision myself.

My agent's power certainly includes the power to accept or reject any medical treatments, including artificial nutrition and hydration. This broad power, in fact, extends to all areas—like reviewing records, or moving me home, to a nursing home, to a hospice house, or wherever she chooses. My agent can enter a DNR or Do-Not-Transfer or any similar kind of order for me, decide about organ donation, autopsy—*all* decisions.

I intend this document as evidence beyond a reasonable doubt of my wishes: I have only one wish—that my agent is allowed to make any and all decisions for me. It does not matter if the medical team agrees with her. It does not matter if that team believes that she is making a decision that, in their view, is not in my best interest or not in accord with what someone believes is my previously-expressed view. I care only about her view. She gets to decide, period. Lastly, I prefer that no one seek to appoint a legal guardian for me for any reason. If such a proceeding somehow happens, I request that my agent be appointed my legal guardian.

Agent's Name ______________________ Phone ______________________
Address ____

First Alternate Agent
Name ______________________
Address ______________________
Phone ______________________

Second Alternate Agent
Name ______________________
Address ______________________
Phone ______________________

Signature ______________________________________ Date ____________

Witness#1 ______________ Date ____________

Witness#2 ______________ Date ____________

(Witness should not be related or financially connected to you).

Notarization On this ________ day of ________, in the year of ________, personally appeared before me the person signing, known by me to be the person who completed this document and acknowledged it as his/her free act and deed. IN WITNESS WHEREOF, I have set my hand and affixed my official seal in the County of ______________________________________,
State of ______________________.

Notary Public ______________ Commission expires ______________

Figure 2. Blank copy of author Bill Colby's personal Durable Power of Attorney for Health Care Decisions.

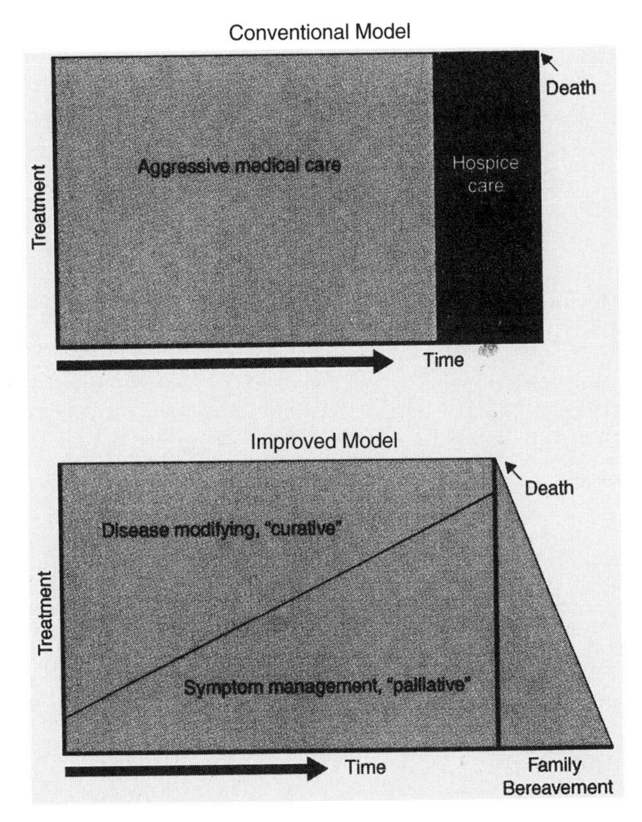

Figure 3. Dr. Joanne Lynn's chart depicting appropriate care near the end of life. Joanne Lynn, *Sick to Death and Not Going to Take It Anymore!* (Berkeley: University of California Press, 2004), 38. (Chart courtesy and copyright of RAND Corporation.)

NOTES

Introduction

1. William H. Colby, *Long Goodbye: The Deaths of Nancy Cruzan* (Carlsbad, CA: Hay House, Inc., 2002), 383.
2. William R. Levesque, et al., "Tube is removed after chaotic day," *St. Petersburg Times*, March 19, 2005, 1A.
3. Anita Kumar, et al., "One by one, options sink," *St. Petersburg Times*, March 18, 2005, 1A; William R. Levesque, et al., "Schiavo: same judges, same result," *St. Petersburg Times*, March 26, 2005, 1A.
4. Joanne Lynn, *Sick to Death and Not Going to Take It Anymore!* (Berkeley: University of California Press, 2004), 67–68; Brown University Center for Gerontology and Health Care Research, "Facts on dying," www.chcr.brown.edu/dying (accessed January 2006).
5. Colby, "5 minutes that can spare a family years of pain," *USA Today*, March 6, 2005, 13A.

Chapter 1

1. Diana Lynne, *Terri's Story: The Court-Ordered Death of an American Woman* (Nashville: Cumberland House Publishing, Inc., 2005); Mark Fuhrman, *Silent Witness: The Untold Story of Terri Schiavo's Death* (New York: Morrow, 2005); Jon B. Eisenberg, *Using Terri: The Religious Right's Conspiracy to Take Away Our Rights* (San Francisco: Harper San Francisco, 2005).
2. Michael Schiavo with Michael Hirsh, *Terri: The Truth* (New York: Dutton, 2006); Mary and Robert Schindler, et al., *A Life That Matters: The Legacy of Terri Schiavo—A Lesson For Us All* (New York: Warner Books, 2006).
3. Arian Campo-Flores, "The legacy of Terri Schiavo," *Newsweek*, April 4, 2005, 24.

4. Allen G. Breed, "Schiavo: before her death became an issue, she had a life," *Kansas City Star*, October 25, 2003, A6.
5. Ibid.
6. Campo-Flores, *Newsweek*, 24.
7. *In re: The Guardianship of Theresa Marie Schiavo, Incapacitated*, No. 90-2908GD-003 (Fla. Pinellas Cir. Ct., Probate Div., February 11, 2000), Greer, J., 1–2. Referenced as "Greer Opinion." Available online at Kathy L. Cerminara & Kenneth W. Goodman, *Key Events in the Case of Theresa Marie Schiavo*, http://www.miami.edu/ethics2/schiavo/timeline.htm (accessed February 2006). Referenced as "Miami Timeline."
8. Deposition of Michael Schiavo, September 27, 1999, 17, in *In re: The Guardianship of Theresa Marie Schiavo, Incapacitated*. Available online at http://www.hospicepatients.org/terri-schindler-schiavo-docs-links-page.html (accessed January 2006). Referenced as "Schiavo Deposition."
9. Trial Transcript, January 24, 2000, 28–29, in *In re: The Guardianship of Theresa Marie Schiavo, Incapacitated*. Available online at http://www.hospicepatients.org/terri-schindler-schiavo-docs-links-page.html (accessed January 2006). Referenced as "Trial Transcript."
10. Schiavo Deposition, 5–6.
11. Jay Wolfson, *guardian ad litem*, "A Report to Governor Jeb Bush and the 6th Judicial Circuit in the Matter of Theresa Marie Schiavo," December 1, 2003, 7. Referenced as "Wolfson Report." Available online at Miami Timeline.
12. Breed, "Schiavo: before her death," *Kansas City Star*, A6.
13. St. Petersburg Police Department Incident Report, February 25, 1990. Available online at Miami Timeline.
14. Trial Transcript, 38–39.
15. Ibid, 39.
16. Fuhrman, *Silent Witness*, 43.
17. Greer Opinion, 2.
18. Trial Transcript, 39.
19. St. Petersburg Police Department Incident Report, February 25, 1990.
20. Personal correspondence with Michael Schiavo, January, 2006.
21. Campo-Flores, *Newsweek*, 24.
22. Wolfson Report, 8.
23. Ibid; Greer Opinion, 2.
24. Trial Transcript, 49.
25. Mike Wilson, "15 years ago, Terri Schiavo's 'last hope'," *St. Petersburg Times*, March 24, 2005, reprinting in its entirety the first article about Terri Schiavo in the paper, from November 15, 1990.
26. Wolfson Report, 8.
27. Lynne, *Terri's Story*, 81; personal correspondence with Michael Schiavo, January, 2006.
28. Ibid, 68.
29. Wolfson Report, 9.
30. Bryan Jennett and Fred Plum, "Persistent vegetative state after brain damage: a syndrome in search of a name," *Lancet*, 1:734–37 (1972). The descriptions of brain function and diagnoses are taken from the following sources: Fred Plum and Jerome B. Posner, *The Diagnosis of Stupor and Coma*, 3rd Ed. (New York: Oxford University Press, 1982), 1–10; J.T. Giacino, et al., "The minimally conscious state: definition and diagnositic criteria," *Neurology*, 58: 349–353

(February 2002); "The Multi-Society Task Force Report on PVS: medical aspects of the persistent vegetative state," *New England Journal of Medicine*, 330: 1499–1508, 1572–1579 (1994).

31. Colby, *Long Goodbye*, 130–32.
32. Wolfson Report, 9.
33. Ibid.
34. Trial Transcript, 53.
35. Wolfson Report, 9.
36. William R. Levesque, "As Schiavo settlement disapeared, so did a relationship: money trail leads to rancor," *St. Petersburg Times*, March 30, 2005, 1A; Greta Van Susteren, "On The Record," Fox News, Feb. 24, 2005. Available online at www.foxnews.como/story/02933,148756,00.html (accessed February 2006).
37. Ibid.
38. William R. Levesque, "Schiavo clash is rooted in cash," *St. Petersburg Times*, November 23, 2003, 1B.
39. William R. Levesque, "As Schiavo settlement disapeared, so did a relationship: money trail leads to rancor," *St. Petersburg Times*, March 30, 2005, 1A.
40. Ibid; Lynne, *Terri's Story*, 70.
41. Greer Opinion, 2.
42. Melanie Ave, David Karp, "After jury award, battle lines drawn," *St. Petersburg Times*, March 23, 2005, 1A; Levesque, "Schiavo clash," *St. Petersburg Times*, 1B.
43. Ibid.
44. Ibid; Lynne, *Terri's Story*, 72–73.
45. Ibid; Levesque, "Schiavo clash," *St. Petersburg Times*, 1B.
46. Melanie Ave, David Karp, "After jury award, battle lines drawn," *St. Petersburg Times*, March 23, 2005, 1A; Lynne, Terri's Story, 72–73; Levesque, "Schiavo clash," *St. Petersburg Times*, 1B.
47. Lynne, *Terri's Story*, 75.
48. The Terri Schindler Schiavo Foundation, "Terri's Story," http://www.terrisfight.org (accessed August 2005, document no longer available online in February 2006).
49. Ibid.
50. Miami Timeline; Wolfson Report, 10.
51. Lynne, *Terri's Story*, 75–76.
52. Ibid.
53. Ibid, 109–110.
54. Ibid.
55. Wolfson Report, 10; Lynne, *Terri's Story*, 92–93.
56. Lynne, *Terri's Story*, 92–93.
57. "Report of Guardian ad litem Richard L. Pearse, Jr.," in *In re: The Guardianship of Theresa Marie Schiavo, Incapacitated*, No. 90-2908GD-003 (Fla. Pinellas Cir. Ct., Probate Div.), Greer, J., December 29, 1998, 2. Available online at http://www.hospicepatients.org/richard-pearse-jr-12-29-98-report-of-guardianadlitem-re-terri-schiavo.pdf (accessed January 2006). Referenced as "Pearse Report."
58. Pearse Report, 3.
59. Ibid, 5.
60. Ibid, 9–13. Mr. Pearse reported that Florida law required clear and convincing evidence that Terri would choose to remove the life support, if she could communicate, before someone speaking for her could authorize removal. Given

his concerns about Michael Schiavo's credibility, Pearse recommended the life support stay in place.

61. Schiavo Deposition, 44–46.
62. Ibid, 48–49.
63. Greer Opinion, 1.
64. Anita Kumar, "Before the circus," *St. Petersburg Times*, April 3, 2005, 1P.
65. David Karp, "Memories diverge on what Terri wanted," *St. Petersburg Times*, March 24, 2005, 1A.
66. Trial Transcript, 73–74.

Chapter 2

1. *In re: The Guardianship of Theresa Marie Schiavo, Incapacitated*, No. 90-2908GD-003 (Fla. Pinellas Cir. Ct., Probate Div., February 11, 2000), Greer, J., 6. Referenced as "Greer Opinion." Available online at Kathy L. Cerminara & Kenneth W. Goodman, *Key Events in the Case of Theresa Marie Schiavo*, http://www.miami.edu/ethics2/schiavo/timeline.htm (accessed February 2006). Referenced as "Miami Timeline."
2. Ibid.
3. David Karp, "Memories diverge on what Terri wanted," *St. Petersburg Times*, March 24, 2005, 1A.
4. Ibid.
5. Diana Lynne, *Terri's Story: The Court-Ordered Death of an American Woman* (Nashville: Cumberland House Publishing, Inc., 2005), 119.
6. Greer Opinion, 5.
7. Julia Quinlan, *My Joy, My Sorrow* (Cincinnati: St. Anthony's Messenger Press, 2005), 106.
8. David Karp, "Memories diverge," *St. Petersburg Times*, 1A.
9. Ibid.
10. Ibid.
11. Greer Opinion, 8–9.
12. Ibid, 9–10.
13. Anita Kumar, "Judge: Schiavo's life can end," *St. Petersburg Times*, February 12, 2000, 1A.
14. Anita Kumar, "Before the circus," *St. Petersburg Times*, April 3, 2005, 1P.
15. Ibid.
16. Anita Kumar, "Woman's parents, husband agree to keep her in hospice," *St. Petersburg Times*, May 11, 2000, 3B.
17. *In re* Schiavo, 780 So. 2d 176 (2nd DCA 2001), *rehearing denied* (Feb. 22, 2001), *review denied*, 789 So. 2d 348 (Fla. 2001)(Case No.: SC01-559), 3. Referenced as "*Schiavo I*." Available online at Miami Timeline. Page citations are to the slip opinion available online.
18. *Schiavo I*, 3–4.
19. Ibid, 4.
20. Ibid, 8.
21. The Schindlers filed a motion for rehearing with the court of appeals, which that court denied on February 22, 2001. They also filed the following motions: in the trial court, asking Judge Greer to recuse himself from the case; in the court of appeals, asking that court to extend the April 20, 2001 date for removal of the feeding tube; and in the Florida Supreme Court, asking that court to review the court of appeals decision. Miami Timeline.

22. Miami Timeline.
23. Miami Timeline.
24. Anita Kumar, "Parents lose fight over life support," *St. Petersburg Times*, April 24, 2001, 1A.
25. Ibid.
26. Jay Wolfson, *guardian ad litem*, "A Report to Governor Jeb Bush and the 6th Judicial Circuit in the Matter of Theresa Marie Schiavo," December 1, 2003, 15. Referenced as "Wolfson Report." Available online at Miami Timeline.
27. Anita Kumar, "Ethical storm swirls after a final meal," *St. Petersburg Times*, April 25, 2001, 1A.
28. The Schindlers also filed an emergency suit with Judge Greer, but that suit was immediately dismissed because it had not been filed within the time limits required by court rules. *In re Schiavo*, 792 So.2d 551 (2nd DCA 2001), 2. Referenced as "*Schiavo II*." Available online at Miami Timeline. Page citations are to the slip opinion available online.
29. *Schiavo II*, 3.
30. Ibid, 9.
31. Ibid.
32. William R. Levesque, "Doctors resume feeding Schiavo," *St. Petersburg Times*, April 27, 2001, 1A; *Schiavo II*, 4.
33. Ibid.
34. Ibid.
35. Miami Timeline.
36. *Schiavo II*, 7.
37. Miami Timeline.
38. *In re Schiavo*, 800 So.2d 640 (2nd DCA 2001), 1. Referenced as "*Schiavo III*." Available online at Miami Timeline. Page citations are to the slip opinion available online.
39. The Schindlers also sought review of Judge Greer's dismissal of the new witnesses. But the court of appeals agreed that the three new witnesses, who claimed to have information about Michael Schiavo's conversations about Terri's wishes, would not affect the initial trial results on that issue. *Schiavo III*, 6.
40. *Schiavo III*, 7.
41. Ibid.
42. Ibid, 12.
43. Miami Timeline.
44. William R. Levesque, "Talks in Schiavo case fail to end family feud," *St. Petersburg Times*, February 14, 2002, 4B.
45. William R. Levesque, "Right-to-die case debated again," *St. Petersburg Times*, October 12, 2002, 3B.
46. *In re Schiavo*, 2002 WL 31817960 (Fla. Cir. Ct. Nov. 22, 2002)(No. 90-2908-GB-003), Greer, J., 4. Referenced as "Greer Opinion II." Available online at Miami Timeline.
47. Greer Opinion II, 4–5.
48. Ibid, 6.
49. Ibid, 6.
50. Ibid, 7.
51. Ibid, 8–9.
52. Miami Timeline.

53. William R. Levesque, "Attorney claims a beating may have caused Schiavo's coma," *St. Petersburg Times*, November 13, 2002, 3B.
54. *In re* Schiavo, 851 So.2d 182 (2nd DCA 2003)(No.2D02-5394), *rehearing denied* (July 9, 2003), *review denied* 855 So.2d 621 (Fla. 2003), 2. Referenced as "*Schiavo IV.*" Available online at Miami Timeline. Page citations are to the slip opinion available online.
55. *Schiavo IV*, 5–6.
56. Ibid, 7.
57. Ibid, 6, 10–12.
58. Miami Timeline.
59. William R. Levesque, "Battles end with quiet removal of feeding tube," *St. Petersburg Times*, October 16, 2003, 1A.
60. William R. Levesque, "Schiavo's family ends legal fight," *St. Petersburg Times*, October 15, 2003, 1A.
61. Randall Terry, "Saving Terri Schiavo," *The Society for Truth and Justice*, http://www.societyfortruthandjustice.com/prod01.htm (accessed January 2006).
62. Ibid.
63. http://www.maranatha.tv, press release, February 14, 2004 (accessed August 2005).
64. Steve Bousquet, "How Terri's Law came to pass," *St. Petersburg Times*, November 2, 2003, 1B.
65. Ibid.
66. Ibid.
67. Ibid.
68. William R. Levesque, et al., "Gov. Bush's order puts Schiavo back on fluids," *St. Petersburg Times*, October 22, 2003, 1A.
69. Bay News 9 Live, Oct. 21, 2003, www.baynews9.com.
70. William R. Levesque, "Schiavo's husband says he'll fight back," *St. Petersburg Times*, October 24, 2003, 1A.
71. Ibid.
72. "Schiavo suspects bulimia caused wife's collapse," *CNN.com*/Law Center, October 28, 2003. Available online at http://www.cnn.com/2003/LAW/10/28/schiavo.lkl/ (accessed January 2006).
73. William R. Levesque, "Schiavo's husband says he'll fight back," *St. Petersburg Times*, 1A; Miami Timeline.
74. Wolfson Report, 33–34.
75. Miami Timeline.
76. *Schiavo v. Bush*, No. 03-008212-CN20 (Fla. Pinellas Cir. Ct., May 5, 2004), Baird, J., 20. Available online at Miami Timeline.
77. Miami Timeline.
78. William R. Levesque, "Justices skeptical of Bush team's defense of 'Terri's Law'," *St. Petersburg Times*, September 1, 2004, 1B.
79. Ibid.
80. *Bush v. Schiavo*, No. SC04-925 (Fla. September 23, 2004), slip op. 11. Available online at Miami Timeline.
81. Ibid, 17.
82. *In re: The Guardianship of Theresa Marie Schiavo, Incapacitated*, No. 90-2908GD-003 (Fla. Pinellas Cir. Ct., Probate Div. February 25, 2005), order denying stay. Available online at Miami Timeline. Referenced as "Stay Order."
83. Miami Timeline.

84. Stay Order, 2.
85. Miami Timeline.
86. *In re Schiavo*, (2nd DCA, March 16, 2005), slip op. 7. Referenced as "*Schiavo V*." Available online at Miami Timeline.
87. Ibid, 10.
88. Miami Timeline.
89. Anita Kumar, et al., "One by one, options sink," *St. Petersburg Times*, March 18, 2005, 1A.
90. Ibid.
91. Anita Kumar, et al., "House scurries on Schiavo bill," *St. Petersburg Times*, March 21, 2005, 1A.
92. Miami Timeline.
93. William R. Levesque, et al., "Tube is removed after chaotic day," *St. Petersburg Times*, March 19, 2005, 1A.
94. Ibid.
95. Kitty Bennett, David Karp, "Four pivotal moments in the case," *St. Petersburg Times*, April 1, 2005, 6A.
96. William R. Levesque, et al., "Tube is removed," *St. Petersburg Times*, 1A.
97. Anita Kumar, et al., "Schiavo tube could be back in Monday," *St. Petersburg Times*, March 20, 2005, 1A.
98. Anita Kumar, et al., "House scurries," *St. Petersburg Times*, 1A.
99. Ibid.
100. Ibid.
101. Ibid.
102. William R. Levesque, "Without a ruling, the wait continues," *St. Petersburg Times*, March 22, 2005, 1A.
103. Ibid.
104. Abby Goodnough, Maria Newman, "Schiavo's parents appeal ruling on feeding tube," *The New York Times*, March 22, 2005. Available online at http://www.theocracywatch.org/terri_appeal_times_mar22_05.htm (accessed February 2006).
105. Miami Timeline.
106. William R. Levesque, et al., "Appeals court awaits on Day 6," *St. Petersburg Times*, March 23, 2005, 1A.
107. Miami Timeline.
108. Adam Liptak, Abby Goodnough, "Schiavo parents appeal again after panel rules against them," *The New York Times*, March 23, 2005. Available online at http://www.theocracywatch.org/terri_parents_times_mar23_05.htm (accessed February 2006).
109. William R. Levesque, et al., "Schiavo case heads to U.S. Supreme Court," *St. Petersburg Times*, March 24, 2005, 1A.
110. Ibid.
111. William R. Levesque, et al., "Schiavo's parents left with few options," *St. Petersburg Times*, March 25, 2005, 1A.
112. William R. Levesque, et al., "Schiavo: same judges, same result," *St. Petersburg Times*, March 26, 2005, 1A.
113. David Karp, et al., "Clash over Schiavo: opinions differ on signs of death," *St. Petersburg Times*, March 28, 2005, 1B.
114. Anne Lindberg, "Pinellas Park, a tale of two cities," *St. Petersburg Times*, March 30, 2005, Neighborhood Times.

115. David Karp, et al., "Clash over Schiavo: opinions differ on signs of death," *St. Petersburg Times*, March 28, 2005, 1B.
116. Abby Goodnough, William Yardley, "Federal judge condemns intervention in Schiavo case," *The New York Times*, March 31, 2005, 14A.
117. Ibid.
118. William R. Levesque, et al., "A struggle to the end, the last hours: for two families, even grief is divided," *St. Petersburg Times*, April 1, 2005, 1A.
119. Ibid.

Chapter 3

1. Alex Leary, Jim Damaske, "The Schiavo saga: grave inscription rekindles old strife," *St. Petersburg Times*, June 22, 2005, 3B.
2. Dr. Jon Thogmartin, Medical Examiner District Six, Pasco & Pinellas Counties, Autopsy of Theresa Schiavo, June 13, 2005, 28. Available online at http://www.co.pinellas.fl.us/forensics; http://reports.tbo.com/reports/autopsy.pdf; or Miami Timeline. Sites accessed January 2006.
3. National Eating Disorders Association, "Bulimia Nervosa," http://www.nationaleatingdisorders.org/p.asp?WebPage_ID=286&Profile_ID=41141 (accessed February 2006).
4. Autopsy of Theresa Schiavo, 28–31.
5. Ibid, 31–34.
6. Ibid.
7. Ibid, 20.
8. Ibid, 14.
9. Ibid, 16.
10. Ibid, 35.
11. Ibid, 34.

Chapter 4

1. The story of Dr. Lown is taken from Bernard Lown, *The Lost Art of Healing* (Boston: Houghton-Mifflin, 1996), 188–212, and from personal interviews with Dr. Bernard Lown, December 2005.
2. Ibid.
3. Bernard Lown, Levine essay, "The 'chair' treatment of acute coronary thrombosis," *Transactions of the Association of American Physicians*, 64:316 (1951).
4. Claude F. Beck, et al., "Ventricular fibrillation of long duration abolished by electric shock," *Journal of the American Medical Association*, 135:985–86 (1947); Igor R. Efimov, "History of Fibrillation and Defibrillation," Washington University, http://efimov.wustl.edu/defibrillation/history/defibrillation_history.htm; Peter Bonadonna, "History of Paramedics," Monroe County Community College, Public Safety Training Center, http://www.monroecc.edu/depts/pstc/backup/parashis.htm (sites accessed January 2006).
5. Hughes W. Day, "History of coronary care units," *American Journal of Cardiology*, 30:405–07 (1972).
6. Ibid.
7. Personal interviews with Dr. Robert Potter, September, November 2005.
8. Ibid.

9. "The EMS Page," Yahoo! Geocities, http://www.geocities.com/HotSprings/Oasis/3346/ems.html (accessed January 2006).
10. Bonadonna, http://www.monroecc.edu/depts/pstc/backup/parashis.htm.
11. Robert Potter interviews, September, November, 2005.
12. National Inventors Hall of Fame, "Forrest M. Bird, Inventor Profile," http://inventors.about.com/gi/dynamic/offsite.htm?site=http://www.invent.org/hall%5Fof%5Ffame/1%5F1%5F6%5Fdetail.asp%3FvInventorID=15 (accessed January 2006).
13. Robert Potter interviews, September, November, 2005.
14. Douglas Harvey, Department of History, University of Kansas, "A Long Weekend in a Long Hot Summer," This Week in KU History, http://www.kuhistory.com/proto/story.asp?id=99 (accessed January 2006).
15. John A. Paraskos, "History of CPR and the role of the national conference,"*Annals of Emergency Medicine*, 22:2, 275–280 (February 1993).
16. The President's Commission on Law Enforcement and Administration of Justice, "Taks Force Report: Science and Technology," The Institute for Defense Analyses (1967). Available online at http://www.911dispatch.com/911/history/index.html (accessed January 2006).
17. Alan Burton, "History of 911," *Dispatch Monthly Magazine* (1995). Available online at http://www.911dispatch.com/911/history/index.html (accessed January 2006).
18. Michael Trebilcock, "City of Miami Department of Fire-Rescue: Our History," http://www.ci.miami.fl.us/fire/history.asp#TOP (accessed January 2006).
19. Sarah Angliss and Colin Uttley, "Science in the Dock: Barnard and the first heart transplant (script)," Spacedog, http://www.spacedog.biz/gscfiles/gscbarnscript.htm (accessed January 2006).
20. Department of Development and Public Affairs, University of Capetown, "30 years on . . . Immunologist remembers world's first heart transplant," *Monday Paper*, 16:34 (Nov. 1997). Available online at http://web.uct.ac.za/depts/dpa/monpaper/97-no34/botha.htm (accessed January 2006).
21. Jennifer Rosenburg, "20th Century History," About.com 20th Century History (December 2003), http://history1900s.about.com/b/a/047759.htm (accessed February 2006); Department of Development and Public Affairs, University of Capetown, "30 years on . . . Immunologist remembers world's first heart transplant," *Monday Paper*.
22. Angliss and Uttley, http://www.spacedog.biz/gscfiles/gscbarnscript.htm.
23. Robert Potter interviews, September, November, 2005.
24. Personal interviews with Dr. Fred Plum, October 2000 and November 2005.
25. Jane Smith, *Patenting the Sun: Polio and the Salk Vaccine* (New York: William Morrow and Co., Inc, 1990), 34.
26. Mary Bellis, "History of the Iron Lung-Respirator," About.com Inventors, http://inventors.about.com/library/inventors/blrespirator.htm (accessed January 2006).
27. Personal interviews with Dr. Fred Plum, October 2000 and November 2005; Fred Plum and Harold G. Wolff, "Observations on acute poliomyelitis with respiratory insufficiency," *Journal of the American Medical Association*, 146: 442–46 (1951); Edmund Sass, "The History of Polio: A Hypertext Timeline," The Polio History Pages, http://www.cloudnet.com/~edrbsass/poliotimeline.htm (accessed January 2006).
28. Ibid (Sass).

29. Bryan Jennett, *The Vegetative State: Medical Facts, Ethical and Legal Dilemmas*, (Cambridge: Cambridge University Press, 2002), 1–4.
30. Bryan Jennett and Fred Plum, "Persistent vegetative state after brain damage: a syndrome in search of a name," *Lancet*, 1:734–37 (1972).
31. Joseph and Julia Quinlan with Phyllis Battelle, *Karen Ann: The Quinlans Tell Their Story* (New York: Doubleday, 1977), 12–13.
32. Ibid, 19–20, 295–96.
33. Ibid, 215.
34. Ibid.
35. Julia Quinlan, *My Joy, My Sorrow* (Cincinnati: St. Anthony's Messenger Press, 2005), 105.
36. Public Law 95-622, 42 U.S.C. 1802 (1978).
37. President's Commission for the Study of Ethical Problems in Medicine and Biomedical and Behavioral Research, *Defining Death: Medical, Legal and Ethical Issues in the Determination of Death*, U.S. Gov't Printing Office, Washington, D.C. (July 1981), 8.
38. Ibid, 24, n.7.
39. President's Commission for the Study of Ethical Problems in Medicine and Biomedical and Behavioral Research, *Deciding to Forego Life-Sustaining Treatment*, U.S. Gov't Printing Office, Washington, D.C. (March 1983).
40. Julia Quinlan, "History, with Julia Quinlan," The Karen Ann Quinlan Hospice, http://www.karenannquinlanhospice.org/history.htm (accessed January 2006).
41. Ibid.
42. William H. Colby, *Long Goodbye: The Deaths of Nancy Cruzan* (Carlsbad, CA: Hay House, Inc., 2002), 27.

Chapter 5

1. UPMC News Bureau, "Our Experts: Thomas E. Starzl, M.D., Ph.D.," http://newsbureau.upmc.com/Bios/BioStarzl.htm; David C. Kaufmann, M.D., FCCM, "The Final Diagnosis—Brain Death," Critical Connections: The Complete News Source for Critical Care Professionals, Society for Critical Care Medicine, http://www.sccm.org/publications/critical_connections/2004_05oct/brain_death.asp (sites accessed January 2006).
2. Ibid.
3. Report of the Ad Hoc Committee of the Harvard Medical School to Examine the Definition of Brain Death, "A definition of irreversible coma," *Journal of the American Medical Association*, 205:337–340 (1968).
4. Joseph E. Murray, *Surgery of the Soul: Reflections on a Curious Career* (Canton, MA: Science History Publications, 2001).
5. Julian Savulescu, "Death, Us and Our Bodies: Personal Reflections," *Journal of Medical Ethics*, 29(3):127–130 (June 1, 2003).
6. Tom L. Beauchamp, LeRoy Walters, *Contemporary Issues in Bioethics*, 2nd ed. (Belmont, CA: Wadsworth Publishing, 1982), 288–293.
7. Kan. Stat. Ann. Sec. 77-202 (Supp. 1971).
8. President's Commission for the Study of Ethical Problems in Medicine and Biomedical and Behavioral Research, *Defining Death: Medical, Legal and Ethical Issues in the Determination of Death*, U.S. Gov't Printing Office, Washington, D.C. (July 1981), 62.
9. Alexander M. Capron and Leon R. Kass, *A Statutory Definition of the Standards*

for Determining Human Death: An Appraisal and a Proposal, 121 U. Pa. L. Rev. 87 (1972).
10. President's Commission, *Defining Death*, 139–40.
11. Public Law 95-622, 42 U.S.C. 1802 (1978); President's Commission, *Defining Death*, iii.
12. Mark Fritz, "Last Rights: How Simple Device Set Off a Fight Over Elderly Care," *The Wall Street Journal*, December 8, 2005, A1.
13. The New Jersey Declaration of Death Act, P.L. 1991, codified as N.J. Stat. Ann. Sec. 26:6A (West 2005).
14. William H. Colby, *Long Goodbye: The Deaths of Nancy Cruzan* (Carlsbad, CA: Hay House, Inc., 2002), 236–242.
15. Marilyn Webb, *The Good Death: The American Search to Reshape the End of Life* (New York: Bantam Books,1997), 170–71.
16. Luis Kutner, *Due Process of Euthanasia: The Living Will, A Proposal*, 44 Ind. L. J. 539 (1969).
17. Webb, *The Good Death*, 170–71.
18. Ibid.
19. Ibid.
20. The National Conference on Commissioners of Uniform State Law, http://www.nccusl.org (accessed January 2006).
21. Colby, *Long Goodbye*, 91–92.
22. Ibid, 236.
23. Charlene Laino, "The Pill turns 40: history of the Pill," MSNBC (1999), *MSNBC.com*, http://www.msnbc.com/modules/pill/default.htm (accessed January 2006).
24. *Griswold v. Connecticut*, 381 U.S. 479 (1965).
25. Ibid.
26. *Roe v. Wade*, 410 U.S. 113 (1973).
27. National Right to Life Committee, "Abortion History," http://www.nrlc.org/abortion/timeline1.html (accessed January 2006).
28. *Cruzan v. Director, Missouri Dep't of Health*, 497 U.S. 261, 270 (1990).
29. Ibid, 269 (quoting an earlier case).
30. *Union Pacific R. Co. v. Botsford*, 141 U.S. 250, 251 (1891).
31. American Hospital Association, "A Patient's Bill of Rights," Chicago, IL, 1972.
32. Colby, *Long Goodbye*, 22.

Chapter 6

1. William H. Colby, *Long Goodbye: The Deaths of Nancy Cruzan* (Carlsbad, CA: Hay House, Inc., 2002), 75–76.
2. Ibid, 122–24.
3. Ibid, 41.
4. Ibid, 288.
5. Ibid, 321.
6. Ibid, 323.
7. *Cruzan v. Director, Missouri Dep't of Health*, 497 U.S. 261, 279–80 (majority opinion); 288 (O'Connor, J., concurring); 309 (Brennan, J., dissenting); 334 (Stevens, J., dissenting) (1990).
8. *Cruzan v. Director, Missouri Dep't of Health*, 283.
9. "Missourians Back the Right to Die," *Columbia Missourian* (August 2, 1990), 1; "Survey on the Right to Die: 92 Percent Say Money for Keeping PVS Patients

Alive Could Be Better Spent," *Internal Medicine World Report* (February 1990), 1–3.

10. Colby, *Long Goodbye*, 374, 385.
11. The Patient Self-Determination Act of 1990, Pub. L. 101-508, codified at 42 U.S.C. 1395.
12. Durable Power of Attorney for Health Care Act of 1991, R.S. Mo. 404.800; Fla. Stat. Ann. Sec. 765.401 (West 2005).

Chapter 7

1. Ronald E. Cranford, "The persistent vegetative state: the medical reality (getting the facts straight)," *Hastings Center Report*, 27–32 (Feb./March 1988), 31.
2. Joseph and Julia Quinlan with Phyllis Battelle, *Karen Ann: The Quinlans Tell Their Story* (New York: Doubleday, 1977), 290–92.
3. "Report of Guardian ad litem Richard L.Pearse, Jr.," in *In re: The Guardianship of Theresa Marie Schiavo, Incapacitated*, No. 90-2908GD-003 (Fla. Pinellas Cir. Ct., Probate Div.), Greer, J., December 29, 1998, 9–11. Available online at http://www.hospicepatients.org/richard-pearse-jr-12-29-98-report-of-guardianadlitem-re-terri-schiavo.pdf (accessed January 2006).
4. At one point the parties attempted mediation, which is actually a useful tool in the judge's arsenal to force battling parties to talk to one another, or at least to communicate through an intermediary. Often it is successful. In the Schiavo/Schindler dispute, it was not. William R. Levesque, "Talks in Schiavo case fail to end family feud," *St. Petersburg Times*, February 14, 2002, 4B.
5. The Patient Self-Determination Act of 1990, Pub. L. 101-508, codified at 42 U.S.C. 1395.
6. Medtronic, Inc., "1949–1960: The Early Years," About Medtronic, http://www.medtronic.com/corporate/1949_1960a.html (accessed January 2006).
7. Gregg Easterbrook, *The Progress Paradox* (New York: Random House, 2003), 46.
8. Ibid.
9. Joanne Lynn, *Sick to Death and Not Going to Take It Anymore!* (Berkeley: University of California Press, 2004), 67–68.
10. Brown University Center for Gerontology and Health Care Research, "Facts on dying," www.chcr.brown.edu/dying (accessed January 2006); Centers for Disease Control and Prevention, National Center for Health Statistics, www.cdc.gov/nchs/fastats/deaths.htm (accessed Janaury 2006); Institute of Medicine report, *Approaching Death: Improving Care at the End of Life* (Washington, D.C.: National Academy Press, 1997), 37–39.
11. Joanne Lynn, "Living Long in Fragile Health: The New Demographics Shape End of Life Care," *Improving End of Life Care: Why Has It Been So Difficult, Hastings Center Special Report* (November/December 2005), S14–18.
12. Centers for Disease Control and Prevention, National Center for Health Statistics, "Deaths/Mortality," http://www.cdc.gov/nchs/fastats/deaths.htm.
13. Lynn, "Living Long in Fragile Health," S16–17.
14. Sharon Kaufman, . . . *And a Time to Die: How American Hospitals Shape the End of Life* (New York: Scribner, 2005), 82–83.
15. Sherwin B. Nuland, *How We Die* (New York: Vintage, 1995), 80–81.
16. Lynn, *Sick to Death*, 26.
17. The President's Council on Bioethics, *Taking Care: Ethical Caregiving in Our*

Aging Society, U.S. Gov't Printing Office: Washington, D.C. (September 2005), 8–9.
18. Ibid.
19. Ibid.

Chapter 8

1. SUPPORT Principal Investigators, "A Controlled Trial to Improve Care for Seriously Ill Hospitalized Patients: The Study to Understand Prognoses and Preferences for Outcome and Risks of Treatment (SUPPORT)," *Journal of the American Medical Association*, 274: 1591–98 (1995).
2. Russell Phillips, et al., "Findings from SUPPORT and HELP: An Introduction," *Journal of the American Geriatrics Society*, 48: S1–3 (2000).
3. Joanne Lynn, "Living Long in Fragile Health: The New Demographics Shape End of Life Care," *Improving End of Life Care: Why Has It Been So Difficult, Hastings Center Special Report* (November/December 2005), S16–17.
4. Joanne Lynn, et al., "Rethinking Fundamental Assumptions: SUPPORT's Implications for Future Reform," *Journal of the American Geriatrics Society*, 48 : S218 (2000).
5. Joanne Lynn, *Sick to Death and Not Going to Take It Anymore!* (Berkeley: University of California Press, 2004), 22–23; Sharon Kaufman, . . . *And a Time to Die: How American Hospitals Shape the End of Life* (New York: Scribner, 2005), 341 n.20; Joanne Lynn, et al., "Prognoses of Seriously Ill Hospitalized Patients on the Days before Death," *New Horizons*, 5: 56–61 (1997).
6. Lynn, *Sick to Death*, 22–23.
7. Nicholas A. Christakis and Elizabeth B. Lamont, "Extent and determinants of error in doctors' prognoses in terminally ill patients: prospective cohort study," *British Medical Journal*, 320: 469–73 (February 19, 2000); Elizabeth B. Lamont and Nicholas A. Christakis, "Prognostic Disclosure to Patients with Cancer near the End of Life," *Annals of Internal Medicine*, 134, 12: 1096–1105 (June 19, 2001).
8. Sandra H. Johnson, "Making Room for Dying: End of Life Care in Nursing Homes," *Improving End of Life Care: Why Has It Been So Difficult, Hastings Center Special Report* (November/December 2005), S37–41.
9. President's Commission for the Study of Ethical Problems in Medicine and Biomedical and Behavioral Research, *Deciding to Forego Life-Sustaining Treatment*, U.S. Gov't Printing Office, Washington, D.C. (March 1983), 52–53.
10. Jan Hoffman, "Doctors' Delicate Balance in Keeping Hope Alive," *New York Times*, December 24, 2005, A1.
11. President's Commission, *Deciding to Forego Life-Sustaining Treatment*, 52–53.
12. Jan Hoffman, *New York Times*, A1.
13. Ibid. Many commentators also note that additional treatments pay far better in the medical reimbursement system than spending the time to have a discussion with the patient about whether that treatment is appropriate. Joanne Lynn, et al., "Rethinking Fundamental Assumptions: SUPPORT's Implications for Future Reform," S218.
14. Peter A. Ubel, "What Should I Do, Doc?," *Archives of Internal Medicine*, 162: 977–80 (May 13, 2002).
15. Ibid.
16. Lynn, *Sick to Death*, 21.
17. Lynn, et al., "Rethinking Fundamental Assumptions," S218–19.

18. Ibid.
19. Ibid.
20. Ibid; SUPPORT Principal Investigators, "A Controlled Trial," *Journal of the American Medical Association*, 1591–98.
21. Council on Ethical and Judicial Affairs, American Medical Association, "Guidelines for the Appropriate Use of Do-Not-Resuscitate Orders," *Journal of the American Medical Association*, 265, 14:1868 (1991).
22. John Paraskos, "History of CPR and the Role of the National Conference," *Annals of Emergency Medicine*, 22:2, 275–80 (February 1993).
23. Council on Ethical and Judicial Affairs, "Guidelines for the Appropriate Use of Do-Not-Resuscitate Orders," 1868.
24. Ibid.
25. Sharon Kaufman, . . . *And a Time to Die: How American Hospitals Shape the End of Life* (New York: Scribner, 2005), 49.
26. Ibid, 48–49.
27. Sherwin B. Nuland, *How We Die* (New York: Vintage, 1995), 39–40.
28. Susan J. Diem, et al., "Cardiopulmonary Resuscitation on Television: Miracles and Misinformation," *The New England Journal of Medicine*, 334, 24: 1578–82 (June 13, 1996); The Robert Wood Memorial Foundation, "CPR: "It's Not Quite Like 'ER'," http://www.rwjf.org/newsroom/featureDetail.jsp?featureID=893&type=3 (accessed February 2006).
29. The Robert Wood Johnson Foundation, "CPR: "It's Not Quite Like 'ER'."
30. Council on Ethical and Judicial Affairs, "Guidelines for the Appropriate Use of Do-Not-Resuscitate Orders," 1868.
31. Ibid, 1868–69; Jim Stoddard, "A Practical Approach to DNR Discussions," *Bioethics Forum*, 14:1, 27–29 (Spring 1998).
32. The Robert Wood Memorial Foundation, "CPR: "It's Not Quite Like 'ER'."
33. President's Commission, *Deciding to Forego Life-Sustaining Treatment*, 237.
34. Ibid, 238.
35. Lynn, et al., "Rethinking Fundamental Assumptions," S219.
36. Ibid.
37. Susan Tolle, et al., "Oregon's Low In-Hospital Death Rates: What Determines Where People Die and Satisfaction with Decisions on Place of Death?," *Annals of Internal Medicine*, 130:8, 681–82 (April 20, 1999); Russell Phillips, et al., "Findings from SUPPORT and HELP: An Introduction," *Journal of the American Geriatrics Society* 48, S1–2 (2000).
38. Tolle, "Oregon's Low In-Hospital Death Rates," 681–85; Susan Hickman, et al., "Hope for the Future: Achieving the Original Intent of Advance Directives," *Improving End of Life Care: Why Has It Been So Difficult, Hastings Center Special Report* (November/December 2005), S26–30; OHSU Center for Ethics in Healthcare, "POLST Paradigm History," http://www.ohsu.edu/ethics/polst/background.shtml (accessed January 2006).
39. Tolle, "Oregon's Low In-Hospital Death Rates," 681–85.
40. Hickman, "Hope for the Future," S28.
41. American Association of Colleges of Nursing, "End-of-Life Nursing Education Consortium," http://www.aacn.nche.edu/elnec/about.htm (accessed January 2006); The EPEC Project: Education in palliative and end-of-life care, http://www.epec.net/EPEC/Webpages/index.cfm (accessed February 2006).
42. Joanne Lynn, et al., "Rethinking Fundamental Assumptions," S218–220.

43. William H. Colby, *Long Goodbye: The Deaths of Nancy Cruzan* (Carlsbad, CA: Hay House, Inc., 2002), 395.
44. Kaufman, . . . *And A Time to Die*, 43.

Chapter 9

1. President's Commission for the Study of Ethical Problems in Medicine and Biomedical and Behavioral Research, *Deciding to Forego Life-Sustaining Treatment*, U.S. Gov't Printing Office, Washington, D.C. (March 1983), 135.
2. The Office of Technology Assessment of the federal Congress in 1987 issued its own report focused on aging and the use of medical technology. In its "Principles for Decisionmaking Regarding the Use of Life-Sustaining Technologies for Elderly Persons" the document stated: "Cognitive function is an important marker of the quality of life." U.S. Congress, Office of Technology Assessment, *Life-Sustaining Technologies and the Elderly*, OTA-BA-306, U.S. Gov't Printing Office, Washington, D.C. (July 1987).
3. The President's Council on Bioethics, *Taking Care: Ethical Caregiving in Our Aging Society*, U.S. Gov't Printing Office, Washington, D.C. (September 2005).
4. Ibid, 103.
5. Ibid, 130, 168–69.
6. Ibid, 229–30.
7. *Annotated Current Opinions of the Council on Ethical and Judicial Affairs of the American Medical Association*, Chicago, IL (1992), 18–19.
8. Ibid, 16–17.
9. President's Council, *Taking Care*, 105.
10. William Hensel, "My Living Will," *Journal of the American Medical Association*, 275, 8: 588 (1996).
11. Ibid.
12. Ibid.
13. President's Council, *Taking Care*, 82–88.
14. Ibid, 194.
15. Ibid, 229.
16. Ibid, 129.
17. *Griswold v. Connecticut*, 381 U.S. 479, 496 (1965); *Prince v. Massachusetts*, 321 U.S. 158, 166 (1944); *Parham v J.R.*, 442 U.S. 584, 602 (1979).
18. President's Council, *Taking Care*, 128.

Chapter 10

1. The President's Council on Bioethics, *Taking Care: Ethical Caregiving in Our Aging Society* U.S. Gov't Printing Office, Washington, D.C. (September 2005), 71, 75–76.
2. Hardin, SB, Yusufaly, YA, "Difficult End-of-Life Treatment Decisions: Do Other Factors Trump Advance Directives?"*Archives of Internal Medicine*, 164: 1531–33 (2004).
3. Charles P. Sabatino, "National Advance Directives: One Attempt to Scale the Barriers," *NAELA Journal* 1: 131–64 (2005), 139.
4. *Cruzan v. Director, Missouri Dep't of Health*, 497 U.S. 261, 278 (1990); and 290 (O'Connor, J., concurring) ("whether a State must also give effect to the decisions of a surrogate decisionmaker . . . may well be constitutionally required to protect the patient's liberty interest.")

Chapter 11

1. William H. Colby, *Long Goodbye: The Deaths of Nancy Cruzan* (Carlsbad, CA: Hay House, Inc., 2002), 380.
2. Colby, *Long Goodbye*, 26.
3. *Cruzan v. Director, Missouri Dep't of Health*, Brief of the American Society of Parenteral and Enteral Nutrition as Amicus Curiae (Sept. 1, 1989), 13–16.
4. Eileen P. Flynn, *Hard Decisions: Forgoing and Withdrawing Artificial Nutrition and Hydration* (Kansas City, MO: Sheed & Ward, 1990), 1–5.
5. Ibid, 1–8.
6. Wikipedia, "Endoscopy," http://en.wikipedia.org/wiki/Endoscopy (accessed January 2006).
7. Dittrick Medical History Center, Case Western Reserve University, "Percutaneous Endoscopic Gastrostomy, 1979," http://www.cwru.edu/artsci/dittrick/site2/museum/artifacts/group-d/peg.htm (accessed January 2006).
8. Colby, *Long Goodbye*, 20.
9. Ibid, 157.
10. *Annotated Current Opinions of the Council on Ethical and Judicial Affairs of the American Medical Association*, Chicago, IL (1992), 18–19.
11. *Cruzan v. Director, Missouri Dep't of Health*, 497 U.S. 261, 279–80 (majority opinion); 288 (O'Connor, J., concurring); 309 (Brennan, J., dissenting); 334 (Stevens, J., dissenting) (1990).
12. Ibid, 288–90 (1990) (O'Connor, J., concurring).
13. Durable Power of Attorney for Health Care Act of 1991, R.S. Mo. 404.800.
14. Joe Millcia, "The Terri Schiavo Case: The 'Tube Doctors': Device's inventors never foresaw ethical dilemma," *The Atlanta Journal-Constitution*, March 26, 2005.
15. Mark Fritz, "Last Rights: How Simple Device Set Off a Fight Over Elderly Care," *The Wall Street Journal*, December 8, 2005, A1.
16. Ibid.
17. Ibid.
18. Ibid.
19. President's Commission for the Study of Ethical Problems in Medicine and Biomedical and Behavioral Research, *Deciding to Forego Life-Sustaining Treatment*, U.S. Gov't Printing Office, Washington, D.C. (March 1983), 75–76.
20. The President's Council on Bioethics, *Taking Care: Ethical Caregiving in Our Aging Society*, U.S. Gov't Printing Office, Washington, D.C. (September 2005), 136.
21. Mark Fritz, "Last Rights: How Simple Device Set Off a Fight Over Elderly Care," *The Wall Street Journal*, December 8, 2005, A1.
22. Thomas E. Finucane, Colleen Christmas, Kathy Travis, "Tube Feeding in Patients with Advanced Dementia," *Journal of the American Medical Association*, 282: 1365–70 (1999); M.R. Gillick, "Rethinking the Role of Tube Feeding in Patients with Advanced Dementia," *New England Journal of Medicine*, 342: 206–10 (2000).
23. Colby, *Long Goodbye*, 125–36; Finucane, *Tube Feeding*, 1368–69 (discussing clincal challenges of feeding a demented patient).
24. America's Second Harvest: The Nation's Food Bank Network, http://www.secondharvest.org (accessed February 2006).

Chapter 12

1. William H. Colby, *Long Goodbye: The Deaths of Nancy Cruzan* (Carlsbad, CA: Hay House, Inc., 2002), 384.

2. CNN Transcripts, March 31, 2005, "Terri Schiavo Dies at Age 41," *CNN.com*, http://transcripts.cnn.com/TRANSCRIPTS/0503/31/nfcnn.01.html (accessed February 2006).
3. LifeSiteNews.com, "Vatican Cardinal: 'Let's Stop with the Euphemisms—They Killed' Terri Schiavo," Vatican City: July 27, 2005, http://www.lifesite.net/ldn/2005/jul/05072702.html (accessed February 2006).
4. Judith Graham, "Schiavo case put priest on hot seat," *Chicago Tribune*, April 24, 2005, Section 4, 1.
5. Stephen Nohlgren, "I'm here because I care," *St. Petersburg Times*, March 30, 2005, 11A.
6. Mitch Stacy, "Religious Groups Take Role In Schiavo Case," Associated Press, March 4, 2005. Available online at ABC News, http://abcnews.go.com/US/wireStory?id=551621 (accessed February 2006).
7. Fr. Richard P. McBrien, "The Schiavo case re-visited," *Tidings Online*, August 5, 2005, http://www.the-tidings.com/2005/0805/essays.htm (accessed February 2006).
8. Mitch Stacy, "Terri Schiavo's alma mater prays for her life," Associated Press, March 15, 2005. Available online at *St. Petersburg Times Online*, http://www.sptimes.com/2005/03/15/news_pf/State/Terri_Schiavo_s_alma_.shtml (accessed February 2006).
9. Mark Washofsky, "A Jewish Guide to the Moral Maze of Hi-Tech Medicine," *Reform Judaism Online: Union for Reform Judaism* (Fall 2005), http://reformjudaismmag.org/Articles/index.cfm?id=1048 (accessed February 2006).
10. Joanne Palmer, "Halachah sheds light on *Schiavo* case," *The Canadian Jewish News: Internet Edition*, December 22, 2005. Available online at http://www.cjnews.com/viewarticle.asp?id=5989 (accessed February 2006).
11. Cathy Grossman, "When life's flame goes out," *USA Today*, October 5, 2005, 1D.
12. David Zweibel, "Accommodating Religious Objections to Brain Death: Legal Considerations, *Journal of Halacha and Contemporary Society* XVII (1989), 49–68, quoted in Robert S. Olick, "Brain Death, Religious Freedom, and Public Policy: New Jersey's Landmark Legislative Initiative," *Kennedy Institute of Ethics Journal*, 1, 4:289–92 (1991).
13. Grossman, "When life's flame goes out," 1D.
14. President's Commission for the Study of Ethical Problems in Medicine and Biomedical and Behavioral Research, *Deciding to Forego Life-Sustaining Treatment*, U.S. Gov't Printing Office, Washington, D.C. (March 1983), 82–83.
15. Ibid, 82–83 & n.114.
16. Pope Pius XII, "The Prolongation of Life" (November 24, 1957), *The Pope Speaks*, 4, 4: 395–96 (Spring 1958).
17. A Science Odyssey: People and Discoveries, "The first successful kidney transplant," http://www.pbs.org/wgbh/aso/databank/entries/dm54ki.html (accessed February 2006).
18. *Satz v. Perlmutter*, 379 So.2d 359 (Fla.1980).
19. President's Commission, *Deciding to Forego Life-Sustaining Treatment*, 82–83.
20. Marilyn Webb, *The Good Death: The American Search to Reshape the End of Life*, (New York: Bantam Books, 1997), 170–71.
21. Joseph and Julia Quinlan with Phyllis Battelle, *Karen Ann: The Quinlans Tell Their Story* (New York: Doubleday 1977), 290–92.
22. President's Commission, *Deciding to Forego Life-Sustaining Treatment*, 88–89 &

n.132, quoting Sacred Congregation for the Doctrine of the Faith, *Declaration on Euthanasia* (June 26, 1980).
23. "Church Teaching on the Duty to Preserve Life, Forgoing Nutrition and Hydration, and Euthanasia," The Catholic Health Association of the United States, St. Louis, MO (June, 2005), 4.
24. Richard A. McCormick, "The *Cruzan* Decision," *Midwest Medical Ethics*, 5, 1/2:3–6 (Winter/Spring 1989).
25. Colby, *Long Goodbye*, 240–41.
26. *Cruzan v. Director, Missouri Dep't of Health*, No. 88-1503, Supreme Court of the United States, Brief of the U.S. Catholic Conference as Amicus Curiae (Oct. 16, 1989), 2 (quoting NCCB Committee for Pro-Life Activities, *Statement on the Uniform Rights of the Terminally Ill Act*, in 16 *Origins* 223 (Sept. 4, 1986)).
27. Colby, *Long Goodbye*, 289–90.
28. Stephen Mumford, *American Democracy and the Vatican: Population Growth and National Security* (Amherst, NY: Humanist Press, 1984), 208–09.
29. Alan S. Lubert, "A Conversation with Mr. & Mrs. Cruzan," *Midwest Medical Ethics* 5, 1:17–20 (Winter/Spring 1989).
30. United States Conference of Catholic Bishops, *Ethical and Religious Directives for Catholic Health Care Services, Fourth Edition* (2001), 56–58. Available online at http://www.usccb.org/bishops/directives.shtml (accessed February 2006).
31. "CHA ethicist looks at shifts in views on nutrition, hydration," *Catholic Health World*, Vol. 21, No. 19 (November 1, 2005). Available online at http://www.chausa.org/Pub/MainNav/News/CHW/Archive/2005/1101/articles/w051101j.htm (accessed February 2006).
32. National Right to Life Committee, "Model Starvation and Dehydration of Persons with Disabilities Prevention Act," http://www.nrlc.org/euthanasia/modelstatelaw.html (accessed February 2006).
33. Kansas House Bill No. 2307, by Committee on Appropriations, Session of 2005, "An Act concerning appointment of guardians and conservators," 2–4 (2005).
34. National Right to Life Committee, "The Will to Live Project," http://www.nrlc.org/euthanasia/willtolive/index.html (accessed February 2006).

Chapter 13

1. Stephen Nohlgren, "I'm here because I care," *St. Petersburg Times*, March 30, 2005, 11A.
2. William H. Colby, *Long Goodbye: The Deaths of Nancy Cruzan* (Carlsbad, CA: Hay House, Inc., 2002), 227.
3. Not Dead Yet: The Resistance, "About Us," http://www.notdeadyet.org/docs/about.html (accessed February 2006).
4. Testimony of Diane Coleman, president of Not Dead Yet, before the Subcommittee on Criminal Justice, Drug Policy and Human Resources of the Committee on Government Reform of the U.S. House of Representatives, Oversight Hearing on "Federal Health Programs and Those Who Cannot Care for Themselves: What Are Their Rights, and Our Responsibilities?" April 19, 2005, http://www.notdeadyet.org/docs/ColemanCongTestmy041905.html (accessed February 2006).
5. Not Dead Yet, "About Us," http://www.notdeadyet.org/docs/about.html.
6. Testimony of Diane Coleman, http://www.notdeadyet.org/docs/ColemanCongTestmy041905.html.

7. *Buck v. Bell, Superintendent of State Colony Epileptics and Feeble Minded*, 274 U.S. 200, 207 (1927).
8. Ibid.
9. Jeffrey Rosen, "One Man's Justice," *New York Times*, December 17, 2000.
10. Ibid.
11. Stephen Jay Gould, "Carrie Buck's daughter: a popular, quasi-scientific idea can be a powerful tool for injustice," *Natural History Magazine*, Museum of Natural History, July/August 2002. Available online at http://www.findarticles.com/p/articles/mi_m1134/is_6_111/ai_87854861 (accessed February 2006).
12. Ibid.
13. Ibid.
14. Ibid.
15. "Charges weighed for parents who let baby die untreated," *New York Times*, April 17, 1982, 7; Barry R. Furrow, et al., *Bioethics: Health Care Law and Ethics, Fourth Ed.* (Eagan, MN: West Group, 2001), 343–44.
16. "Charges weighed for parents who let baby die untreated," *New York Times*, April 17, 1982, 7; C. Everett Koop, *KOOP: The Memoirs of America's Family Doctor* (New York: Random House, 1991), 240–61.
17. Koop, *KOOP: The Memoirs*, 75.
18. Dr. C. Everett Koop, Statement before Hearing on Handicapped Newborns, Subcommittee on Select Education, Committee on Education and Labor, U.S. House of Representatives (September 16, 1982), cited in President's Commission for the Study of Ethical Problems in Medicine and Biomedical and Behavioral Research, *Deciding to Forego Life-Sustaining Treatment*, U.S. Gov't Printing Office, Washington, D.C. (March 1983), 219–20 & n. 81.
19. Ibid.
20. 42 U.S.C.§5102 (1986); Furrow, et al., *Bioethics*, 343–44.
21. President's Commission, *Deciding to Forego Life-Sustaining Treatment*, 202–03.
22. Ibid, 197.
23. Elisabeth Rosenthal, "As More Tiny Infants Live, Choices and Burden Grow," *New York Times*, September 29, 1991, 1.
24. Ibid.
25. President's Commission, *Deciding to Forego Life-Sustaining Treatment*, 199–200.
26. Paul Raeburn, "A Second Womb," *New York Times*, August 14, 2005; personal interview with Dr. John Muraskas, February 2006.
27. *Bouvia v. Superior Court*, 225 Cal. Rptr. 297 (Ct. App. 1986).
28. Not Dead Yet, press release dated December 20, 1996, http://www.notdeadyet.org/docs/prel1.html (accessed February 2006).

Chapter 14

1. C. Everett Koop, *KOOP: The Memoirs of America's Family Doctor* (New York: Random House, 1991), 293 (Surgeon General Report summary).
2. *Gonzales, Attorney General v. Oregon*, 546 U.S. ___ (2006), slip op. 28. Available online at http://www.law.cornell.edu/supct/pdf/04-623P.ZO (accessed February 2006).
3. *Gonzales, Attorney General v. Oregon*, 546 U.S. ___ (2006), slip op. 25 (Scalia, J., dissenting). Available online at http://www.law.cornell.edu/supct/pdf/04-623P.ZD (accessed February 2006).
4. *Washington v. Glucksberg*, 521 U.S. 702, 712–13 (1997).
5. Ibid, 715.

6. Ibid, 706–07.
7. Lisa Belkin, "Doctor Tells of First Death Using His Suicide Device," *New York Times*, June 6, 1990, A1.
8. Michael Betzold, *Appointment with Doctor Death* (Troy, MI: Momentum Books, Ltd., 1993), 41–46.
9. Belkin, "Doctor Tells of First Death," *New York Times*, A1.
10. Dirk Johnson, "Kevorkian Faces A Murder Charge In Death On Video," *New York Times*, November 26, 1998.
11. Archives search for "Dr. Jack Kevorkian," done on http://www.nytimes.com on December 28, 2005.
12. Johnson, "Kevorkian Faces A Murder Charge," *New York Times*; Mike Wallace, "A Letter from Dr. Kevorkian," *New York Review of Books*, 48, 11 (July 5, 2001).
13. CBS News, "Parole Board Denies Kervorkian," December 22, 2005, http://www.cbsnews.com/stories/2005/12/22/national/main1160151.shtml?CMP=OTC-RSSFeed&source=RSS&attr=HOME_1160151 (accessed February 2006).
14. Johnson, "Kevorkian Faces A Murder Charge," *New York Times*.
15. *Washington v. Glucksberg*, 521 U.S. 702 (1997); *Vacco v. Quill*, 521 U.S. 793 (1997).
16. *Glucksberg*, 735.
17. Barbara Coombs Lee, "Observations on the First Year of Oregon's Death with Dignity Act," *Psychology, Public Policy, and Law*, 6, 2:268 (June 2000); Oregon Department of Human Services, "Seventh Annual Report on Oregon's Death with Dignity Act, (March 10, 2005), 6. Available online at http://egov.oregon.gov/DHS/ph/pas/ar-index.shtml (accessed February 2006).
18. Testimony of former Oregon Governor Barbara Roberts before the California Assembly Judiciary Committee on the California Compassionate Choices Act A.B. 654, April 12, 2005.
19. Oregon Department of Human Services, "Seventh Annual Report," 7–9; *see also* Death with Dignity National Center, "Safeguards of the Law," http://www.deathwithdignity.org/historyfacts/ (accessed February 2006).
20. Coombs Lee, "Observations," *Psychology, Public Policy, and Law*, 276–78; *see also* Death with Dignity National Center, http://www.deathwithdignity.org
21. Oregon Department of Human Services, "Seventh Annual Report," 20–21.
22. Ibid.
23. Testimony of former Oregon Governor Barbara Roberts before the California Assembly Judiciary Committee on the California Compassionate Choices Act A.B. 654, April 12, 2005.
24. Ibid.
25. Coombs Lee, "Observations," *Psychology, Public Policy, and Law*, 286–87.
26. Ibid.
27. Oregon Department of Human Services, "Seventh Annual Report," 6.
28. Marcia Angell, "Keep alive the right to die," *Los Angeles Times*, October 4, 2005.
29. *Washington v. Glucksberg*, No. 96-110, Supreme Court of the United States, Brief of the American Medical Association, et al. as Amici Curiae (November 12, 1996), 1.
30. Kant Patel, "Euthanasia and Physician-Assisted Suicide Policy in the Netherlands and Oregon: A Comparative Analysis," *Journal of Health & Social Policy*, 19, 1:39–40 (2004).

31. Ibid, 43.
32. Leon R. Kass, *Life, Liberty and the Defense of Dignity*, (New York: Encounter Books, 2002), 207–08.
33. Stephen Drake, "Those with disabilities wonder who will next be deemed worthless," *Kansas City Star*, November 2, 2003, B5.
34. The Nightingale Alliance, "Fast Facts," http://www.nightingale alliance.org/cgi-bin/home.pl?section=3 (accessed February 2006).
35. Physicians for Compassionate Care Educational Foundation, May 6, 2004 Press Release, http://www.pccef.org/press/press18.htm (accessed February 2006).
36. Lee, "Observations," *Psychology, Public Policy, and Law*, 283–85.
37. Kenneth R. Stevens, "Comment on Ganzini and Dobscha regarding Comparing Rates of Physician-Assisted Suicide in Oregon with that of Other States," *The Journal of Clinical Ethics* 15, 2:363–64 (2004).
38. Donald G. McNeil, Jr., "First Study on Patients Who Fast to End Lives," *New York Times*, July 31, 2003.
39. *Washington v. Glucksberg*, No. 96-110, Supreme Court of the United States, Brief of the American Medical Association, et al. as Amici Curiae (November 12, 1996), Appendix B, Opinions of the Council on Ethical and Judicial Affairs 2.211—Physician Assisted Suicide, issued Dec. 1993, updated June, 1996.

Chapter 15

1. Terrence Youk, *Pioneers of Hospice: Changing the Face of Dying*, videotape, Madison-Deane Initiative of the Visiting Nurse Association of Chittenden and Grand Isle Counties, Vermont (2005). Available online at www.pioneersofhospice.org (accessed February 2006).
2. Jamie Thompson, "Juggler says, 'God told me to come,'" *St. Petersburg Times*, March 31, 2005, 14A.
3. Joanne Lynn, Joan Harrold, *Handbook for Mortals: Guidance for People Facing Serious Illness* (New York: Oxford University Press, 1999), 130–36.
4. Ceci Connolly, "At Schiavo's Hospice, a Return to Routine; Scars of 'The Siege' Linger for Staff at Florida Facility," *The Washington Post*, June 18, 2005, A1.
5. Marcia Lattanzi-Licht, John Mahoney, Galen W. Miller, *The Hospice Choice: In Pursuit of a Peaceful Death* (New York: Fireside Books, 1998), 44–45.
6. St. Christopher's Hospice, http://www.stchristophers.org.uk/page.cfm/link=496 (accessed February 2006).
7. Helena Katz, "A career of compassion," *McGill Reporter*, Nov. 6, 1997, 1; Youk, *Pioneers of Hospice*.
8. President's Commission for the Study of Ethical Problems in Medicine and Biomedical and Behavioral Research, *Deciding to Forego Life-Sustaining Treatment*, U.S. Gov't Printing Office, Washington, D.C. (March 1983), 17.
9. Youk, *Pioneers of Hospice*.
10. The Connecticut Hospice, Inc.,http://www.hospice.com/cthospice/about.html (accessed February 2006); Youk, *Pioneers of Hospice*.
11. Youk, *Pioneers of Hospice*.
12. Ibid.
13. St. Christopher's Hospice, http://www.stchristophers.org.uk/page.cfm.
14. Katz, *McGill Reporter*, 1.
15. B. Jennings, T. Ryndes, C. D'Onofrio, M.A. Baily, "Access to Hospice Care: Expanding Boundaries, Overcoming Barriers," *Hastings Center Report* (March–April 2003), S6.

16. Youk, *Pioneers of Hospice.*
17. Elisabeth Kübler-Ross, *On Death and Dying* (New York: Macmillan, 1974, twelfth printing), back cover.
18. Youk, *Pioneers of Hospice.*
19. Jennings, "Access to Hospice," *Hastings Center Report*, S6.
20. Personal interviews with Dr. Robert Milch, December 2005.
21. Lattanzi-Licht, *The Hospice Choice*, 51–53.
22. National Hospice and Palliative Care Organization, "NHPCO 2004 Facts and Figures," http://www.nhpco.org/files/public/Facts_Figures_for2004data.pdf (accessed February 2006); personal interviews with NHPCO staff, January 2006.
23. Ibid.
24. Ibid.
25. Lattanzi-Licht, *The Hospice Choice*, 48–51.
26. Youk, *Pioneers of Hospice.*
27. Joanne Lynn, *Sick to Death and Not Going to Take It Anymore!* (Berkeley: University of California Press, 2004), 67–68.
28. American Medical Association EPEC Project, Education for Physicians on End-of-life Care, "Plenary 1: Gaps in End-of-life Care," 7–8 (1999).
29. National Hospice and Palliative Care Organization, "NHPCO 2004 Facts and Figures."
30. Jennings, "Access to Hospice," *Hastings Center Report*, S11.
31. Lattanzi-Licht, *The Hospice Choice*, 51–53.
32. Center to Advance Palliative Care, "Frequently Asked Questions," http://www.capc.org/about-capc/faqs (accessed February 2006); Robin Marantz Henig, "The Struggle to Create the Good Death," *The New York Times Magazine*, August 7, 2005, 26, 30–31.
33. Ibid.
34. Ibid.
35. Ibid.
36. Connolly, "At Schiavo's Hospice," *The Washington Post*, A-1.
37. Stephen Nohlgren, "Beyond the Schiavo case: back to normal," *St. Petersburg Times*, April 2, 2005, 1B.
38. Personal interview with Mary Labyak, January 2006.
39. Maggie Callanan, Patricia Kelley, *Final Gifts* (New York: Bantam Books, 1993).
40. Personal interview with Mary Labyak, January 2006.
41. Youk, *Pioneers of Hospice.*

Chapter 16

1. Lance Armstrong with Sally Jenkins, *It's Not About the Bike: My Journey Back to Life* (New York: Berkley Books, 2000), 1.
2. Terrence Youk, *Pioneers of Hospice: Changing the Face of Dying*, videotape, Madison-Deane Initiative of the Visiting Nurse Association of Chittenden and Grand Isle Counties, Vermont (2005). Available online at www.pioneersofhospice.org (accessed February 2006).

BIBLIOGRAPHY AND ADDITIONAL READING

Lance Armstrong with Sally Jenkins, *It's Not About the Bike: My Journey Back to Life* (New York: Berkley Books, 2000)

Jean-Dominique Bauby, *The Diving Bell and the Butterfly* (New York: Vintage Books, 1998)

Tom L. Beauchamp, LeRoy Walters, *Contemporary Issues in Bioethics*, 2nd ed. (Belmont, CA: Wadsworth Publishing, 1982)

Michael Betzold, *Appointment with Doctor Death* (Troy, MI: Momentum Books, Ltd., 1993)

Mary Kay Blakely, *Wake Me When It's Over: A Journey to the Edge and Back* (New York: Ballantine, 1989)

Ira Byock, *Dying Well: Peace and Possibilities at the End of Life* (New York: Riverhead Books, 1997)

Ira Byock, *The Four Things That Matter Most: A Book About Living* (New York: Free Press, 2004)

Maggie Callanan, Patricia Kelley, *Final Gifts* (New York: Bantam Books, 1993)

Arthur L. Caplan, et al., *The Case of Terri Schiavo: Ethics at the End of Life* (Amherst, NY: Prometheus Books, 2006)

William H. Colby, *Long Goodbye: The Deaths of Nancy Cruzan* (Carlsbad, CA: Hay House, Inc., 2002)

Joan Didion, *The Year of Magical Thinking* (New York: Knopf, 2005)

Hank Dunn, *Hard Choices for Loving People* (Herndon, VA: A&A Publishers, Inc., 1994)
Stephen Dunn, *Different Hours* (New York: W.W. Norton & Company, 2000)
Ronald Dworkin, *Life's Dominion* (New York: Vintage Books, 1994)
Gregg Easterbrook, *The Progress Paradox* (New York: Random House, 2003)
Jon B. Eisenberg, *Using Terri: The Religious Right's Conspiracy to Take Away Our Rights* (San Francisco: Harper San Francisco, 2005)
Marc Etkind, *. . .Or Not to Be: A Collection of Suicide Notes* (New York: Riverhead Books, 1997)
Anne Fadiman, *The Spirit Catches You and You Fall Down* (New York: Farrar, Straus and Giroux, 1997)
Peter G. Filene, *In the Arms of Others: A Cultural History of the Right-to-Die in America* (Chicago: Ivan R. Dee, 1998)
Eileen P. Flynn, *Hard Decisions: Forgoing and Withdrawing Artificial Nutrition and Hydration* (Kansas City, MO: Sheed & Ward, 1990)
Michael Foucault, *The Birth of the Clinic: An Archaeology of Medical Perception* (New York: Vintage Books, 1994)
Mark Fuhrman, *Silent Witness: The Untold Story of Terri Schiavo's Death* (New York: Morrow, 2005)
Francis Fukuyama, *Our Posthuman Future* (New York: Farrar, Straus and Giroux, 2002)
Barry R. Furrow, et al., *Bioethics: Health Care Law and Ethics, Fourth Ed.* (Eagan, MN: West Group, 2001)
Harold S. Kushner, *When Bad Things Happen to Good People* (New York: Anchor, 2004, paperback reissue)
Barbara Coombs Lee, *Compassion In Dying: Stories of Dignity and Choice* (Troutdale, OR: NewSage Press, 2003)
Fran Moreland Johns, *Dying Unafraid* (San Francisco: Synergistic Press, 1999)
Bill Hancock, *Riding with the Blue Moth* (Champaign, IL: Sports Publishing, LLC, 2005)
Steven L. Jeffers, *Sacred Oasis In Illness* (Overland Park, KS: SMMC Foundation, 2001)
Bryan Jennett, *The Vegetative State: Medical Facts, Ethical and Legal Dilemmas* (Cambridge: Cambridge University Press, 2002)
Fenton Johnson, *Geography of the Heart: A Memoir* (New York: Washington Square Press, 1996)
Sharon Kaufman, *. . . And a Time to Die: How American Hospitals Shape the End of Life* (New York: Scribner, 2005)
Leon R. Kass, *Life, Liberty and the Defense of Dignity* (New York: Encounter Books, 2002)
C. Everett Koop, *KOOP: The Memoirs of America's Family Doctor* (New York: Random House, 1991)
Elisabeth Kübler-Ross, *On Death and Dying* (New York: Macmillan, 1974, twelfth printing)
Marcia Lattanzi-Licht, John Mahoney, Galen W. Miller, *The Hospice Choice: In Pursuit of a Peaceful Death* (New York: Fireside Books, 1998)
Bernard Lown, *The Lost Art of Healing* (Boston: Houghton-Mifflin, 1996)
Thomas Lynch, *The Undertaking: Life Studies from the Dismal Trade* (New York: Penguin Books, 1997)
Joanne Lynn, Joan Harrold, *Handbook for Mortals: Guidance for People Facing Serious Illness* (New York: Oxford University Press, 1999)

Joanne Lynn, *Sick to Death and Not Going to Take It Anymore!* (Berkeley: University of California Press, 2004)
Diana Lynne, *Terri's Story: The Court-Ordered Death of an American Woman* (Nashville: Cumberland House Publishing, Inc., 2005)
Beth Witrogen McLeod, *Caregiving: The Spiritual Journey of Love, Loss, and Renewal* (New York: John Wiley & Sons, Inc., 1999)
Alan Meisel and Kathy Cerminara, *The Right to Die: The Law of End-of-Life Decision-making, 3rd ed.* (New York: Aspen, 2004)
Robin Metz, *Unbidden Angel* (Merrick, New York: Cross-Cultural Communications, 1999)
Virginia Morris, *Talking About Death* (Chapel Hill, NC: Algonquin Books, 2001)
Stephen Mumford, *American Democracy and the Vatican: Population Growth and National Security* (Amherst, NY: Humanist Press, 1984)
Joseph E. Murray, *Surgery of the Soul: Reflections on a Curious Career* (Canton, MA: Science History Publications, 2001)
Sherwin B. Nuland, *Doctors: The Biography of Medicine* (New York: Vintage Books, 1988)
Sherwin B. Nuland, *How We Die: Reflections on Life's Final Chapter* (New York: Vintage Books, 1995)
Mary Pipher, *Another Country: Navigating the Emotional Terrain of Our Elders* (Riverhead Books, 2000)
Fred Plum and Jerome B. Posner, *The Diagnosis of Stupor and Coma, 3rd Ed.* (New York: Oxford University Press, 1982)
Stephen G. Post, *The Moral Challenge of Alzheimer's Disease* (Baltimore: The John's Hopkins University Press, 1995)
Joseph and Julia Quinlan with Phyllis Battelle, *Karen Ann: The Quinlans Tell Their Story* (New York: Doubleday, 1977)
Julia Quinlan, *My Joy, My Sorrow* (Cincinnati: St. Anthony's Messenger Press, 2005)
Mary Roach, *Stiff: The Curious Lives of Human Cadavers* (New York: W.W. Norton & Company, 2003)
Michael Schiavo with Michael Hirsh, *Terri: The Truth* (New York: Dutton, 2006)
Mary and Robert Schindler, et al., *A Life That Matters: The Legacy of Terri Schiavo—A Lesson For Us All* (New York: Warner Books, 2006)
David Shenk, *The Forgetting: Alzheimer's: Portrait of an Epidemic* (New York: Doubleday, 2001)
Jane Smith, *Patenting the Sun: Polio and the Salk Vaccine* (New York: William Morrow and Co., Inc, 1990)
Wesley J. Smith, *Culture of Death: The Assault on Medical Ethics in America* (San Francisco: Encounter Books, 2000)
Dalton Trumbo, *Johnny Got His Gun* (New York: Bantam Books, 1939)
Marilyn Webb, *The Good Death: The American Search to Reshape the End of Life* (New York: Bantam Books,1997)
Terry Tempest Williams, *Refuge: An Unnatural History of Family and Place* (New York: Vintage Books, 1991)
Edward O. Wilson, *On Human Nature* (Cambridge, MA: Harvard University Press, 1978)

RESOURCES

AARP
601 E Street, NW
Washington, DC 20049
888/687-2277
www.aarp.org

Administration on Aging
Washington, DC 20201
202/619-0724
www.aoa.dhhs.gov

Aging with Dignity
PO Box 1661
Tallahassee, FL 32302
888/594/7437
www.agingwithdignity.org
(Provides Five Wishes document)

AIDS Hotline
800/342-2437 or 800/227-8922
(Operated by the Center for Disease Control and Prevention)

ALS Association
27001 Agoura Road, Suite 150
Calabasas Hills, CA 91301-5104
800/782-4747
www.alsa.org

Alzheimer's Association
225 North Michigan Ave.
Chicago, IL 60601-7633
800/272-3900
www.alz.org

Alzheimer's Disease Education and Referral Center (ADEAR)
PO Box 8250
Silver Springs, MD 20907
800/438-4380
www.alzheimers.org

Alzheimer's Disease and Related Disorders Association
919 N Michigan Avenue, Suite 1100
Chicago, IL 60611
800/272-3900
www.alz.org

American Association of Retired Persons (AARP)
601 E. Street, NW
Washington, DC 20049
800/424-3410
www.aarp.org

American Academy of Hospice and Palliative Medicine
4700 W. Lake Ave.
Glenview, IL 60025
847/375-4731
www.aahpm.org

American Association of Homes and Services for the Aging
2519 Connecticut Ave., NW
Washington, DC 20008-1520
202/783-2242
www.aahsa.org

American Bar Association Commission on Law and Aging
740 15th St., NW
Washington, DC 20005-1022
202/662-8690
www.abanet.org/aging/

American Chronic Pain Association
PO Box 850
Rocklin, CA 95677
800/533-3231
www.theacpa.org

American College of Physicians
190 N Independence Mall West
Philadelphia, PA 19106-1572
800/523-1546 X2600
www.acponline.org

American Dietetic Association
120 South Riverside Plaza, Suite 2000
Chicago, IL 60606-6995
800/877-1600
www.eatright.org

American Geriatrics Society
350 Fifth Ave., Suite 801
New York, NY 10118
800/563-4916
www.americangeriatrics.org

American Hospital Association
One North Franklin
Chicago, IL 60606
312/422-3000
www.aha.org/aha

American Medical Association
515 N. State Street
Chicago, IL 60610
800/621-8335
www.ama-assn.org

American Nurses Association
8515 Georgia Ave., Suite 400
Silver Spring, MD 20910
800/274-4262
www.nursingworld.org

American Society of Bioethics and Humanities
4700 W. Lake Ave.
Glenview, IL 60025-1485
847/375-4745
www.asbh.org

American Society for Parenteral and Enteral Nutrition (A.S.P.E.N.)
8630 Fenton Street, Suite 412
Silver Spring, MD 20910
800/727-4567
www.nutritioncare.org

American Pain Foundation
201 North Charles Street, Suite 710
Baltimore, MD 20201-4111
888/615-7246
www.painfoundation.org

American Society of Aging
833 Market Street, Suite 511

San Francisco, CA 94103
800/537-9728
www.asaging.org

The American Society of Law, Medicine & Ethics
765 Commonwealth Ave., Suite 1634
Boston, MA 02215
617/262-4990
www.aslme.org

Boston University School of Public Health
715 Albany Street
Boston, MA 02118
617/638-4640
www.bu.edu/dbin/sph

Cancer Care, Inc.
275 7th Avenue
New York, NY 10001
800/813-4673
www.cancercare.org

Cancer Information Services (National Cancer Institute)
www.cancer.gov
800/422-6237

Caring Connections
1700 Diagonal Road, Suite 625
Alexandria, VA 22314
www.caringinfo.org
800/658-8898 (Free state-specific health care planning documents for download, and advice)

Center on an Aging Society
Health Policy Institute
Georgetown University
2233 Wisconsin Ave., NW
Washington, DC 20007
202/687-9840
www.aging-society.org

Center to Advance Palliative Care
1255 Fifth Ave., Suite C2
New York, NY 10029
212/201-2670
www.capc.org

Center for Bioethics and Health Law
University of Pittsburgh
3708 Fifth Ave., Suite 300
Pittsburgh, PA 15213-3405
412/647-5700
www.pitt.edu/~bioethic

Center for Practical Bioethics
Harzfeld Building
1111 Main Street, Suite 500
Kansas City, MO 64105-2116
800/344-3829
www.practicalbioethics.org

Department of Health and Human Services
200 Independence Ave., SW
Washington, DC 20201
877/696-6775
www.hhs.gov

Department of Veterans Affairs
810 Vermont Ave., NW
Washington, DC 20420
800/827-1000
www.va.gov

Family Caregivers Alliance
180 Montgomery St., Suite 1100
San Francisco, CA 94104
800/445-8106
www.caregiver.org

Funeral Consumers Alliance
33 Patchen Road
South Burlington, VT 05403
800/765-0107
www.funerals.org

Genetic Alliance: Help Line
4301 Connecticut Avenue, NW

Washington, DC 20008
800/336-4363
www.geneticalliance.org

Growth House: Guide to Death, Dying, Grief, Bereavement, and End-of-Life Resources
www.growthhouse.org
(Website resource)

The Hastings Center
21 Malcolm Gordon Road
Garrison, NY 10524-5555
845/424-4040
www.thehastingscenter.org

Hospicelink (Hospice Education Institute)
190 Westbrook Road
Essex, CT 06426-1510
800/331-1620
www.hospiceworld.org

Hospice and Palliative Nurses Association
One Penn Center West,
Suite 229
Pittsburgh, PA 15276
412/787-9301
www.hpna.org

Hospice Foundation of America
1621 Connecticut Ave., NW
Washington, DC 20009
800/854-3402
www.hospicefoundation.org

Kennedy Institute of Ethics at Georgetown University
Georgetown University
Washington, DC 20057
202/687-8099
www.kennedyinstitute.george
town.edu

The Mayday Pain Project
www.painandhealth.org
(Website resource)

Medicare Rights Center
1460 Broadway, 17th floor
New York, NY 10036
800/333-4114
www.medicarerights.org

National Academy of Elder Law Attorneys, Inc. (NAELA)
1604 North Country Club Road
Tucson, AZ 85716
520/881-4005
www.naela.org

National Alliance for Caregiving
4720 Montgomery Lane,
5th floor
Bethesda, MD 20814
301/718-8444
www.caregiving.org

National Family Caregivers Association
10400 Connecticut Ave.,
Suite 500
Kensington, MD 20895
800/896-3650
www.thefamilycaregiver.org

National Hispanic Council on Aging
1341 Connecticut Ave., NW
Washington, DC 20036
202/429-0787
www.nhcoa.org

National Hospice and Palliative Care Organization (NHPCO)
1700 Diagonal Road, Suite 625
Alexandria, VA 22314
800/658-8898 (hospice referrals)
703/837-1500 (other questions)
www.nhpco.org

National Institutes of Health
9000 Rockville Pike

Bethesda, MD 20892
301/496-4000
www.nih.gov

National Indian Council on Aging
10501 Montgomery Blvd., NE
Albuquerque, NM 87111
505/292-2001
www.nicoa.org

National Institute on Aging
Building 31, Room 5C27
31 Center Drive, MSC 2292
Bethesda, MD 20892
301/496-1752
www.nia.nih.gov

National Library of Medicine
8600 Rockville Pike
Bethesda, MD 20894
888/346-3656
www.nlm.nih.gov

Senior Corps
1201 New York Ave., NW
Washington, DC 20525
202/606-5000
www.seniorcorps.org

Visiting Nurses Association of America
99 Summer St.
Boston, MA 02110
888/866-8773 x221
www.vnaa.org

INDEX